Intersectional Feminism in the Age of Transnationalism

Intersectional Feminism in the Age of Transnationalism

Voices from the Margins

Edited by
Olga Bezhanova and Raysa E. Amador

LEXINGTON BOOKS
Lanham • Boulder • New York • London

Published by Lexington Books
An imprint of The Rowman & Littlefield Publishing Group, Inc.
4501 Forbes Boulevard, Suite 200, Lanham, Maryland 20706
www.rowman.com

6 Tinworth Street, London SE11 5AL, United Kingdom

British Library Cataloguing in Publication Information Available

Library of Congress Control Number: 2020949430

ISBN: 978-1-7936-1943-3 (cloth)
ISBN: 978-1-7936-1945-7 (pbk)
ISBN: 978-1-7936-1944-0 (electronic)

To my family.
—Raysa E. Amador.

In loving memory of Graciela Giordano, friend, feminist, scholar,
and a real-life Mafalda. Te has ido, pero nunca te olvidaremos.
—Olga Bezhanova.

Contents

List of Figures

Acknowledgments

I thank Adelphi University for its support during my sabbaticals, faculty awards for research travel, and technical assistance. I also want to thank Ms. Carmen Castellón for her help and support and patience. I am grateful to the reviewers Dr. Nick Carbó, Dr. Ana María Hernández, Dr. Sara Aponte-Olivieri, and Dr. Jorge Rosario-Vélez for their useful comments and suggestions. I want to thank the outstanding contributors for the many revisions in the preparation of the final manuscript. Their research, in the form of chapters, has resulted in a powerful and important book.

I have been able to devote ourselves to this work thanks to *Los Nuestros*: Rufino, Raysana, Rufi, Ana, Gabriel, Carolina, Santi, María de los Angeles, Ana Rosa, and Arístico whose voices echo through these pages and to Aristides and Ana Amador whose spirits embrace us all.

Above all, I would like to express my gratitude to Lexington Books' editors Judith Lakamper, Becca Beurer, and Shelby Russell who adamantly supported us. Their patience, support, and their belief in this project and unflagging confidence in us as editors influenced our efforts throughout the text's various stages of development.

Brindamos to our collaboration and friendship, which has sustained us during the 2020 COVID-19 pandemic, and everything that this book represents for us.

—Raysa E. Amador

This edited book was born at the session held by Feministas Unidas as part of the fiftieth Annual NeMLA Convention that took place in Washington, DC, in March of 2019. Feministas Unidas is a coalition of feminist scholars of Spanish, Spanish American, Luso-Brazilian, Afro-Latin American, and US Hispanic and Latino Studies. Our coalition has existed since 1979 and has supported and promoted the scholarly activities of several generations of feminist scholars of Hispanic Studies. As the current treasurer and record-keeper of Feministas Unidas, I have, for the past few years, served as the organizer of the annual session of our association at the NeMLA Convention. Feministas Unidas strives to offer a dedicated space to feminist scholars in our field of knowledge to talk about the directions that our scholarship takes and the ways in which we can address the challenges that we face both as feminists and as representatives of a field that has long been marginalized in US academia and that is currently under a great stress from the austerity measures adopted by many colleges. It became clear during our spirited discussion at the convention that the ways in which intersectional feminism interacts with neoliberal transnationalism are of great importance to today's feminist theory. This is why when my coparticipant in the session, Raysa E. Amador, suggested we look into the possibility of working together on an edited book on this subject, I knew this would be an important and promising project for us to undertake.

It was an enormous pleasure to work with Raysa E. Amador on this book. We have enjoyed a perfect synergy, and our book demonstrates that great things can happen when women come together to work on advancing feminist thought.

This project would not be possible without the wonderful opportunities created by Feministas Unidas for feminist scholars to meet, develop links of solidarity, create mentoring relationships and deep friendships. I am also very grateful to the Northeast Modern Languages Association that has been very hospitable to our association of feminist scholars of Hispanic Studies.

My research assistant Jacob Graves provided invaluable help with the editing of the book, and I want to thank him for his hard work and dedication to the project. Jacob's work on this edited book was made possible by the Undergraduate Research and Creative Activities program of the Southern Illinois University at Edwardsville. Laura Pawlow, the coordinator of this program, works extraordinarily hard to make sure that researchers at SIUE can involve undergraduate students in our scholarly activities.

An enormous debt of gratitude is owed to my wonderful friends Regina VanOverschelde, Maria Kontoyianni, and Fridegonde Klouvi, who are amazing, strong women and a great inspiration in everything I do.

My journey as a feminist began when, as a small child, I had to listen to my father endlessly repeat, "The most important thing for a woman is to be able to make her own money so that she never has to depend on some guy." My mother, who is a descendant of a long line of female teachers in our family, taught me the importance of having a strong voice and making it heard. My sister Marina is an unwavering example of strength, resilience, and courage even in very harsh circumstances. My husband, who became a fan of my feminist writings long before we met, inspires much of my feminist activism today.

Much of the work on this book was done as we were quarantined during the COVID-19 pandemic. I want to thank my four-year-old daughter Klara who lightened the load of my transition to the role of departmental chair (which had to occur as I was working on this book) with observations such as, "I'm glad you are the boss, Mommy. Why is it that only women are the boss? Can men be the boss sometimes, too?" The future of feminism is in good hands.

—Olga Bezhanova

Introduction

Transnationalism and Intersectional Feminism—Convergence and Conflict

Olga Bezhanova

Much of the work on this book on transnationalism and the degree to which it is compatible with intersectional feminism was done as the COVID-19 pandemic disrupted our lives and made us even more conscious than before of planetary interconnectedness. In its global reach, COVID-19 has been compared to the pandemic that devastated the planet almost exactly a century earlier and that is still known to us under the name of 'the Spanish flu.' The complex dynamic of international relations of the moment made the association between Spain and this deadly strain of influenza possible, even though the illness did not originate there.[1] As scholars of Hispanic Studies, therefore, we are aware of the ways that global catastrophes, of which pandemics are only one example, are narrativized and placed in the service of already existing power relations. We are yet to appreciate the full consequences of COVID-19 but it is already clear that, like any highly disruptive event of a planetary significance, the pandemic exposed the tensions between the global and the national as well as the national and the local. At the same time, the pandemic and our reactions to it highlighted the continued relevance of the categories of sex, race, and class and the intersections between them.

The impact of COVID-19 is unevenly distributed by both biological sex and its social expression through gender. The pandemic causes a significantly larger mortality in men than in women, with the death rates showing that over 60% of victims claimed by the disease are male.[2] At the same time, the secondary effects of the pandemic have been acutely felt by women and girls. The policy brief released by the Women Headquarters of the United Nations on April 9, 2020, traces the exponential growth in gender-based violence as a result of the quarantine measures undertaken by many governments to combat the pandemic.[3] The brief also discusses the unique ways in which the pandemic is undermining women's economic gains:

Emerging evidence on the impact of COVID-19 suggests that women's economic and productive lives will be affected disproportionately and differently
from men. Across the globe, women earn less, save less, hold less secure jobs,
are more likely to be employed in the informal sector. They have less access to
social protections and are the majority of single-parent households. Their capacity to absorb economic shocks is therefore less than that of men.[4]

The pandemic is also having a disparate effect along racial and ethnic lines.
In early April of 2020, Aletha Maybank, the chief health equity officer and
vice president of the American Medical Association, issued a statement
calling on the public authorities in the United States to release the information on the racial and ethnic impacts of the pandemic.[5] There is evidence,
for instance, that African Americans are disproportionately affected by
the pandemic, yet the response to this aspect of the crisis has been lacking. A preprint paper titled "Assessing Differential Impacts of COVID-19
on Black Communities" that reflected the results of a study funded by the
Public Policy Office of the Foundation for AIDS Research concluded, for
instance, that "nearly twenty-two percent of US counties are disproportionately black and they accounted for 52% of COVID-19 diagnoses and 58%
of COVID-19 deaths nationally . . . Social conditions, structural racism,
and other factors elevate risk for COVID-19 diagnoses and deaths in black
communities."[6]

These disparities exist on a global scale, as well. COVID-19 has demonstrated that the capacity to concentrate on mitigating the effects of the pandemic as the most pressing issue of the day is a luxury that some countries
and regions cannot afford. As the coronavirus started reaching East Africa, for
instance, it has become clear that for many people in the region concerns over
the pandemic will have to take second place to the devastation wrought by the
largest infestation of locusts that countries of East Africa have experienced
in seventy-five years.[7] The difficulty of getting the protective equipment, the
medical supplies, and the trained personnel that many countries faced at the
height of the COVID-19 pandemic was aggravated, in East Africa, by the
need to make extraordinary efforts to prevent swarms of locusts from moving to the parts of the continent that are less prepared to battle the infestation
of these insects. The solidarity usually practiced by African countries in the
face of such calamities is undermined by the need to maintain social distancing. As Keith Cressman, a senior locust forecasting officer with the United
Nations' Food and Agriculture Organization put it, "with travel restrictions
in place, experts can't get there to train people up. And even if they could get
there, social distancing means you can't fill up rooms for lessons on locust
control."[8] Social distancing is a privilege that comes at a greater price for
individuals and countries that exist in permanent scarcity.

In developed countries, growing class divides became visible as a result of the divergent reactions to workplace shutdowns among those whose jobs can be moved into "the Cloud" and those who are tethered to physical locations by the nature of the work that they perform. The COVID-19-related quarantines, which many perceive as a nuisance, are, in fact, a privilege that is inaccessible to those who already live in precarious situations. As Ingar Solty, a senior fellow for Peace and Security Policy at the Rosa-Luxemburg-Stiftung, observed:

> It is the workers who are risking infections by going to work, who are risking infecting their elder and sick relatives . . . It is also they who tend to live in cramped living conditions. It is therefore they who are running a much higher risk of stress, marital strife and domestic violence . . . It is thus they who are forced to choose whether to not work and become evicted or go to work and risk killing their elder relatives either through infections they bring home or through having their own children infect them.

In the post-COVID-19 era, it is very likely that class divides will deepen as the global economy enters into a recession and desperate job seekers attempt to prove their usefulness in the world that is still reeling from the pandemic.[9]

As the newly unemployed and increasingly desperate protesters started to express their disagreement with the effectiveness of extended quarantines, it has become clear that there is little sympathy for their plight among those who can work remotely and can afford the luxury of an indefinite term of self-isolation. As Glenn Harlan Reynolds observed in a *USA Today* article in late April, "there really are two Americas here: Those still getting a paycheck from government, corporations or universities, and those who are unemployed, or seeing their small businesses suffer due to shutdowns. And the America still getting paid is, so far, not showing a whole lot of sympathy for the America that isn't." Of course, COVID-19 did not create the class divide between those who have embraced the digitalization of the economy and those whose professions and economic stability have been wiped out to make space for the digital economy.[10] These class divisions have been growing globally throughout the past three decades and have culminated in the populist political tide of the recent years.[11] The pandemic has made them more visible than ever, making it clear that globally begotten ills are more easily borne by those who, at least for the moment, have found their place in the global economy.

A study released in early March of 2020 by Well Being Trust, a charitable organization based in Oakland, California, which has been studying the effects of the opioid epidemic on the public health in the United States, predicts that 'deaths of despair' (a concept denoting the heightened mortality that results from suicides, alcoholism, and drug addiction in the wake of the isolating and economically detrimental effects of globalization) are likely to increase in number dramatically as the economic effects of the pandemic and the social disruption it caused become more evident. The study projects between 28,000 and 150,000 additional 'deaths of despair' that will result from the devastation wrought by the pandemic-related shutdowns.[12] These sad developments will not be limited to the United States, of course, nor will they be at their worst in this country. Swiss psychiatrists Wolfram Kawohl and Carlos Nordt warn that the psychological impact of these disruptions will be unevenly distributed, causing the greatest harm to the already marginalized populations globally and within each society: "The downsizing of the economy and the focus of the medical system on the COVID-19 pandemic can lead to unintended long-term problems for a vulnerable group on the fringes of society."[13] Kawohl and Nordt project up to 9,570 additional suicides per year globally as a result of the deteriorating economic conditions worldwide in the wake of the pandemic-related quarantines.[14]

The impoverishment resulting from the pandemic-related disruptions to the global economy poses an even greater risk for the countries that are already suffering from extreme poverty. In the Western hemisphere, Haiti, with over a third of its entire gross domestic product dependent on the money that Haitians residing abroad send home to support their families, has been especially badly impacted. As the neighboring Dominican Republic declared a state of emergency on March 19, 2020, many of the Haitians who lived and worked in the country found themselves among the first to lose work and be forced to repatriate as the borders between the two countries closed.[15] Other countries in the hemisphere whose economies are heavily reliant on exporting their workforce overseas are encountering the same reduction in national revenue as a result of border closures in response to the pandemic. The heavy dependence of the economies in Central America and the Caribbean on their capacity to export 'human resources' mimics the bleeding, in the colonial and postcolonial eras, of Latin America's "open veins" of everything that can be "transmuted into European—or later United States—capital."[16] Neoliberal globalization has transformed the labor force of the countries in the region into a 'natural resource' and has used the transnationalization of this resource to thwart the capacity of workers both in countries that export and those that import migrant laborers to organize and demand better working conditions. When workers are obligated to migrate in order to make a living and support their families, they experience displacement not only from the localities that are familiar to them but also from the collective dimension of their identity as part of a labor force. Instead, they are forced to adopt the neoliberal identity of an entrepreneurial self that seeks to maximize its individual opportunities through geographical mobility at the expense of familial, cultural, and linguistic rootedness and worker solidarity.

As large-scale catastrophes of the past half century have tended to do, the COVID-19 pandemic strengthened the neoliberalizing projects that had already been in place. To give an example, Costa Rica, a country whose healthcare system is among the best in Central America, experienced the lowest COVID-related mortality rates in the region. Still, the financial elites of the country have used this difficult moment to push for the flexibilization of worker contracts that would erode the hard-won gains of the country's labor movements.[17] In Mexico, Alfonso Ramírez Cuéllar, the president of MORENA, has questioned the excessive reach of the austerity measures undertaken by the government that, according to Ramírez Cuéllar, are endangering its capacity to conduct environmental, agricultural, industrial, and financial policy.[18] Since in many places large public gatherings are prohibited to slow the transmission rates of the coronavirus, it becomes impossible for workers to organize protests against these measures. There is little doubt that the high costs of pandemic-related quarantines will be recouped through a variety of austerity measures that will further weaken welfare protections. The World Health Organization is conscious of this possibility, and its European director Hans Kluge has issued a call to the leaders of European countries to avoid repeating the sad history of administering austerity cuts to healthcare systems and social programs that had characterized the EU's response to the global economic crisis of 2008–2009.[19] It is also highly likely that the damage wrought by the pandemic will be used to justify, for a long time to come, a variety of cost-cutting measures that will increase global inequality and advance the neoliberal assault on the concept of state sovereignty.

As we observe the disparate effects of the COVID-19 pandemic on different genders, races, regions, and socioeconomic groups, it is becoming clear that an intersectional analysis of the effects of COVID-19 will be necessary to address the aftermath of the pandemic. Who will be addressing the aftermath, however? Which institutions do we expect to protect us during and after the pandemic? One of the effects of this crisis has been a realization that we still rely on the institutions of our respective nation-states to protect us from globally generated disasters. Globalization has weakened the nation-state model, and catastrophes of the caliber of COVID-19 highlight the consequences of this process. As Philip Bobbitt warned in 2003, the nation-state model of governance becomes delegitimized every time it is demonstrated to be impotent in the face of global threats: "No nation-state can protect its society from transnational perils, such as ozone depletion, global warming, and infectious epidemics. And yet guaranteeing national security, civil peace through law, economic development and stability, international tranquility and equality, were the principal tasks of the nation-state."[20] Once the

COVID-19 quarantines end and life resumes its course (at least to a degree), the already existing trends toward the disempowerment of the nation-state will be strengthened by the demonstrable weakness of national governments around the world in the face of the pandemic. Especially striking in this context has been the contrast between the rapid spread of the deadly virus and the slow-motion response of the democratic governments of developed nations that are constrained by "political interventions driven by consensus [that] appear slow, coarse, and boring" in comparison to the frenetic activity of the global information networks which most of us use to access news about this and other crises.[21]

The delegitimization of the nation-state model of governance is not a new development, of course. It has accompanied the remaking of the world economy along the lines of the neoliberal globalization that has been taking place since the 1970s. In place of the nation-state system of governance that has been dominant since the nineteenth century, a new system of governmentality has begun to form. It does not yet have a settled name but has been termed, by various scholars, as "a market-state," "a postnational state," and, following the line of reasoning proposed by Francis Fukuyama, "a post-historic society."[22] As nation-states wither under the assault of globalizing forces, the term 'transnationalism' becomes particularly useful to refer to the multitude of phenomena that occur in the tangible and intangible spaces between the weakened nation-states. Transnationalism is a result of globalization but the two terms should not be confused: "Transnationalism overlaps globalization but typically has a more limited purview. Whereas global processes are largely decentered from specific national territories and take place in a global space, transnational processes are anchored in and transcend one or more nation-states."[23] Simply put, transnational phenomena are a small part of a large process we know as globalization.

Transnationalism has attracted a lot of scholarly attention in the past few decades. There have been many debates about the precise meaning of the term 'transnational' and the way it differs from concepts with partially overlapping meaning, such as multicultural, transcultural, transborder, and global. While there are important differences between the phenomena denoted by these terms, they all arise from the reality of the weakening of the nation-state and its institutions as a result of the transformations in the global economy that have occurred since the late 1970s. In this volume, we have decided to forego an extensive discussion of terminology and have, instead, concentrated on different manifestations of transnational phenomena and their interactions with intersectional feminist scholarship. The contributions to our volume discuss such varied topics as works of fiction by Edwidge Danticat, Judith Ortiz-Cofer, and Diamela Eltit; visual art of Laura Aguilar and Maruja Mallo; films directed by Lucrecia Martel; a TV series based on a novel by María Dueñas; art–activism of Ani Ganzala and Zinha Franco; and the philosophical thought of Gloria Anzaldúa. Yet they all proceed from the belief in the continued usefulness of intersectionality as a valuable category of critical analysis that is particularly necessary at the time when the effects of neoliberal globalization are undermining many familiar categories of critical inquiry.

For the most part, academic treatment of transnationalism betrays a clear sympathy toward the rise in transnational phenomena. Not only is the term 'transnational' in vogue, but it is also often professionally beneficial to academics to describe the realities that it denotes favorably and mention the term frequently.[24] Moreover, as scholars of the Humanities, we pay particular attention to art, a form of human activity that benefits from transcending borders and experiencing a freedom of geographical mobility and other forms of movement. Several chapters in this volume discuss the ways in which artists have used their experiences of transnational displacement and the rise in transnational digital networks to their advantage. As feminist academics, however, we are well aware of the multitude of ways in which globalization harms marginalized populations at the same time as it offers increased opportunities to those who already enjoy a privileged status. Like the capacity to use the COVID-19 quarantines to enhance one's personal brand through an intensified online presence, the possibility of using transnational displacements to the advantage of one's artistic or academic career is the purview of the few. A truly intersectional analysis is only possible if we take into account the variety of ways in which a transnationalization of politics, economy, and the daily life perpetuates different forms of oppression. An unconditional acceptance of the effects of globalization—of which the rise in transnational phenomena is one—stands in the way of a truly intersectional approach which, by definition, is based on the belief that racialized, gender-based, class-based, and other forms of oppression deserve to be acknowledged and addressed.

The tensions between the transnational and the intersectional are well known and have been at the heart of the debates in feminist scholarship for some time. The very fixedness of the identity categories which give rise to an intersectional analysis disturbs the privileging of fluidity and boundless malleability that accompanies globalization: "Intersectionality relies on the production and reproduction of fixed identity categories that are tethered to the apparatuses of the nation-state, which is itself a problematic category and social formation, in order to make interventions."[25] The problematic nature of the nation-state model of governmentality is well known, as is its dependency on creating external and internal Others which are typically gendered and racialized. The impulse to "break from nation-centric frames of analysis" that has animated much of critical approaches to the effects of the withering away of the nation-state model constitutes a well-justified reaction to the otherizing and often extremely violent effects of nationalism.[26]

There is, however, no reason to assume that, once the nation-state is weakened to the point of losing its monopoly on violence, a form of statehood that succeeds it will be less unforgiving toward gendered and racialized groups. Before we begin to celebrate the erosion of nations' foundations by transnational flows, we should ask who the real beneficiaries of this process are likely to be. As Leslie Sklair pointed out at the beginning of this century, globalization has resulted in a planet-wide realignment of global systems of power: "Capitalist globalization, and thus effective power in the global system, is increasingly in the hands of a transnational capitalist class (TCC) comprising four fractions: those who own and control the major corporations and their local affiliates, globalizing bureaucrats and politicians, globalizing professionals, and consumerist elites."[27] An intersectional analysis needs to be conscious of the ways in which this newly emerged supranational class system is nourishing inequality. It also has to take into account that the new global elite articulates and normalizes a discourse that advances its interests at the expense of those it dispossesses.

The popularity of transnationalism as not only an object of scholarly study but also as a phenomenon considered to be largely positive coincides with capitalism's transition away from what Zygmunt Bauman termed the "solid phase" of capitalism.[28] This form of capitalism, also known as industrial capitalism or Fordism, had found in the nation-state a form of governmentality that was perfectly suited to facilitate the rapid expansion of capital throughout the nineteenth and the first half of the twentieth century. This form of statehood provided capital with the workforce that, in its attachment to a particular territory, mimicked capital's dependence on the physical location of the large, unwieldy machinery housed in factories. The disciplinary apparatus of the nation-state created compliant, sedentary workers and punished those who resisted being tied down: "Throughout the solid stage of the modern era, nomadic habits remained out of favour. Citizenship went hand in hand with settlement, and the absence of 'fixed address' and 'statelessness' meant exclusion from the law-abiding and law-protected community."[29] The compulsory comprehensive system of education provided by the nation-state molded the labor force of the industrial capitalist era with a view to create a high degree of cultural and linguistic uniformity among workers and school them into the conveyor-belt mentality of a factory production.

The overlap between the interests of capital and the ways in which nation-states create "the imagined community of the nation" was limited to the initial stages of development of the industrial capitalism.[30] In the last fifty years, technological and digital advances weakened and, in many cases, abolished the territorial groundedness of capital. The nation-state, however, is incapable of assuming as fluid a nature as capital has. The increasing speed of capital's movement created a new logic of capital accumulation that now privileges lack of rootedness over sedentariness. As it sheds its attachment to a particular territory, capital frees itself from the constraints of national politics and, as a result, "nations are losing their economic value."[31] The slow-motion folding of nation-state institutions, as well as the weakening of constraints on the free movement of capital and labor across national borders, creates fresh opportunities for enrichment that benefit capital holders at the expense of those who rely on national welfare programs. One example of this phenomenon can be found in the austerity measures that have accompanied the neoliberal realignment of national economies in the wake of the global economic crisis of 2008–2009.[32]

As Heidi Hartmann points out, "capital creates ideology."[33] An entire ideological apparatus exists to school the populace into accepting, and even welcoming, the new reality that arises from capital's changing needs. The often-uncritical view of the rise in transnational phenomena that is evident in most discussions of transnationalism is part of an ideological shift that normalizes this new stage in the development of capitalism. Neoliberalism, as this form of capitalism has been termed, makes the economic relations that it produces seem natural and unavoidable by molding every form of social relations to suit its ethos.[34] In order to function, a globalized neoliberal economy needs a certain kind of subjectivity that will interiorize the precepts of neoliberalism to such a degree that they would seem commonsensical and in need of no questioning. As Jim McGuigan observes, "the neoliberal self is connected to a generational structure of feeling, a selfhood counter-posed to the old social-democratic self."[35] One of the characteristics of this neoliberal self is "compulsory individualization" that positions everybody as an entrepreneur managing his or her own self as a brand and bearing full responsibility for any contretemps experienced on the way to economic success.[36] According to Byung-Chul Han, "twenty-first-century society is no longer a disciplinary society, but rather an achievement society . . . Its inhabitants are no longer 'obedience-subjects' but 'achievement-subjects.' They are entrepreneurs of themselves."[37] In this model, each individual interiorizes a disciplining and castigating stance vis-à-vis the self, engaging in self-blame and experiencing isolating feelings of shame whenever one fails to achieve success in administering oneself as a business venture.

A perception of the self as a business enterprise subverts any possibility of solidarity, given that competition is an integral part of entrepreneurship. If every individual is an entrepreneur of the self, he or she will be obligated to see others as competitors for perennially scarce resources. Once this model of selfhood is interiorized, the very identity of human beings begins to mimic the characteristics that have currency in the world of business. As the

needs of capital have shifted, these characteristics have undergone a significant change. As Richard Sennett points out, the collapse of Bretton Woods
agreements in the early 1970s led the world of business to begin privileging
short-term gains over long-term investments.[38] As a result, the very structure
of a business enterprise changed to reward fluidity over stability: "Stability
seemed a sign of weakness, suggesting to the market that the firm could not
innovate or find new opportunities or otherwise manage change . . . Now the
willingness to destabilize one's own organization sent a positive signal."[39]
Eventually, this mentality started seeping into realms that exist at a remove
from the world of profit-making. The neoliberal self-attempts to mimic the
increasingly fluid nature of capital by striving to disrupt fixed identity categories and achieve a state where no obstacles exist to an uninterrupted fluidity.
A successful brand—which, within this worldview, is what an individual
should always attempt to become—needs to be ready for constant mutation.
After all, as branding experts remind us, the most important thing one needs
to know to be successful at marketing is that "it's all fluid."[40] The neoliberal
entrepreneurs of the self cannot afford to ignore these marketing principles
as they construct their sense of self and its relationship with the world and
with others.

As Laurence Minsky and Ilan Geva put it in their book on global brand
management, "brands need to become active, not reactive, ahead of the
changes to succeed and survive. Organizations need to make the brand a
center of gravity and be prepared for an ever-shifting reality."[41] The belief in
the value of constant mutation has become an organizing idea in the world of
business. "In order to survive, successful brands have to adapt or die," asserts
Michael Hodgson, a designer and a branding expert, in a chapter titled "The
Only Constant: Change" of his book on the use of brand logos in marketing.[42]
The more human beings conceive of themselves as business enterprises in
need of a careful administration—even if they do not use these exact terms
to describe their sense of self—the more likely they are to see a boundless
capacity to embrace change as an aspirational goal. Human beings are not
corporations, though, and constant shape-shifting comes at a large personal
cost. The marketization of the self and its mode of relating to others turns
everybody into a "lonely, self-concerned and self-centered shopper who has
adopted the search for the best bargain as a cure for loneliness . . . a character for whom the swarm of shopping mall customers is the sole community
known and needed."[43]

The adoption of the neoliberal mentality that defines an individual as
an enterprise leads to a degradation of the concepts of the social and the
political. Once human beings begin to see themselves and others as objects
of consumption that are subjected to the laws of supply and demand, product
optimization, and brand-building, the nature of human relations changes,

privileging exploitation over a search for a genuine, nonutilitarian under-standing of each other. A long-term engagement with the polity and the com-munity gives way to striving for instant gratification. Sociability is emptied of much of it meaning by the rise of the 'antisocial social media' that have "fostered the deterioration of democratic and intellectual culture around the world."[44] The lure of instant popularity peddled by social media platforms reinforces the tendency to see other human beings in consumerist terms: "The fading of sociality skills is boosted and accelerated by the tendency, inspired by the dominant consumerist life mode, to treat other humans as objects of consumption and to judge them after the pattern of consumer objects by the volume of pleasure they are likely to offer."[45] If we approach this mode of sociality from a feminist perspective, it becomes clear that the consumeriza-tion of human relations reinforces the traditional objectification of women.[46] Alongside the incontestable advances achieved by the third and the fourth waves of feminist activism, the "pervasive consumerization of everyday life, near-total commodification of culture, information society, loss of mean-ing and identities, decaying community life, withering of the lifeworld, and expanding conformist culture" that accompany globalization are creating a set of challenges that will require a significant readjustment in terms of femi-nist discourse.[47]

As Hester Eisenstein points out, "the contemporary women's movement facilitated the growth and spread of corporate globalization" in ways that are often missed in celebratory accounts of today's feminism.[48] Twenty-first-century feminism, especially the variety originating in the English-speaking world, is "readily transnationalized, that is rendered transnational culture, because it is a fundamentally mediated and commodified discourse and set of material practices."[49] It is accessible to the cohort that Simidele Dosekun terms "globally 'scattered' feminine subjects who have the material, discur-sive, and imaginative capital to access and to buy into it."[50] This strain of fem-inism, however, is frequently out of bounds for those who lack such capital. Intersectional feminist scholars should be wary of the many ways in which the rhetoric of feminist liberation is co-opted to advance the interests of the social class that is most comfortable with the advances of neoliberalism.

As John Patrick Leary says in his dictionary of late-capitalist newspeak, neoliberalism is the word people often use "to name everything bad about the contemporary world."[51] In a similar way, frequent references to neolib-eral feminism express a dissatisfaction with the ways in which the corporate world is exploiting a newfound affinity with feminist vocabulary and with some of the goals of women's rights movements. As Michaele Ferguson reminds us, however, 'neoliberal feminism' is not a term that any group of feminists has claimed for itself but, rather, is the sort of terminology that is used to signal a distance from a phenomenon one does not support: "Since we have not witnessed a self-described neoliberal feminist manifesto, or a group self-designated as neoliberal feminist, scholars must necessarily engage in interpretive analysis when they claim that a set of cultural and political phenomena are evidence of something they call neoliberal feminism."[52] As a result, a strain of critical theory has appeared that presents neoliberal feminism "as an uncanny impostor, the product of neoliberalism's cynical cooptation of true feminism [and] feminists as passive and helpless in the face of the seemingly irresistible and omnipotent force of neoliberalism."[53] The reality is far more complex, however. In recent decades, some of the most powerful market actors on the global arena have adopted the feminist rhetoric of fighting against sexism, promoting women's financial independence, and alleviating female poverty.[54] Their actions are not destroying worldwide structures of gender oppression—nor can anybody genuinely expect corporations to strive toward that goal—yet it is undeniable that many women benefit from these initiatives.

The *rapprochement* between the corporate world and feminism has not been one-directional. The changes that this development has brought to feminism can be summarized as follows: "(a) the co-optation of feminism into neoliberal economic projects, (b) the integration of feminism into neoliberal ideology, and (c) the interweaving of feminist ideas into rationalities and technologies of neoliberal governmentality."[55] A fruitful critique of these developments consists not in an outright denial of their capacity to advance the interests of *some* or even *many* women but in an application of an intersectional lens that demonstrates the class- and race-based limitations of this form of female advancement. Neoliberal globalization undermines female solidarity by granting extraordinary possibilities of advancement to certain cohorts of women at the expense of other female groups. This gap is particularly evident in the way in which we look at transnational developments.

The deterritorialized supranational elites that have arisen through the readjustment of planet-wide class structures as a result of globalization often rely on the concept of cosmopolitanism to lend an aura of glamor to their abandonment of local, territorially bound allegiances. The embrace of cosmopolitanism by the more privileged cohort of feminist thinkers has given rise to a widespread discontent on the part of the feminists who question the often Orientalizing and neoimperialist aspects of this phenomenon. Caren Kaplan, for instance, offered the following definition of cosmopolitan feminism:

> In certain globalized feminist discourses . . . a kind of cosmopolitanism is generated that produces and recuperates forms of orientalism, old and new. Cosmopolitanism, with its promise of freedom to move about the world and its interest in the mixture of difference, calls out to many feminists in the present moment . . . That travel is never innocent, however, is not acknowledged fully in

cosmopolitanism. Feminist travel enacts its own imperialisms often in the name of personal or gender liberation.[56]

Intersectionality can be of invaluable help in creating a degree of critical distance between feminist thought and an unqualified embrace of cosmopolitanism. Approaching the discussion of the liberating aspects of moving freely around the globe from the vantage point of social class makes it clear that "liberated subjects [who] travel in the differentiated spaces of the global economy" belong to a specific social stratum that has much to gain from equating feminist liberation with unfettered global travel.[57] At the same time, even the women who possess the resources that enable them to access the kind of feminist vindication that comes with cosmopolitan globe-trotting are not exempt from paying a heavy price exacted by neoliberal fluidity. Solidarity is undermined by the rise of "the new forms of sociality [that privilege] a growing network of contacts among fragile subjects, dense but tenuous nodes connected with the help of elaborate technological tools."[58] Loneliness, isolation, and the loss of many meaningful forms of community constitute some of the costs of an alliance between feminism and neoliberal globalization.

Feminists' increasing reliance on the libertarian and free-marketeer vocabulary of the primacy of individual choice is one of the most notable consequences of this alliance. It has inspired much of the celebratory feminism of the 1990s "that hailed young women in particular as free and confident agents with supposedly infinite choice" and that saw the neoliberal rhetoric of choice as potentially liberating.[59,60] Neoliberalism positions an individual not as a coherent whole but as a collection of interchangeable components that can be swapped in and out at will to maximize the individual's functioning in a constantly changing economy. The idea that a trajectory of a human life is a series of freely pursued, unmediated individual choices lies at the core of the neoliberal mentality: "The very concept of the good life has been taken apart, broken down into a succession of isolated preferences. The underlying idea is that both our personal identities and our societies lack a stable structure—and that this is a good thing."[61] Seeing each human being as a product only of his or her own rational, informed choices negates every individual's rootedness in his or her material circumstances. Ultimately, the neoliberal philosophy of 'choice' undermines any possibility of a meaningful feminist action. All that remains of feminism is the capacity of a handful of women to enrich themselves in the neoliberal economy by making the correct individual choices.[62]

What is particularly curious about the fast spread of the neoliberal mentality is that there is no longer any area of life that exists at too great a remove from the world of economics to avoid being infected by this *Weltanschauung*:

Unlike previous iterations of *homo economicus* in which an economic rationality was brought to bear only on situations with possible economic outcomes, the
neoliberal subject is entrepreneurial in most spheres of life, taking on activities
seemingly divorced from economic transactions as modes of enterprise . . .
The successful neoliberal individual therefore mirrors the successful corporation by being capable of consistent growth, effective competition, and flexible
adaptation.[63]

The flexible adaptation that neoliberalism requires of individuals is, of
course, heavily gendered and racialized. It privileges those who are unbur-
dened by the need to care for others and can obtain access to the often-costly
resources that facilitate professional, geographic, and other kinds of mobility.
These resources can include professional (re)training, psychotherapy to coun-
teract the detrimental effects of constant change, the financial wherewithal to
maintain family links in spite of geographic displacement, and the capacity to
secure an easy, safe, and legal crossing of national borders in pursuit of better
professional opportunities or leisurely travel.

In the words of Arlene Dávila, "strategies of flexibility through mobility
across nation-states favor those with resources and capital."[64] The geographic
mobility of the elite strata of workers in the financial, creative, and knowledge industries differs vastly from that of the agricultural migrant workers,
women in the reproductive and sex industries, low-wage service sector
employees, or climate and war refugees. In many cases, the forced displacement of the latter facilitates the easy and enjoyable mobility of the former.
What the two groups share, however, is an increased rootlessness which—
whether perceived by the workers themselves as pleasurable or tragic—is a
result of the capital's need for an ever-increasing speed of movement that
encounters no boundaries. Even the global economic crisis of 2008–2009, a
development which shook the foundations of the neoliberal consensus of the
preceding three decades, proved unable to place any limits on the capital's
demand for ever-increasing mobility: "The preference for mobility has not
waned; neoliberalizing projects still thrive on the notion that the more fleeting
and mobile the capital or the group, the more value it should be given and
the more incentives created to protect it. The result is hierarchies of mobili-
ties."[65] The increasing hierarchization of individuals on the basis of their
capacity comfortably to inhabit the world of fluidity thwarts social mobility.
Moving across boundaries of class proves more and more difficult as inequality reaches staggering numbers.[66] A truly intersectional view of the causes of
inequality cannot avoid taking into consideration issues of social class and
economic dispossession within the global economy.

There is no reason to believe that the world of academia would prove
immune to the lure of participating in the articulation and dissemination of a

set of ideas that benefit capital. In the early years of the twenty-first century, the readiness of academics in developed countries to embrace the idea that 'it is all fluid' became clearly visible. The dismantling of any obstacles that nation-states can still place in the way of the rapid movement of capital has become crucial to capital's never-ending search for expansion. As Bauman points out, "we are witnessing the revenge of nomadism over the principle of territoriality and settlement. In the fluid stage of modernity, the settled majority is ruled by the nomadic and exterritorial elite. Keeping the roads free for nomadic traffic and phasing out the remaining check-points has become the meta-purpose of politics."[67] Given the reluctance of US academia to notice transnationalism's utility to global capitalism, one has to wonder if this has become, in many cases, the meta-purpose of a significant part of scholarship, as well.

Academics do not belong to the same social stratum as financial elites, yet our existence is, by its nature, nomadic both in geographic and intellectual terms. While often underprivileged economically (especially in the case of the growing cohort of contingent workers in academia), we are part of a transnational community of scholars and often rely on globally dispersed networks of professional, affective, and relational support. Hence, academics are well positioned to be less sensitive to the drawbacks of deterritorialization and geographic fluidity than to their advantages. At the same time, the Humanities, a field of study to which the contributors to this volume belong, is particularly embattled in the increasingly corporate world of academia.[68] The belief that we have much to gain and little to lose from embracing the deterritorializing aspects of neoliberal fluidity might have inspired at the least some of the willingness to occupy a conciliatory position toward these phenomena.

In *Feminism Without Borders*, Chandra Mohanty suggests that, in the world of the increasingly mobile capital, "our minds must be as ready to move as capital is, to trace its paths and to imagine alternative destinations."[69] Mohanty's words perfectly encapsulate the demands that neoliberalism places on human beings. In order to be successful in the global economy where capital moves at a lightning speed, individuals must be prepared to abandon any form of attachment to a particular territory, identity, set of beliefs, or a way of being in the world in order to accommodate "capital's need to have access to a rootless labor force that is ready to sever all attachments and move anywhere at a short notice in search of increasingly precarious employment."[70] The chasm between those who have the economic, cultural, social, linguistic, and so on capital needed to at least attempt mimicking the rapid movement of financial flows in the global economy—be it in a physical way through immigration or intellectually, in the manner proposed by Mohanty—and those who lack such capital cannot fail to increase the already staggering levels of inequality.

A truly intersectional analysis is only possible if we keep in mind that the costs exacted by the need constantly to "be as ready to move as capital is" differ, depending on a multitude of factors, with race and gender being among the most prominent.[71] As Mallika Dutt points out, "for women of color/immigrant women/Third World women, it is necessary to engage with culture in a multi-dimensional way such that we simultaneously acknowledge its liberating and oppressive aspects."[72] As we celebrate the liberating potential of such aspects of the neoliberal culture as social media, transnationalism, and the disturbance of fixed identity categories, we need to be careful to avoid losing sight of their oppressive aspects. Strategies of surveillance through social media; the undermining of the welfare protections that a weakened nation-state can offer; and the high psychological, emotional, social, and economic costs of mutability are some of the negative factors that we have to consider in a discussion of transnationalism.

At the same time, we have to avoid slipping into a facile condemnation of those who use familiar attachments to stable identity categories to shield themselves from the often devastating effects of the rapid movement of capital. For instance, immigrants often resist the calls to maximize their value on the global labor market by erasing any allegiance to the nation of their origin. It is precisely the strength of their national attachments that for many immigrants, especially those most lacking in educational and cultural capital, provides an "'identity reservoir' one cannot be stripped of, whatever the difficulty one may face in the country of settlement."[73] Moreover, in the face of traumatic ruptures that migration entails for all but the deterritorialized elites, "one's persistent national identity is the basis for personal consistency."[74] The capacity painlessly to relinquish one's attachment to an imagined community of a nation is a by-product of significant privilege.

The belief in the importance of constantly engaging in feats of intellectual, emotional, psychological, and professional agility has permeated every sphere of life in the neoliberal societies of the present day. In his analysis of the link between the rising rates of depression in developed countries and the ubiquitous nature of the belief in the merits of fluidity, sociologist Alain Ehrenberg describes this phenomenon as follows:

> In all areas—be they working life, family, or school—the world was changing its rules. Gone were mechanical obedience, discipline, and moral conformity; they had shifted to flexibility, change, quickness of reaction, and so on. Self-control, flexibility of mind and feeling, and the capacity for action meant that each individual had to be up to the task of constantly adapting to a changing world that was losing its stable shape, becoming temporary, consisting of ebb and flow, something like a snakes-and-ladders game. The social and political game was not so easy to read any more. These institutional transformations

made it seem as if each person, even the humblest and the lowest of the lot, had to take on the job of *choosing* and *deciding* everything.[75]

What this fantasy of an all-powerful individual who can overcome every obstacle through will and ingenuity conceals is the collapse of welfare institutions. These institutions came into existence with the consolidation of the nation-state model and have been withering away as fluid capital renders nations less relevant. At the close of the twentieth century, Mallika Dutt resumed this process as follows: "Emphasis on the 'market' as the answer to all economic problems, in conjunction to unfettered capital mobility, has led to the growing power of transnational corporations and a corresponding decline in the role of the state."[76] The watershed moment in these developments arrived with the signing of NAFTA and General Agreement on Tariffs and Trade which "further consolidated the power of transnational corporations and eviscerated state sovereignty."[77]

In the twenty years that have passed since the writing of Dutt's essay, these trends have become even more pronounced and have galvanized, in different parts of the world, a variety of ultranationalist movements that are capturing the discontent arising from the weakening of the nation-state model of governance by global capital. In a 2004 article titled "Transnationalism in Question," Waldinger and Fitzgerald speak to the pitfalls of an unthinking celebration of transnationalism that has characterized much—if not most—of the scholarly treatment of the subject:

> Unfortunately, the scholars of immigrant transnationalism have been too fond of the phenomenon they study to notice [its] unpleasant aspects. Were it otherwise, they would surely not have veered so far toward celebrating the phenomenon they purported to analyze, depicting transnationalism as subversive and transnationals as grassroots actors challenging the hegemony of states and global capitalism "from below."[78]

There is little reason to believe that global capital could be undermined or threatened by a phenomenon it provoked in its efforts to dismantle state controls on the movement of capital and labor. The permeability of borders—for capital as well as the labor force that it is convenient for capital to displace at any given moment—is subversive only inasmuch as anything that advances the goals of neoliberal capitalism can be.

As Hans Lauge Hansen reminds us, an embrace of cosmopolitanism, globalization, and contiguous phenomena is a defensive strategy stumbled upon by the global Left, demoralized by the collapse of the Soviet-inspired alternatives to neoliberal capitalism:[79] "Cosmopolitanism can be understood as a political strategy of the left that has been paralyzed by the neoliberal hegemony and globalizing discourses. Instead of insisting on changing the system and collective values, it limited itself to the defense of human rights within the framework of the institutions of the parliamentary democracies of the West."[80] Of course, these institutions also weaken under the assault of the flows of global capital, so even this limited sphere of activity gradually loses its relevance.

Another crucial factor that we need to take into consideration is that the explosive success of the far-right, ultranationalist movements around the globe is, in itself, part of the transnational undermining of national sovereignty:

> Those reactions fully belong to the phenomenon, to be ignored only at the price of implicating oneself in a subject of which one should uniquely be a student. By limiting the transnational field of study to the generally pacific activities of groups whose cause may appear noble or innocuous, scholars obscure the conditions that foster or limit the full range of long-distance nationalisms in both receiving and sending contexts.[81]

By concentrating on the positive effects of transnationalism, we run the danger of seeing the rise of such far-right groups as a pathology instead of an integral part of the dismantlement of the nation-state model of governance and, just as importantly, of the devaluation of national attachments. Recognizing that such movements fully belong to the transnational moment does not constitute an endorsement of their odious beliefs. To the contrary, a meaningful program of counteracting such movements can be articulated only through an exhaustive analysis of the conditions that bring them into existence.

In many ways, the celebration of transnationalism in academic circles is a result of a dissatisfaction with the frequent failure of the nation-state model of governmentality to accommodate the demands of marginalized minorities. Speaking about the overlap between the struggles for national liberation and the fight for gender equality in many second- and third-world nations, Ella Shohat correctly observes that "the decolonization of the nation has not led to the decolonization of heterosexual women and gays and lesbians from patriarchy and homophobia."[82] National liberation has not resulted in an improvement in the position of women in the newly independent states of the global South or the nations formed more recently after the collapse of the USSR. To the contrary, marginalized communities of women, ethnic and racial groups, and sexual minorities have, more often than not, seen their demands cast as a threat to the unity of the nation in the nationalistic discourses that agglutinate the 'imagined community' of the nation.[83] The disillusionment with nationalism's capacity to accommodate the demands of these marginalized groups has often led their members to look sympathetically at the globalizing processes that weaken nation-states.[84]

There also exists a belief that the oversized presence of the United States at the epicenter of scholarship can be diminished through embracing a transnational approach. It is for this reason that the term 'transnational' is sometimes used to refer to a search for a non-US-centric lens of critical analysis. The importance of finding an approach that does not privilege a viewpoint centered on the United States and is not inspired by US-based interests and concerns cannot be overstated. In particular, the field of Hispanic Studies should not perpetuate a situation where the neoimperialist adventures of the United States in the Spanish-speaking world are recreated on the level of scholarship. It has long become clear, however, that "discarding the nation-state as a unit of analysis does not automatically dislodge a US-centric epistemic approach."[85] This is not surprising, given that the United States has been the primary exporter of neoliberal theory and praxis to regions around the world since the 1970s. Latin America, in particular, "served as a laboratory in which the neoliberal system had gestated" as the United States put in place—or attempted to do so—neoliberal regimes throughout the countries of South and Central America.[86] There is no reason to assume that neoliberalism, and the transnational push that it inspires, would be in any significant way hostile to the geopolitical and economic interests of the United States.

One of the effects of the deprivileging of the nation-state as a useful epistemological category has been "the emergence and expansion of interdisciplinary fields of study within the academy [which] have produced a move away from older approaches to international studies that used the nation-state as a foundational analytical and political lens."[87] In recent years, Western academia has seen a dramatic rise in inter- or multidisciplinary programs of study, projects, and initiatives. Their defenders position these programs as more congruent with the spirit of the times than the academic programs that arose when the nation-state model of governmentality was gaining strength: "Like national borders, disciplinary borders too are out of synch with . . . transnational movements" understood as "the worldwide movements and dislocations of people associated with the development of 'global' or 'transnational' capitalism."[88] This interdisciplinary turn in academia, however, is often used as a mechanism of neoliberal austerity. In the two decades that passed since the writing of Shohat's text, the increasingly corporatist structure of the Western higher education systems has attempted to replicate, within the academy, globalization's erasure of national borders. Appeals to the need for interdisciplinary studies in academia often serve as a justification for diverting funds toward "individual cross-disciplinary hires who serve an 'umbrella' function by bridging two or more disciplines and thus performing work previously assigned to two or three faculty."[89] In the field of Hispanic

Studies, efforts to "reevaluate language as something other than a purely national construct tied to a rooted national identity" have placed no barriers to reductions in tenure lines, an ever-shrinking job market, or a cratering of an already limited number of funding opportunities for research.[90] Given that academic departments dedicated to the study of national literature came into existence with the rise of the nation-state, there is no reason to assume they will not cease to exist altogether once the disempowerment of the nation-state is complete.[91]

In the realm of modern language departments across North America, the interdisciplinary turn within academia is often used to justify job searches that require expertise in different fields and a capacity to teach two or even more languages.[92] The emergence of "border studies" as an academic specialization is also in line with the turn away from the nation-state as the basic category of organizing academic units within university.[93] We have to ask ourselves, however, to what extent the emerging model of weakening or even shutting down programs organized according to the national literatures model (Spanish Studies, French Studies, German Studies, etc.) and substituting them with a collection of "ethnic studies tracks" within larger English departments is beneficial to our disciplines. At the same time, an increasing focus on border-crossing as not only an area of scholarly interest but an academic track or program is sometimes used to funnel resources, tenure-track positions, and funding away from Hispanic (or Spanish) Studies departments. If the focus of scholarly attention shifts toward border-crossing as the most interesting issue about Hispanic communities, we run the risk of creating a vision of the Spanish-speaking world as offering little of value outside of its encounters with the United States. Instead of offering a larger space within academia to non-US cultures and to the discourses arising from the concerns that are specific to them, 'the transnationalist turn' has normalized a worldview that serves US-centric interests and justifies austerity.

Throughout the 1990s and early 2000s, feminist scholarship in the United States and Western Europe has been largely inclined to view transnationalism in positive terms. There are, of course, objective reasons that push feminist scholars toward embracing a transnational approach. As Shohat points out, "the global nature of the colonizing process, the global flow of transnational capital, and the global reach of contemporary communications technologies virtually oblige the multicultural feminist critic to go beyond the restrictive framework of the nation-state as a unit for analysis."[94] The welcoming approach to the border-erasing effects of the globalization and to the weakening of the nation-state model of governance that has characterized the early stage of transnational feminism often fails to take into account the experiences of the marginalized groups that are most heavily impacted by the displacements effectuated by the rapid movement of global capital.[95] As Ranjoo

Sedou Herr reminds us, the negative effects of the neoliberal globalization accrue, first and foremost, to the women of the underdeveloped societies.[96] Other than the barriers that nation-states can still place in the way of global capital, there seem to be no real obstacles to the continued battering of the most disadvantaged by the constantly changing needs of global capitalism: "Nationalism may have a positive role to play in this struggle; if Third World governments, backed up by their people, were to effectively resist economic incursions of worldwide 'neoliberalism,' then perhaps hardships suffered by Third World women due to economic globalization could be alleviated, if not prevented."[97] Nation-states are vastly imperfect, yet globalization adopts all of their imperfections while adding many that are uniquely its own.

Transnational feminism has sometimes fallen into the trap of serving as "global capitalism's fellow traveler."[98] There is a clear need to address the limitations of the transnationalist approach to feminism in a way that would question the neoliberal emphasis on individual freedom and consumer choice as the central aspirational goals of feminist activism. Our volume seeks to fill this gap by adopting the intersectional approach based on recognizing "the interactions of multiple power structures (including race, sexuality, class, and ability)" to create structures of oppressions.[99] Contributions to the volume analyze a variety of artistic genres and modes of feminist expression and include work by female—and feminist—scholars at different stages of their academic journey. We believe that the somewhat uneven structure of the contributions is a small price to pay for creating a volume that is inclusive of not only established Hispanists but also budding feminist scholars in our discipline. The editors made no special effort to select only female authors for this volume but neither did we resist this possibility once it became clear that all of the submitted pieces were authored by women. We have dedicated the first part of the volume to the chapters that study prose (essay, novel, and short story), the second to television and film, and the third to visual and performing arts.

The first chapter in the book discusses Gloria Anzaldúa's *Borderlands/La Frontera: The New Mestiza* (1987), which has long become a canonical text for those who are interested in studying the concepts of transborder liminality and migrant identity formation. In her chapter "Border Trouble: Anzaldúa's Margins" Leslie Bary discusses the ways in which Anzaldúa's vision of liminality has been reified and idealized in critical discourse. The popularity of Anzaldúa's book among scholars has led to the emergence of critical texts that do not take into account the geographical and temporal situatedness of Anzaldúa's thinking. Borderlands are in vogue, and there is a premium on applying the terminology inspired by Anzaldúa to a variety of subjects, texts, and artifacts without a deep engagement with the thinker's ideas. Bary's chapter offers a more nuanced reading of Anzaldúa that gives justice to this crucial feminist thinker of the late twentieth century while reminding us of the need to engage with Anzaldúa's work on a deeper level. There are many as yet untapped depths in Anzaldúa's work, and Bary's analysis invites us to explore them.

Sowmya Ramanathan's chapter titled "Tuning In: Intimacy and Networks in Diamela Eltit's *Fuerzas especiales*" discusses a novel by a leading Chilean writer that concentrates on the experiences of those who have been discarded by the neoliberal economy and pushed into spaces that are "dumping grounds for the misformed and deformed products of fluid modern society."[100] Eltit's novel traces the ways in which cyber-space creates an illusion that endless self-optimization can help all individuals prove their usefulness to neoliberal economy. While cybernetworks flatten relationships and empty human identities of their contextual meanings, networks of digitally unmediated human affect and experience have a subversive potential that can inform resistance to neoliberal practices. Ramanathan's analysis exists in the intersections between gender and social class, illuminating the relationship between economic and gender-based marginalizations.

"Transculturation and the Body: Edwidge Danticat and Judith Ortiz Cofer" by Raysa E. Amador analyzes short stories by two immigrant writers whose artistic production mimics the characteristics of a transnational space to explore the costs and the complexities of immigrant displacement. Edwidge Danticat was born in Haiti but left the country to join her immigrant parents in New York in early adolescence. Danticat's success as an English-language writer in the United States led Izabella Penier to refer to the author as "a spokesperson for the one million Haitians living in exile in the United States."[101] Danticat herself, of course, never claimed the title of a spokesperson for other Haitians. She writes in English and was educated at some of the most elite institutions of higher learning,[102] which necessarily sets the writer apart from many other Haitian émigrés. Still, Danticat's work is crucial in that it is written in "a new language: that of the newly exiled Caribbean subject in the era of globalization."[103] The critics' insistent use of the word 'exile' in reference to an immigrant (and not, in any meaningful sense of the word, an exile) like Danticat demonstrates that the work the writer does to bring to light the complexities of immigrant experience is of crucial importance. Judith Ortiz Cofer, the second writer whose work Amador discusses in her chapter, is a Puerto Rican who had left Puerto Rico for the conterminous United States at an even younger age than Danticat. Like Danticat, Ortiz Cofer created works of literature that exist in the intersection of a female and a migratory perspective. As Amador demonstrates in her analysis, Ortiz Cofer pays particular attention to the depiction of her characters' bodies because the body gives some sense of an anchoring to individuals who are severed from their countries, families, and communities.

Barbara Minter's chapter "'Postfeminist Supergirl' Turned Superspy: Crossing Borders and New Identities in *El tiempo entre costuras*" analyzes a Spanish television series based on a best-selling novel by author María Dueñas that has enjoyed an enormous popularity in Spain and overseas. Not only is a novel itself a transnational publishing phenomenon but the TV series based on it exalts border-crossing as a way of overcoming gender-based oppression even in the context of the Spanish Civil War and the early stages of the Franco regime in Spain. The popularity of both the novel and the TV series points to the attractiveness of a certain vision of female 'empowerment' to large audiences, one which can be projected onto the past and explored safely in the context of events long gone. Sira Quiroga, the protagonist of the series, easily crosses borders not only between states but also between gender roles and professions as she successfully performs her duties as both a seamstress and an international spy. The series' popularity with the viewers brought Antena 3, the channel that produced the series, its greatest success in twelve years.[104] The "transnational masquerade at once implausible and seductive" that lies at the heart of the series allows the viewers to explore the anxieties generated by the increasing transnationalization of existence today in a safe and contained space of a glamorous TV series.[105] The 'supergirl' characteristics of Sira—whose name is appropriately reminiscent of the all-knowing and always helpful Siri, the virtual assistant of Apple's smart devices—create a vision of a flawless femininity that characterizes the female "achievement-subjects" who give themselves over to "*compulsive freedom*[106]—that is, to the *free constraint* of maximizing achievement."[107] *El tiempo entre costuras*, thus, offers ample opportunities to analyze intersections between gender, culture, and national belonging in Spanish television.

In her chapter titled "Lucrecia Martel's Salta Trilogy: A (Trans)National Bildungsroman of Female Sexuality," Java Singh analyzes a film trilogy by a leading Argentinean film director Lucrecia Martel. Singh's focus is on the degree to which it is possible to create artistic narratives that will highlight transnationally recognizable concerns without erasing local issues and regional histories. This is a crucial question that has to be asked whenever we attempt to approach the transnational. The cultural, financial, and technological hegemony of the Western Anglophone world easily exports its concerns and positions them as globally relevant, often leaving little space for the issues that are indigenous to cultures that lack such dominance. The financial and intellectual elites of nonhegemonic cultures who benefit from neoliberal globalization adopt the idiosyncrasies of the Anglophone trendsetters as a marker of privileged class belonging. Singh's analysis of Martel's Salta trilogy highlights the conflict between the interests of such an elite and the concerns of those who, by nature of their impoverishment and racial identity, do not benefit from globalization. Singh demonstrates that it is the feminist and anticapitalist thrust of Martel's films that makes them relevant to audiences outside of Argentina.

"Reimagining the *Borderlands:* Intersectionality and Transnational Queering of Laura Aguilar's Self-Portrait *Three Eagles Flying*" by Rosita Scerbo discusses a self-portrait titled *Three Eagles Flying* by Laura Aguilar, a feminist Chicana photographer. Aguilar's visual art is particularly relevant to our volume in that it brings to the fore the complex relationships between different kinds of marginalized identities. At the same time, Scerbo's use of Anzaldúa's idea of Borderlands demonstrates how this complex concept, studied at length in the first chapter of our volume, can be of use in approaching Laura Aguilar's art. As she traces the evolution of the concept of intersectionality throughout the work of different generations of feminist scholars, Scerbo demonstrates that it is still eminently useful for discussing the work of contemporary artists who work on the crossroads between different identities.

María Alejandra Zanetta discusses the work of Maruja Mallo, one of the leading painters of the Spanish avant-garde. As many Spanish artists, Mallo was forced into exile during the Spanish Civil War. Her travels in South America brought the painter into contact with Candomblé, a syncretic religion practiced in Brazil and Uruguay that integrates a variety of elements derived from African cultures. Mallo's Candomblé-inspired art seeks to find a way to transcend patriarchal limitations. Zanetta's chapter is titled "The Transformative Experience of the New Continent in Maruja Mallo's Art" and it explores the ways in which the artist's work was impacted by her encounter with the spiritual richness of the Americas. The transnational experience of her forced exile strengthened Mallo's interest in the vision of human identity as essentially fluid. Mallo created her artwork before the concept of fluidity was appropriated by neoliberal capitalism, and Zanetta's analysis of the painter's artistic trajectory offers an enlightening glimpse into the history of the twentieth-century transnationalism and fluidity.

Candomblé—and the possibilities it offers for art and activism—lies at the heart of the chapter titled "Technologies of Affective Solidarity: Salvador, Brazil's Ani Ganzala and Zinha Franco" by Naomi Pueo Wood. The legacy of Candomblé-inspired artistic practices has been of great use to Brazilian artists and activists Zinha Franco and Ani Ganzala who are developing ways for black female artists to connect and support each other. Franco and Ganzala oppose neoliberal competitiveness and foster communities of care among female artivists. Wood's chapter explores the challenges faced by female, black, and queer artists who exist at the intersection of gender, race, and sexuality and who create technologies of survival that arise from the history of their communities.

In the creation of our book, we have been wary of "the dangers of producing US-centered conceptions of the transnational."[108] To obviate this danger, we have included in our book authors who are immigrants to the United States as well as authors who reside abroad. All of the scholars who have contributed to the book belong to a marginalized and rapidly shrinking field of study that is dedicated to analyzing the cultural production of the Hispanic world. In our work on this boo, we have proceeded from the belief that intersectionality is a useful term that enriches feminist analysis. Paying attention to the intersectional proves indispensable to a discussion of the ways in which feminist vindication is put in question by the neoliberal exaltation of constant movement and boundless fluidity.

Recent years have seen many debates over the degree to which the concept of intersectionality continues to be useful. We believe, however, that the drive constantly to dethrone categories of analysis and find better or more precise ones can stem from the consumerist mentality that neoliberalism thrives on and that has come to dominate academia. As Brittney Cooper has argued,

> [the] need to displace intersectionality while claiming a desire to keep it intact in some greatly altered form is absolutely a function of market-driven, neoliberal forms of academic knowledge production and the sense that academics must always say something new. It is therefore bizarre when critics suggest that it is intersectionality itself, and not the impulses seeking to displace intersectional frames, that acts as a tool of neoliberal collusion, despite a continuing need for its political project within institutions.[109]

Of course, intersectionality will only continue to be useful as a category of truly feminist analysis if we prevent it from being claimed by the world of corporate branding that has already appropriated and emptied of meaningful content such terms as 'diverse' or 'multicultural.'[110] In the work on our volume, we have attempted to demonstrate the continued relevance of intersectionality and the ways in which it can inform critical approaches that are wary of neoliberal exploitation.

NOTES

1. Ryan A. Davis, *The Spanish Flu: Narrative and Cultural Identity in Spain, 1918* (New York: Palgrave Macmillan, 2013): 6–7.

2. "Provisional Death Counts for Coronavirus Disease (COVID-19)," National Center for Health Statistics, Centers for Disease Control and Prediction, Accessed on April 15, 2020. https://www.cdc.gov/nchs/nvss/vsrr/COVID19/index.htm

3. *Policy Brief: The Impact of COVID-19 on Women*, UN Women Headquarters, April 9, 2020, https://reliefweb.int/sites/reliefweb.int/files/resources/policy-brief-the-impact-of-covid-19-on-women-en.pdf, 13–14.

4. *Policy Brief*, 4.

5. Aletha Maybank, "Why Racial and Ethnic Data on COVID-19's Impact Is Badly Needed," American Medical Association, April 8, 2020, https://www.ama-assn.org/about/leadership/why-racial-and-ethnic-data-covid-19-s-impact-badly-needed

6. Gregorio Millett et al. "Assessing Differential Impacts of COVID-19 on Black Communities," *amfAR, Foundation for AIDS Research* Pre-print version, May 5, 2020, https://ehe.amfar.org/Assessing%20Differential%20Impacts%20of%20COVID-19%205-3-20_final.pdf

7. Matt Simon, "Africa's Huge Locust Swarms Are Growing at the Worst Time," *Wired* April 16, 2020, https://www.wired.com/story/africas-huge-locust-swarms-are-growing-at-the-worst-time/

8. Simon, Africa's Huge Locust Swarms.

9. Robin Cohen, "The Virus: Class Dimensions of Mobility and Immobility," *GRFDT: Global Research Forum on Diaspora and Transnationalism*, April 8, 2020, https://grfdt.com/Upload/Publication/10127_Virus%20Class.pdf, 5–6.

10. The phenomenon known as the "digitalization of the economy" has been defined as "a process of expansion and penetration of digital technologies into entire spheres of the economy of the post-industrial society during the past two decades" (Mikhailov and Kopylova 27).

11. Roger Eatwell's and Matthew Goodwin's 2018 volume *National Populism: The Revolt Against Liberal Democracy* offers an in-depth discussion of this process.

12. Serena Gordon, "Coronavirus Pandemic May Lead to 75,000 'Deaths of Despair' from Suicide, Drug and Alcohol Abuse, Study Says," *CBS News,* May 8, 2020, https://www.cbsnews.com/news/coronavirus-deaths-suicides-drugs-alcohol-pandemic-75000/

13. Wolfram Kawohl and Carlos Nordt, "COVID-19, Unemployment, and Suicide," *Lancet Psychiatry* 7 (May 2020), https://www.thelancet.com/action/showPdf?pii=S2215-0366%2820%2930141-3, 390.

14. Kawohl and Nordt, "COVID-19, Unemployment," 389.

15. Carlos R. Altuna Tezanos, "Haití: Acorralado entre hambruna y la pandemia," *Listín Diario: El periódico de los Dominicanos,* May 2, 2020, https://listindiario.com/las-mundiales/2020/05/02/615707/haiti-acorralado-entre-hambruna-y-la-pandemia

16. Eduardo Galeano, *Open Veins of Latin America: Five Centuries of the Pillage of a Continent*, trans. Cedric Belfrage, 25th ed. (New York: Monthly Review P, 1997): 20.

17. David Díaz Arias and Ronny Viales Hurtado, "Centroamérica: neoliberalismo y COVID-19," *Geopolítica(s), Revista de estudios sobre espacio y poder* 11 (2020): 57–58.

18. "Austeridad ya es un problema: líder de Morena," *Diario de Chiapas,* June 6 2020, https://diariodechiapas.com/portada/austeridad-ya-es-un-problema-lider-de-morena/127659

19. "La OMS hace un llamamiento para 'evitar la austeridad' y los recortes en sanidad tras la Crisis," *La Vanguardia,* May 28, 2020, https://www.lavanguardia.com

/vida/20200528/481435711802/oms-llamamiento-evitar-austeridad-recortes-sanidad -coronavirus.html

20. Philip Bobbitt, *The Shield of Achilles: War, Peace, and the Course of History* (New York: Anchor Books, 2003): 228.

21. César Rendueles, *Sociophobia: Political Change in the Digital Utopia*, trans. Heather Cleary. (New York: Columbia UP, 2013): 131.

22. Bobbitt, *The Shield of Achilles*, xxvii; Jürgen Habermas, *The Postnational Constellation: Political Essays*, ed. and trans. Max Pensky (Cambridge, MA: MIT Press, 2001): 61; César Molinas, *Qué hacer con España: del capitalismo castizo a la refundación de un país* (Barcelona: Destino, 2013): 115.

23. M. Kearney, "The Local and the Global: The Anthropology of Globalization and Transnationalism," *Annual Review of Anthropology* 24 (1995): 548.

24. As Roger Waldinger and David Fitzgerald pointed out in 2004, "with sympathizers, if not adherents, of the transnationalist view at the helm of three scholarly journals (Diaspora, Identities, and Global Networks); an international center on transnational communities based at Oxford University; and a legion of supportive books, articles, and dissertations pouring out across the social sciences, the transnationalist moment would seem to be now. One hesitates to be left standing in the station when the train is so obviously departing" (1181).

25. Brittney Cooper, "Intersectionality," In *The Oxford Handbook of Feminist Theory*, ed. Lisa Disch and Mary Hawkesworth (New York: Oxford UP, 2016): 396.

26. Leela Fernandes, *Transnational Feminism in the United States: Knowledge, Ethics, and Power* (New York and London: New York UP, 2013): 5.

27. Fernandes, *Transnational Feminism in the United States*, 144.

28. Zygmunt Bauman, *Liquid Modernity* (Cambridge: Polity, 2000): 57.

29. Bauman, *Liquid Modernity*, 13.

30. Benedict Anderson, *Imagined Communities: Reflections on the Origins and Spread of Nationalism* (London/New York: Verso, 2006, [1983]): 25.

31. Richard Sennett, *The Culture of New Capitalism* (New Haven & London: Yale UP, 2006): 18.

32. Olga Bezhanova, *Literature of Crisis: Spain's Engagement with Liquid Capital* (Lewisburg: Bucknell UP, 2017): xix, xxiv–xxvii.

33. Heidi I Hartmann, "The Unhappy Marriage of Marxism and Feminism: Towards a More Progressive Union," In *Women and Revolution: A Discussion of the Unhappy Marriage of Marxism and Feminism*, ed. L. Sargent (Boston: South End P, 1981): 45.

34. Neoliberalism is a complex term that critics continue to debate. However, there is a consensus that "the neoliberal model is predicated on a minimalist state—withdrawal of the state from the process of economic and social development and its replacement with the 'free market'" (Petras and Veltmeyer 2007: 241). The function of the state within this model is to facilitate the free movement of capital and exercise vigilance over the subjects who might constitute a destabilizing presence in a neoliberal society. As a result of the national governments' withdrawal from many of their regulatory functions, "the state increasingly shifts the responsibility it took up in early modernity of administering pastoral care to the state's population and shifting its care

to private corporations. Indeed, the state operates increasingly in their interests leaving individuals incredibly exposed to the vagaries of the market" (Ventura 2012: 16).

35. Jim McGuigan, *Neoliberal Culture* (London: Palgrave Macmillan, 2016): 131.

36. McGuigan, 129.

37. Byung-Chul Han, *The Burnout Society*, trans. by Erik Butler. (Stanford: Stanford UP, 2015. [2010]): 8.

38. Sennett, *The Culture of New Capitalism*, 37–40.

39. Sennett, *The Culture of New Capitalism*, 41.

40. Laurence Minsky and Ilan Geva, *Global Brand Management: A Guide on Development, Building and Managing an International Brand* (London/New York: Kogan Page, 2020): 167.

41. Minsky and Geva, *Global Brand Management*, 35.

42. Michael Hodgson, *Recycling and Redesigning Logos: A Designer's Guide to Refreshing and Rethinking Design* (Rockport: Quayside, 2010): 30.

43. Zygmunt Bauman, *Liquid Love* (Cambridge: Polity, 2003): 69.

44. Siva Vaidhyanathan, *Antisocial Media: How Facebook Disconnects Us and Undermines Democracy* (New York: Oxford UP, 2018): 3.

45. Bauman, *Liquid Love*, 75.

46. Although social media are often hailed as a vehicle of political activism and liberation, they are owned by enormously rich and powerful corporations that derive profit from the economic model known as "surveillance capitalism" (Zuboff 7). The admirers of the supposedly liberating potential of social media often forget that this potential is more easily reached by those who possess the educational, linguistic, and cultural capital needed to become the successful entrepreneurs of the self through collecting virtual connections and signs of approval and popularity on social media. This form of capitalist profit accumulation "operates through the unprecedented asymmetries in knowledge and the power that accrues to knowledge" (Zuboff 11). At the same time, the model of sociability offered by Facebook, Twitter, and Instagram is based on an illusion of togetherness sought out by the alienated neoliberal subjects who inhabit the imagined communities of social media apps. As César Rendueles remarks, "deep down, the social effervescence of digital media is inessential, decorative. It is useless at fostering what our shared existence should: taking care of one another" (25).

47. Su H. Lee, *Debating New Social Movements: Culture, Identity, and Social Fragmentation* (Lanham: UP of America, 2007): 23.

48. Hester Eisenstein, "A Dangerous Liaison? Feminism and Corporate Globalization," *Science & Society* 69, no. 3 (July 2005): 488.

49. Simidele Dosekun, "For Western Girls Only?" *Feminist Media Studies* 15, no. 6 (2015): 961.

50. Dosekun, "For Western Girls Only?" 966.

51. John Patrick Leary, *Keywords: The New Language of Capitalism* (Chicago: Haymarket Books, 2018): 13.

52. Michaele L. Ferguson, "Neoliberal Feminism as Political Ideology: Revitalizing the Study of Feminist Political Ideologies," *Journal of Political Ideologies* 22, no. 3 (2017): 223.

53. Ferguson, "Neoliberal Feminism as Political Ideology," 223.

54. Among the examples of pro-women initiatives undertaken by some of the most powerful market players Prügl lists "Goldman Sachs' 10,000 Women initiative, which partners with business schools around the world in order to bring business training to women entrepreneurs and help them scale up their operations; the World Economic Forum's Women Leaders and Gender Parity Program which seeks to make visible gender gaps in economic and political spheres, increase the number of women in decision-making, and provide a forum for discussing gender equality issues; the Nike Foundation's effort to popularise The Girl Effect . . . investing in girls' health and education" (616).

55. Elisabeth Prügl, "Neoliberalising Feminism," *New Political Economy* 20, no. 4 (2015): 617.

56. Caren Kaplan, "Hillary Rodham Clinton's Orient: Cosmopolitan Travel and Global Feminist Subjects," *Meridians: Feminism, Race, Transnationalism* 2, no. 1 (2001): 220.

57. Kaplan, "Hillary Rodham Clinton's Orient," 226.

58. Rendueles, *Sociophobia*, 23.

59. Stéphanie Genz and Benjamin A. Brabon. *Postfeminism: Cultural Texts and Theories.* 2nd ed. (Edinburgh UP, 2018): 8.

60. There are few issues that are more crucial to the feminist theory and praxis than a woman's right to control her reproductive system. Without this crucial capacity, no gender equality exists. At the same time, an unqualified support for reproductive rights need not entail an uncritical acceptance of the neoliberal rhetoric of 'choice' that has accompanied this struggle in societies with stronger neoliberal traditions. As Matthew Eagleton-Pierce has remarked, "at first glance, to focus on terms such as 'choice,' 'global' or 'investment' may appear slightly odd for such words are surely unremarkable objects of analysis. The neoliberal perspective given to each term lies alongside many other meanings, some of which will be comparatively neutral. Yet it is through such processes that the neoliberal vocabulary cultivates a form of power . . . The neoliberal spirit of capitalism is able to increase its attractiveness and complicate the strategies of its critics" (xviii).

61. Rendueles, *Sociophobia*, 113–14.

62. An example of this phenomenon is Oprah Winfrey who, throughout her long career, has consistently linked feminism and "individuals' right to pursue their self-interest without constraints" (Peck 41). Winfrey's popularity gave rise to the phenomenon of a successful female entrepreneur who uses her oversize presence in traditional and digital media to inform less successful women that their hardships stem from the subpar choices they make in administering their lives.

63. Rachel Smith Greenwald, *Affect and American Literature in the Age of Neoliberalism* (New York: Cambridge UP, 2015): 37.

64. Arlene Dávila, *Culture Works: Space, Value, and Mobility across the Neoliberal Americas* (New York & London: New York UP, 2012): 17.

65. Dávila, *Culture Works*, 16.

66. As Thomas Piketty notes in *Capital in the Twenty-First Century*, "since the 1970s, income inequality has increased significantly in the rich countries, especially

the United States . . . This process has generated deep anxiety in the emerging countries and even deeper anxiety in the rich countries" (15). The reason for this disparity in the intensity of antiglobalization feelings is that "the expansion of international trade, the mobility of capital and labor (notably for the most skilled), and the spread of technological innovation have partially bridged the gap between the wealthiest countries and the developing countries. But, at the same time, they have also contributed to a change in income distribution within these economies . . . The international mobility of top skills and the growth of global trade have meant that across the world the high end of the wage distribution falls in line with that of the countries where economic elites are the best compensated" (Bourguignon 3–4). In other words, the improvement in the standard of living of the transnational class of the highly mobile has come at the expense of the increasing poverty of those who lack such mobility. There is every incentive for this highly deterritorialized group to use its considerable cultural and intellectual capital to promote a positive view of globalizing processes.

67. Bauman, *Liquid Modernity*, 13.

68. As Charli Valdez demonstrates in her analysis of the state of the Humanities in the United States, since the neoliberalization of the US economy began in the 1970s, "the national decline in the humanities has been a commonly recognized and unchecked problem . . . Enrollments are off, funding is down, and tenure-line staffing has precipitously dropped" (193). Valdez's solution to this problem is to structure her teaching in a way that will "further disrupt [the students'] sense of nationalism" through an exploration of the "deterritorialized hyperspace" of social media (201) and an engagement with the experiences of transborder communities. Valdez's teaching strategies are both fascinating and highly useful, yet the question remains of whether the Humanities can truly be rescued by embracing such profoundly neoliberal phenomena as deterritorialization, social media, and border-crossing. Once we are fully "detached from the hegemony of national culture" (Valdez 201), it might prove harder than we currently expect to defend the continued existence of academic programs in 'national languages and cultures' to which the contributors to this volume belong and that constitute a significant part of the current degree offerings in the Humanities.

69. Chandra Tolpade Mohanty, *Feminism without Borders: Decolonizing Theory, Practicing Solidarity* (Durham & London: Duke UP, 2003): 251.

70. Bezhanova, *Literature of Crisis*, xxiii.

71. Mohanty, *Feminism without Borders*, 251.

72. Mallika Dutt, "Reclaiming a Human Rights Culture: Feminism of Difference and Alliance," In *Talking Visions: Multicultural Feminism in a Transnational Age*, ed. Ella Shohat (New York: MIT Press, 1998): 232.

73. Paolo Boccagni, "Private, Public or Both? On the Scope and Impact of Transnationalism in Immigrants' Everyday Lives," In *Diaspora and Transnationalism: Concepts, Theories and Methods*, ed. Rainer Bauböck and Thomas Faist (Amsterdam: Amsterdam UP, 2010): 189.

74. Boccagni, "Private, Public or Both?" 189.

75. Alain Ehrenberg, *The Weariness of the Self: Diagnosing the History of Depression in the Contemporary Age*, trans. by Enrico Caouette, Jacob Homel,

David Homel, and Don Winkler (Montreal & Kingston: McGill-Queen's UP, 2010. [1998]): 185

76. Dutt, "Reclaiming a Human Rights Culture," 226.

77. Dutt, "Reclaiming a Human Rights Culture," 226.

78. Roger Waldinger and David Fitzgerald, "Transnationalism in Question," *American Journal of Sociology* 109, no. 5 (March 2004): 1185.

79. Translation from Spanish is mine.

80. Hans Lauge Hansen (2016) "Modos narrativos en la memoria de los movimientos militantes," In *Militancias radicales. Narrar los sesenta y setenta desde el siglo XXI*, ed. Cecilia González and Aránzazu Sarría Buil (Buenos Aires/Madrid: Postmetropolis Editorial/Protohistoria Ediciones, 2016): 90.

81. Waldinger and Fitzgerald, "Transnationalism in Question," 1185–86.

82. Ella Shohat, "Introduction," In *Talking Visions: Multicultural Feminism in a Transnational Age*, ed. Ella Shohat (New York: MIT Press, 1998): 12.

83. The ways in which nations are imagined as patriarchal families that place women in subjugated roles have been exhaustively analyzed by feminist critics. Ranjoo Sedou Herr offers an indispensable overview of the feminist scholarship on the subject in her article on the prospects of nationalist feminism (136–39).

84. Ranjoo Sedou Herr, "The Possibility of Nationalist Feminism," *Hypatia* 18, no. 3 (Fall 2003): 135.

85. Fernandes, *Transnational Feminism in the United States*, 6.

86. Darío Salinas Figueredo, "Democratic Governability in Latin America: Limits and Possibilities in the Context of Neoliberal Domination," In *Imperialism, Neoliberalism and Social Struggles in Latin America*, ed. Richard A. Dello Buono and José Bell Lara (Leiden: Brill, 2007): 89.

87. Fernandes, *Transnational Feminism in the United States*, 2–3.

88. Shohat, "Introduction," 1.

89. Terry Ginsberg, "Contemporary Interdisciplinary Studies and the Ideology of Neoliberal Expansion," *Arab Studies Quarterly* 33, no. 3–4 (2011): 143.

90. Heike Scharm and Natalia Matta-Jara, "Introduction," In *Postnational Perspectives on Contemporary Hispanic Literature*, ed. Heike Scharm and Natalia Matta-Jara (Gainesville: UP of Florida, 2017): 5.

91. Nil Santiáñez, "Space, Subjectivity, and Literary Studies in the Age of Globalization," In *Postnational Perspectives on Contemporary Hispanic Literature*, ed. Heike Scharm and Natalia Matta-Jara (Gainesville: UP of Florida, 2017): 45.

92. Here is an example from a recent job ad in Spanish: "The Department of Literature and Languages at The University of Texas at Tyler invites applications for a tenure-track Assistant Professor in Spanish and French beginning fall 2020 . . . Responsibilities include, but are not limited to, teaching Spanish and French language and culture, occasionally peninsular literature or linguistics to English and Spanish majors, research and publication, learning outcome assessment, and local community outreach for service learning" (*Chronicle of Higher Ed*, https://chroniclevitae.com/jobs/0000506980-01).

93. In recent years, a number of English Literature departments started hiring assistant professors with degrees in Hispanic Studies. Some recent examples include

"The English Department at the University of Redlands seeks a tenure-track assistant professor of Chicanx/Latinx literary and cultural studies, with expertise in media and/or visual culture, to begin Fall 2020," "The Department of English Language and Literature at Southern Illinois University Edwardsville (SIUE) is seeking an Assistant Professor with research specialization in Global Literatures, with a focus on Latinx literatures, border studies, and/or indigenous literary studies," "The Department of English at Baylor University seeks a dynamic and creative scholar specializing either in African American literature or in Latino/a or Hispanic American literature." https://academicjobs.wikia.org/wiki/Ethnic_American_Literature_2019

94. Shohat, "Introduction," 7.

95. Many of the definitions of transnationalism that have had great currency in critical discourse suffer from concentrating on the experiences of the privileged minority and eliding those of the less privileged groups. Paolo Boccagni points out that the widely accepted definition of transnational attitudes that was proposed by Haller and Landolt in 2005 and which posits "feeling equally at home in both countries" as a marker of a truly transnational experience (Haller and Landolt 1200, 1203) suitably applies only to a restricted and "self-selective minority of 'cosmopolitans'" (191). As an ontological category, 'the transnational' has only too often been colonized by the preferences and concerns of the globe-trotting cosmopolitan elite whose interests do not intersect with those of, to give an example, economic immigrants from Ecuador to Italy whose transnational experiences Boccagni describes in his enlightening piece: "Reaffirming one's national identity, whether as an obvious fact or as a source of pride, is a means of distinction from the all-embracing identity of 'immigrants' . . . that one feels being imposed by the receiving society. Whatever regret or disenchantment regarding the 'ever worsening' situation in Ecuador, one's persistent national identity is the basis for personal consistency in the face of the drastic changes that result from migration" (Boccagni 189).

96. Herr, "The Possibility of Nationalist Feminism," 145–46.

97. Herr, "The Possibility of Nationalist Feminism," 146.

98. Laura Briggs, "Transnational," In *The Oxford Handbook of Feminist Theory*, ed. Lisa Disch and Mary Hawkesworth (New York: Oxford UP, 2016): 994.

99. Eizabeth Losh and Jacqueline Wernimont. *Bodies of Information: Intersectional Feminism and the Digital Humanities* (Minneapolis: U of Minnesota P, 2019): 5.

100. Bauman, *Liquid Love*, 116.

101. Izabella Penier, "The Formation of Female Migratory Subjects in Edwidge Danticat's *Krick? Krack!*" *Gender Studies* 10 (December 2010): 53.

102. Danticat holds an undergraduate degree from Barnard College and a Master of Fine Arts in Creative Writing from Brown University.

103. Martin Munro, "Introduction: Borders," In *Edwidge Danticat: A Reader's Guide*, edited by Martin Munro (Charlottesville and London: U of Virginia P, 2010): 8.

104. Greenwald, *Affect and American Literature*, 91.

105. Greenwald, *Affect and American Literature*, 97.

106. Here and in the rest of the quote, italics are the author's.

107. Han, *The Burnout Society*, 11.
108. Fernandes, *Transnational Feminism in the United States*, 18.
109. Cooper, "Intersectionality," 393–94.
110. For the corporate world, a nominal dedication to diversity has served as a convenient tool to improve corporate branding and defend against possible criticism: "Gender mainstreaming and diversity management are two technologies that . . . have helped adapt feminist ideas to neoliberal rationalities, making new gender identities and gender difference productive for outcomes ranging from economic growth to business profit" (Prügl 620). Far from being capable of disrupting the process of neoliberalization, these concepts allow the corporate world to justify many of its exploitative practices. As Arlene Dávila points out, we should avoid reproducing "an empty and symbolic politics of multicultural representation" and keep in mind that "far from an added-on ornament that 'softens' or ameliorates the social inequalities of neoliberal policies, culture becomes imperative to their production" (189).

BIBLIOGRAPHY

Altuna Tezanos, Carlos R. "Haití: Acorralado entre hambruna y la pandemia." *Listín Diario: El periódico de los Dominicanos*, May 2, 2020. Accessed May 10, 2020. https://listindiario.com/las-mundiales/2020/05/02/615707/haiti-acorralado-entre-hambruna-y-la-pandemia

Anderson, Benedict. *Imagined Communities: Reflections on the Origins and Spread of Nationalism*. London/New York: Verso, 2006. [1983]

"Austeridad ya es un problema: líder de Morena." *Diario de Chiapas*, June 6 2020. Accessed June 7, 2020. https://diariodechiapas.com/portada/austeridad-ya-es-un-problema-lider-de-morena/127659

Bauman, Zygmunt. *Liquid Modernity*. Cambridge: Polity, 2000.

———. *Liquid Love*. Cambridge: Polity, 2003.

Bezhanova, Olga. *Literature of Crisis: Spain's Engagement with Liquid Capital*. Lewisburg: Bucknell UP, 2017.

Bobbitt, Philip. *The Shield of Achilles: War, Peace, and the Course of History*. New York: Anchor Books, 2003.

Boccagni, Paolo. "Private, Public or Both? On the Scope and Impact of Transnationalism in Immigrants' Everyday Lives." In *Diaspora and Transnationalism: Concepts, Theories and Methods*, edited by Rainer Bauböck and Thomas Faist, 185–204. Amsterdam: Amsterdam UP, 2010.

Bourguignon, François. *The Globalization of Inequality*. Translated by Thomas Scott-Railton. Princeton and Oxford: Princeton UP, 2015.

Briggs, Laura. "Transnational." In *The Oxford Handbook of Feminist Theory*, edited by Lisa Disch and Mary Hawkesworth, 991–1009. New York: Oxford UP, 2016.

Cohen, Robin. "The Virus: Class Dimensions of Mobility and Immobility." *GRFDT: Global Research Forum on Diaspora and Transnationalism* April 8, 2020. Accessed April 21, 2020, 1–6. https://grfdt.com/Upload/Publication/10127_Virus%20Class.pdf

Cooper, Brittney. "Intersectionality." In *The Oxford Handbook of Feminist Theory*, edited by Lisa Disch and Mary Hawkesworth, 385–406. New York: Oxford UP, 2016.

Crenshaw, Kimberlé Williams. "From Private Violence to Mass Incarceration: Thinking Intersectionality about Women, Race, and Social Control." *UCLA Law Review* 59 (2012): 1419–72.

Dardot, Pierre and Christian Laval. *The New Way of the World: On Neo-Liberal Society*. Translated by Gregory Elliott. London: Verso, 2013. [2009]

Dávila, Arlene. *Culture Works: Space, Value, and Mobility across the Neoliberal Americas*. New York & London: New York UP, 2012.

Davis, Ryan A. *The Spanish Flu: Narrative and Cultural Identity in Spain, 1918*. New York: Palgrave Macmillan, 2013.

Díaz Arias, David and Ronny Viales Hurtado. "Centroamérica: neoliberalismo y COVID-19." *Geopolitica(s). Revista de estudios sobre espacio y poder* 11 (2020): 53–9.

Dosekun, Simidele. "For Western Girls Only?" *Feminist Media Studies* 15, no. 6 (2015): 960–75.

Dutt, Mallika. "Reclaiming a Human Rights Culture: Feminism of Difference and Alliance." In *Talking Visions: Multicultural Feminism in a Transnational Age*, edited by Ella Shohat, 225–46. New York: MIT Press, 1998.

Eagleton-Pierce, Matthew. *Neoliberalism: The Key Concepts*. London & New York: Routledge, 2016.

Eatwell, Roger and Matthew Goodwin. *National Populism: The Revolt against Liberal Democracy*. London: Penguin Books, 2018.

Ehrenberg, Alain. *The Weariness of the Self: Diagnosing the History of Depression in the Contemporary Age*. Translated by Enrico Caouette, Jacob Homel, David Homel, and Don Winkler. Montreal & Kingston: McGill-Queen's UP, 2010. [1998]

Eisenstein, Hester. "A Dangerous Liaison? Feminism and Corporate Globalization." *Science & Society* 69, no. 3 (July 2005): 487–518.

Ferguson, Michaele L. "Neoliberal Feminism as Political Ideology: Revitalizing the Study of Feminist Political Ideologies." *Journal of Political Ideologies* 22, no. 3 (2017): 221–35.

Fernandes, Leela. *Transnational Feminism in the United States: Knowledge, Ethics, and Power*. New York and London: New York UP, 2013.

Galeano, Eduardo. *Open Veins of Latin America: Five Centuries of the Pillage of a Continent*. Translated by Cedric Belfrage. 25th ed. New York: Monthly Review P, 1997.

Ginsberg, Terry. "Contemporary Interdisciplinary Studies and the Ideology of Neoliberal Expansion." *Arab Studies Quarterly* 33, no. 3–4 (2011): 143–52.

Genz, Stéphanie and Benjamin A. Brabon. *Postfeminism: Cultural Texts and Theories*. 2nd ed. Edinburgh UP, 2018.

Gordon, Serena. "Coronavirus Pandemic May Lead to 75,000 'Deaths of Despair' from Suicide, Drug and Alcohol Abuse, Study Says," *CBS News*, May 8, 2020. Accessed May 10, 2020. https://www.cbsnews.com/news/coronavirus-deaths-su icides-drugs-alcohol-pandemic-75000/

Habermas, Jürgen. *The Postnational Constellation: Political Essays*, edited and translated by Max Pensky. Cambridge, MA: MIT Press, 2001.

Haller, William and Patricia Landolt. "The Transnational Dimensions of Identity Formation: Adult Children of Immigrants in Miami." *Ethnic and Racial Studies* 28, no. 6 (November 2005): 1182–214.

Han, Byung-Chul. *The Burnout Society*. Translated by Erik Butler. Stanford: Stanford UP, 2015. [2010].

Hansen, Hans Lauge. "Modos narrativos en la memoria de los movimientos militantes." In *Militancias radicales. Narrar los sesenta y setenta desde el siglo XXI*, edited by Cecilia González and Aránzazu Sarría Buil, 87–106. Buenos Aires/ Madrid: Postmetropolis Editorial/Protohistoria Ediciones, 2016.

Hartmann, Heidi I. "The Unhappy Marriage of Marxism and Feminism: Towards a More Progressive Union." In *Women and Revolution: A Discussion of the Unhappy Marriage of Marxism and Feminism*, edited by L. Sargent, 43–70. Boston: South End P, 1981.

Herr, Ranjoo Seodu. "The Possibility of Nationalist Feminism." *Hypatia* 18, no. 3 (Fall 2003): 135–60.

Hodgson, Michael. *Recycling and Redesigning Logos: A Designer's Guide to Refreshing and Rethinking Design*. Rockport: Quayside, 2010.

Kaplan, Caren. "Hillary Rodham Clinton's Orient: Cosmopolitan Travel and Global Feminist Subjects." *Meridians: Feminism, Race, Transnationalism* 2, no. 1 (2001): 219–40.

Kawohl, Wolfram and Carlos Nordt. "COVID-19, Unemployment, and Suicide." *Lancet Psychiatry* 7 (May 2020): 389–90. https://www.thelancet.com/action/sh owPdf?pii=S2215-0366%2820%2930141-3

Kearney, M. "The Local and the Global: The Anthropology of Globalization and Transnationalism." *Annual Review of Anthropology* 24 (1995): 547–65.

"La OMS hace un llamamiento para "evitar la austeridad" y los recortes en sanidad tras la crisis." *La Vanguardia*, May 28, 2020. Accessed June 8, 2020. https://www .lavanguardia.com/vida/20200528/481435711802/oms-llamamiento-evitar-auster idad-recortes-sanidad-coronavirus.html

Leary, John Patrick. *Keywords: The New Language of Capitalism*. Chicago: Haymarket Books, 2018.

Lee, Su H. *Debating New Social Movements: Culture, Identity, and Social Fragmentation*. Lanham: UP of America, 2007.

Losh, Eizabeth and Jacqueline Wernimont. *Bodies of Information: Intersectional Feminism and the Digital Humanities*. Minneapolis: U of Minnesota P, 2019.

Marciniak, Katarzyna, Anikó Imre, and Áine O'Healy. "Mapping Transnational Feminist Media Studies." In *Transnational Feminism in Film and Media*, edited by Katarzyna Marciniak, Anikó Imre, and Áine O'Healy, 1–18. New York: Palgrave Macmillan, 2007.

Maybank, Aletha. "Why Racial and Ethnic Data on COVID-19's Impact Is Badly Needed." American Medical Association. Last modified April 8, 2020. https:// www.ama-assn.org/about/leadership/why-racial-and-ethnic-data-covid-19-s-impac t-badly-needed

McGuigan, Jim. *Neoliberal Culture*. London: Palgrave Mcmillan, 2016.

Mikhailov, A. M. and A. A. Kpylova. "Relationship Between the Economy Digitalization and the 'Knowledge' Production Factor." In *Digital Age: Chances, Challenges and Future*, edited by Svetlana Ashmarina, Marek Vochozka, and Valentina Mantulenko, 27–38. Switzerland: Springer, 2020.

Millett, Gregorio et al. "Assessing Differential Impacts of COVID-19 on Black Communities." *amfAR, Foundation for AIDS Research* Pre-print version. May 5, 2020. Accessed May 7, 2020. https://ehe.amfar.org/Assessing%20Differential%20Impacts%20of%20COVID-19%205-3-20_final.pdf

Minsky, Laurence and Ilan Geva. *Global Brand Management: A Guide on Development, Building and Managing an International Brand*. London/New York: Kogan Page, 2020.

Mohanty, Chandra Tolpade. *Feminism without Borders: Decolonizing Theory, Practicing Solidarity*. Durham & London: Duke UP, 2003.

Molinas, César. *Qué hacer con España: del capitalismo castizo a la refundación de un país*. Barcelona: Destino, 2013.

Munro, Martin. "Introduction: Borders." In *Edwidge Danticat: A Reader's Guide*, edited by Martin Munro, 1–12. Charlottesville and London: U of Virginia P, 2010.

Peck, Janice. *The Age of Oprah: Cultural Icon for the Neoliberal Era*. New York: Routledge, 2016.

Penier, Izabella. "The Formation of Female Migratory Subjects in Edwidge Danticat's *Krick? Krack!*" *Gender Studies* 10 (December 2010): 51–63.

Petras, James and Henry Veltmeyer. "Social Movements and the State: Political Power Dynamics in Latin America." In *Imperialism, Neoliberalism and Social Struggles in Latin America*, edited by Richard A. Dello Buono and José Bell Lara, 239–59. Leiden: Brill, 2007.

Piketty, Thomas. *Capital in the Twenty-First Century*. Translated by Arthur Goldhammer. Cambridge, MA/London: Belknap P of Harvard UP, 2014.

Policy Brief: The Impact of COVID-19 on Women. UN Women Headquarters. Last modified April 9, 2020. 1–20. https://reliefweb.int/sites/reliefweb.int/files/resources/policy-brief-the-impact-of-covid-19-on-women-en.pdf

"Provisional Death Counts for Coronavirus Disease (COVID-19)." National Center for Health Statistics. Centers for Disease Control and Prediction. Accessed April 15, 2020. https://www.cdc.gov/nchs/nvss/vsrr/COVID19/index.htm

Prügl, Elisabeth. "Neoliberalising Feminism." *New Political Economy* 20, no. 4 (2015): 614–31.

Puar, Jasbir. *Terrorist Assemblages: Homonationalism in Queer Times*. Durham and London: Duke UP, 2007.

Rendueles, César. *Sociophobia: Political Change in the Digital Utopia*. Translated by Heather Cleary. New York: Columbia UP, 2013.

Reynolds, Glenn Harlan. "Protests Show Two Americas—Those Who Lost Their Jobs and Those Still Getting Paid." *USA Today* April 21, 2020. Accessed April 25, 2020. https://www.usatoday.com/story/opinion/2020/04/21/behind-protests-two-americas-one-unemployed-and-one-gets-paychecks-column/5167453002/

Salinas Figueredo, Darío. "Democratic Governability in Latin America: Limits and Possibilities in the Context of Neoliberal Domination." In *Imperialism, Neoliberalism and Social Struggles in Latin America*, edited by Richard A. Dello Buono and José Bell Lara, 85–102. Leiden: Brill, 2007.

Santiáñez, Nil. "Space, Subjectivity, and Literary Studies in the Age of Globalization." In *Postnational Perspectives on Contemporary Hispanic Literature*, edited by Heike Scharm and Natalia Matta-Jara, 29–45. Gainesville: UP of Florida, 2017.

Scharm, Heike and Natalia Matta-Jara. "Introduction." In *Postnational Perspectives on Contemporary Hispanic Literature*, edited by Heike Scharm and Natalia Matta-Jara, 1–26. Gainesville: UP of Florida, 2017.

Sennett, Richard. *The Culture of New Capitalism*. New Haven & London: Yale UP, 2006.

Shohat, Ella. "Introduction." In *Talking Visions: Multicultural Feminism in a Transnational Age*, edited by Ella Shohat. New York: MIT Press, 1998.

Simon, Matt. "Africa's Huge Locust Swarms Are Growing at the Worst Time." *Wired* April 16, 2020. Accessed April 20, 2020. https://www.wired.com/story/africas -huge-locust-swarms-are-growing-at-the-worst-time/

Sklair, Leslie. "Democracy and the Transnational Capitalist Class." *Annals of the American Academy of Political and Social Science* 581 (May 2002): 144–57. http: //citeseerx.ist.psu.edu/viewdoc/download?doi=10.1.1.468.8043&rep=rep1&type= pdf

Smith, Paul Julian. *Dramatized Societies: Quality Television in Spain and Mexico*. Liverpool: Liverpool UP, 2016.

Smith Greenwald, Rachel. *Affect and American Literature in the Age of Neoliberalism*. New York: Cambridge UP, 2015.

Solty, Ingar. "COVID-19 and the Western Working Classes." *Rosa Luxemburg Siftung* March 20, 2020. Accessed April 21, 2020. https://www.rosalux.de/en/publ ication/id/41800/covid-19-and-the-western-working-classes?cHash=cb941bdafc3 bd1b3cb07bd3b86c877aa

Tabulawa, Richard. "Interdisciplinarity, Neoliberalism and Academic Identities: Reflections on Recent Developments at the University of Botswana." *Journal of Education* 69 (2017): 11–42.

Vaidhyanathan, Siva. *Antisocial Media: How Facebook Disconnects Us and Undermines Democracy*. New York: Oxford UP, 2018.

Valdez, Charli. "Critical Race Theory, Transborder Theory, and Code Switching in the Trump Years." *Critical Theory and the Humanities in the Age of the Alt-Right*, edited by Christine M. Battista and Melissa R. Sande, 193–210. New York: Palgrave Macmillan, 2019.

Ventura, Patricia. *Neoliberal Culture: Living with American Neoliberalism*. Farnham/Burlington: Ashgate, 2012.

Waldinger, Roger and David Fitzgerald. "Transnationalism in Question." *American Journal of Sociology* 109, no. 5 (March 2004): 1177–95.

Zuboff, Shoshana. *The Age of Surveillance Capitalism: The Fight for a Human Future at the New Frontier of Power*. New York: Public Affairs, 2019.

Part I

ESSAY, NOVEL, AND SHORT STORY

Chapter 1

Border Trouble

Anzaldúa's Margins

Leslie Bary

Yo no soy americano
pero comprendo el inglés

—Traditional, Zacatecas/California

Por más que la gente me juzgue texano
Yo les aseguro que soy mexicano

—Pepe Guízar

Ay ay ay, soy mexicana de este lado

—Anzaldúa

Gloria Anzaldúa's *Borderlands/La Frontera: The New Mestiza*,[1] a key literary and theoretical contribution to Chicana literature as well as feminist, borderlands, and queer studies, among other disciplines, gained immediate broad popularity in the United States with the multiculturalism of the 1990s.[2] It is now a classic of decolonial studies, well cited in the English-speaking world and available in Spanish translation since 2016. The work generates wide-ranging discussions, and much has been written on the implications of Anzaldúa's hybrid subject for solidarity. *Borderlands/La Frontera*'s hypercanonical status and its progressive diffusion across the globe have created something of an echo-effect in scholarship, as its relevance to a new geographical area, or another field or project is discovered, and the text is introduced to a new audience. Anzaldúa's writing from *This Bridge Called My Back*[3] forward, and Chicana feminism more broadly, are meant to be transdisciplinary and to invoke global solidarity, as Sonia Saldívar-Hull explains

41

in her introduction to the second edition of *Borderlands/La Frontera*[4] and in her landmark work *Feminism on the Border*.[5] Yet this broad appeal means that a good deal of writing on Anzaldúa is intended to introduce and explain more than to analyze or critique.

Some contexts and aspects of Anzaldúa's book, including the connections it makes with sacred, maternal spaces and ancient, non-Western knowledge, as well as its implicit response to Octavio Paz's discussion of the figure of Malintzin in *El laberinto de la soledad*[6] have by now been very well, even exhaustively interpreted. Many liberal scholars and first worlders, as well as some of those who position themselves further on the left or speak from the global South, see the text as revealing and affirming, and consider the plural self it posits a healing alternative to modern subjectivity. As her collaborator AnaLouise Keating[7] and numerous other scholars have pointed out, Anzaldúa's borderlands are not only loci of geopolitical struggle and cultural layering, but also generative spaces "where activism and spirituality converge to produce new knowledge"[8] in the interest of cultural and psychic healing, as well as decolonization at other levels. Central to this project is the act of "crossing," challenging one's perspective, shattering the modern/colonial subject, and opening horizons, to enable a dialogic reconfiguration of our faltering world.

Anzaldúan "border gnosis"[9] has had resonance far beyond both the United States "Third World" contexts addressed in *This Bridge Called My Back* and the US-Mexico borderlands evoked in *Borderlands/La Frontera*. Critics have considered Anzaldúa's philosophy in relation to Caribbean thought,[10] and her relevance to decolonial projects and transnational feminism in France[11] and Spain.[12] Her writing sheds light on the borderlands formed by the Pale of Settlement and later, the Soviet Union and the West,[13] and is used as counterpoint in work on the India-Pakistan border[14] and the Israel-Palestine one.[15] This enthusiasm has to do in part with the mainstreaming of intersectional feminism and anticolonialism, the importance of the hybrid subject in postcolonial theory, the broad applicability of the border metaphor, and the near universalism of *nepantla*,[16] especially as elaborated in Anzaldúa's later work, as a space of cultural and spiritual transformation.

Walter Mignolo has attributed to Anzaldúa the creation of "a space-in-between *from where to think* rather than a hybrid space *to talk about*, a hybrid thinking-space of Spanish/Latin American and Amerindian legacies as the condition of possibility for Spanish/Latin American and Amerindian postcolonial theories."[17] The hybrid "thinking-space," however, is less new for Latin America, and even for the United States, than this quotation suggests. The anonymous composers of the *Popol Vuh*, as well as Guamán Poma de Ayala, Juan Francisco Manzano, Silviano Santiago, and W. E. B. DuBois, just to name a few, all thought from hybrid spaces, although the first four did not write in English. All of their work reveals what Mignolo calls the "colonial difference" and "works toward [its] restitution."[18] Of course, all of these figures enact and interpret hybridity and "in-betweenness" differently, and Anzaldúa's *nepantla* is, among other things, a strategy to heal the painful psychic split DuBois's "double consciousness" indicates. Nonetheless, the deep roots of Anzaldúan hybridity not only in the experience of the US-Mexico borderlands but in the intellectual traditions in which some of her key Mexican references are steeped, are worth excavating and highlighting, despite the fact that the Chicano tradition deploys the concept of *mestizaje* to quite different ends than the Latin American one does.[19]

I do not here question the purpose of Anzaldúa's project or validity of the interest it has generated. I do consider certain problems with the reification of the liminal model, in the critical and theoretical response to *Borderlands/ La Frontera* as much as in the text itself. Does Anzaldúa's invocation of *mestizaje* replicate more conservative, and not always successful efforts at coalition-building? Regarding the book's later reception, is decoloniality sufficient as a political stance? These questions are central, since *Borderlands/ La Frontera* aims to nurture a new, insurgent consciousness. I am also reading Anzaldúa as a scholar of Latin America, for whom the Río Grande is a northern, not a southern border. The references underpinning her multifaceted writing look different from here, and its situatedness as a product of the United States and a response to the situation there is more evident. This is not a criticism, it being my view that the fact that *Borderlands/La Frontera* evokes and speaks from a concrete region and political situation, not from every borderland everywhere, is a strength and not a weakness, and enhances the enduring value of the text.[20] "The U.S.-Mexican border *es una herida abierta* where the Third World grates against the first and bleeds," writes Anzaldúa, drawing an analogy between land and body.[21] The borderlands are metaphor and mindscape, but also a specific place; specificity matters in literature as well as in politics, as I will argue below.

The Latin American Studies-based work on Anzaldúa is somewhat obscured by the preponderance of readings made from American Studies and international English-language perspectives. One of my objectives in this essay is to bring readings that problematize the borderlands as a space of negotiation and transformation to greater light. Especially since the text uses Mexican material, refers to discussions of Mexican and *mestizo* identity embedded in continent-wide discussions, and is a classic not only in US literature but also in world literature of anticolonial struggle and emergent identities, it merits study in the Latin American context as well as the United States and world or "transnational" ones. Furthermore, the border in literary studies has become more porous than it was when *Borderlands/La Frontera* was first published. The overlapping between the literatures of both Americas, and scholarly awareness of its extent, have deepened. In this sense as well Anzaldúa's book, although situated in the United States, speaking originally to a US audience, and now widely read across the Anglophone world, merits further attention from a Latin Americanist point of view. This matters greatly in a context where, on the one hand, English-speaking readers do not always recognize that Latin American writing is not "U.S. Latino" and on the other, the work of scholars like Rodrigo Lazo[22] and Kirsten Silva Greusz[23] shows how closely imbricated with Spanish America the United States has been since its inception.

Borderlands/La Frontera inscribes a US perspective by the geographical space it traces out, its Chicano nationalist symbology, and its participation in debates on feminism, race, and postmodernism in the form these were taking in the United States at the time of its writing. But it is also deeply informed by Anzaldúa's reading in modern Mexican philosophy.[24] It also has literary antecedents in Gabriela Mistral's Indianizing stance and queering of the *mestizo* trope,[25] as well as Rosario Castellanos's use of the term "Nepantla" (written with an initial capital) to name "el no lugar de lo femenino, portador del lenguaje y de la escritura,"[26] and to frame the crossing of national borders, and problematize sex and gender roles.[27] As Josefina Saldaña-Portillo,[28] Sheila Marie Contreras,[29] and B. V. Olguín[30] have demonstrated, the neoindigenist discourse of Chicana/o nationalism is as problematic as its southern sources. Olguín goes on—devastatingly—to show how, from eighteenth-century practices to representations in Mexican American, Chicana/o nationalist texts and beyond, Californios and Tejanos, Mexican Americans and Chicanos have constructed hegemonic, anti-Indian *mestizo* identities, and collaborated in the settler colonialist project. What happens to "Chicana/o indigenist claims to subaltern abjection-as-counterhegemonic agency" and "resistance paradigms in Chicano/a literary studies" in the wake of this recovered knowledge is one of the questions he asks.[31]

I opened with epigraphs from two classic *corridos* and a *corrido*-like line from *Borderlands/La Frontera*'s opening poem. The "Corrido de Joaquín Murrieta," whose origins Luis Leal[32] traced to mid-nineteenth-century Zacatecas (Mexico), is sung throughout the Southwest. It tells of the border-crossing, identity-confounding outlaw, avenger of California Mexicans in the Gold Rush era. The song begins with Murrieta declaring that he is not "American," but has learned to speak English. He later specifies that he is also not a foreigner, since California belongs to Mexico; his documentation is his baptismal certificate, slung across his *sarape*. The second *corrido*, by songwriter Pepe Guízar (Guadalajara, Jalisco, 1912-Mexico City, 1980), riffs on the issue of mistaken identity. The singer assures us he was born on the Mexican side of the border, although he is taken for Texan further south. His dress and mien are misread in central Mexico, where the northern borderlands are overlooked, and conflated with territory now in the United States. Both *corridos* dramatize doublings and folds in national space and identity, and their characters, equipped to navigate this terrain, embody its complexity. At the same time, the speakers insist on their Mexican identity and location within Mexico—in Murrieta's case, even in what has become US territory. I want to expand our geographical setting southward, following Robert Irwin's observation that Anzaldúa's borderlands elide the Mexican side in the same way the US-based field of borderlands studies does,[33] and to look back in time, underscoring the plays on split and double identities that have been made as long as the United States and Mexico have shared their shifting boundary. I also present them in contrast to Anzaldúa's border subject, fractured in a way they are not and also fuller of possibilities. "I am a bridge stretched / between the worlds of the Anglo and the wetback," she writes in this poem.[34] She connects geographies, temporalities, facets of being. On "this thin edge of / barbwire," she aims at change.[35]

Are these border identities "transnational" in the current sense of migration and identification beyond nation? Not entirely, although they bear study in transnational frames. Their strength comes from their sense of place, even when that place straddles national borders and is embedded in routes leading abroad. All are asserting minority identities in ancient lands now located in modern Mexico and the United States, and their travels are within that home. In the *corridos* the hybridized speakers are affirming national identities, not questioning them or leaving them behind. Anzaldúa's multilayered identity is also a situated one, despite affiliations that transcend place. By giving voice to that identity, she aims to alter national consciousness in the United States. At the same time, in a paradoxical movement, she is transforming that identity, giving birth to a new *mestiza* subject. This subject formation has proven highly attractive to theorists focused on intercultural hybridity and cosmopolitan migration, more interested in the new form than in the ground from which it rose. Yet the stories and poems set in South Texas, that fill large sections of the book and locate it there, are not tales of the past—they are happening now.

José David Saldívar has called Anzaldúa's new *mestiza* consciousness "outernational" and "diversalist" rather than transnational and universalist, saying it participates in a "critical cosmopolitanism from below."[36] He situates her work carefully in its contexts at the borders of the United States and in its planetary affiliations with decolonial projects. Yet Anzaldúa's Mexican and South American sources align her, across borders, with postimperial projects that are not always subaltern. This connection is intriguing, as the language of her subaltern project in the United States replicates some of the impasses that inhere in postimperial, but not necessarily counterhegemonic projects further south.

LIMINALITY

Anzaldúa's "new *mestiza*" is theorized in *Borderlands/La Frontera* as the liminal subject of a decolonizing project. Liminal and "hybrid" models of the subject allow the possibility of representation and agency, but base these on multiple and partial rather than unified identities. Such models are for this reason commonly invoked in studies of colonial literatures both before and after formal decolonization, as well as minority and other "marginal" literatures and cultures, as bases for constructing counterhegemonic, rather than simply oppositional identities and discourses.[37]

Scholars such as Linda Gordon have examined the ways in which the concept of "difference" in feminist scholarship can function to evade conflict rather than grapple with social divisions. "Difference," Gordon suggests, evokes "more specific and more critical concepts such as privilege, contradiction, conflict of interest, even oppression and subordination" only to elide them.[38] Similar concerns motivate my contention here that the concept of liminality is often used too loosely, without sufficient recognition of the heterogeneity of the liminal space and the widely differing degrees of oppression suffered and power wielded therein. The attention to liminal, interstitial, and hybrid subject-positions of the past several decades has represented an important theoretical advance. But having named liminality as an attractive alternative to the homogeneity of the traditionally centered subject (whether this subject acts as oppressor or in resistance), it is important to consider that liminality too can have a variety of contents and uses. Those of us who are in a position to choose where and how we enter the liminal space(s) must remember that not all of its inhabitants have these options. I am thinking, for instance, of the immigrants who enter this country after being displaced by war elsewhere, and who here are allowed neither assimilation nor a stable space in which to recreate some of their cultural practices. In the context of globalization, I am thinking of minority cultures that are fractured by modernization without having access to its benefits. I am thinking of Alberto Moreiras's question in *The Exhaustion of Difference*, "What if that indeterminate space of in-between-ness should prove to be, not the purveyor of a new historical coherence, but rather a *mestizo* space of incoherence . . .?"[39] I am concerned about the idealization of liminality and its conversion into yet another universalizing discourse.

There is now a large critical bibliography which explicates, contextualizes, and debates *Borderlands/La Frontera*; Anzaldúa's book has also attained a central place in the canon of several academic disciplines. I am interested in the book here because it is a well-known text which provides very strong examples of both the advantages and the pitfalls of constructing a counterhegemonic discourse on the basis of liminality. While my respect for

Anzaldúa's project is significant and I am intrigued especially by the darker, less conciliatory dimensions of her work, I critique here some implications of the "border" identity she constructs. I wish to show that Anzaldúa's liminal subject, which takes part in a tradition that theorizes *mestizaje* (meaning racial but also cultural mixing) as a basis for Latin American cultural identity, offers both a promising critique of the unitary subject and a possible way out of the impasses of essentialism. But *Borderlands/La Frontera*, like the theories of *mestizaje* upon which it draws, ultimately rests upon a nostalgia for wholeness which works against liminality's own aims. When the "borderlands" become a central metaphor, what margins slip out of view? Can every border stand-in for every other?

By speaking of a nostalgia for wholeness, I do not mean to diminish the importance of forging an identity and claiming a voice—articulated in terms of wholeness and centering at some points in Anzaldúa's text—for subjects who, as Nancy K. Miller puts it, are not "burdened by too much Self, Ego, Cogito."[40] It seems to me, for instance, that the search for a mythic home that in some ways structures the text reflects a desire for spiritual sustenance, not for a centered subjectivity in the Cartesian sense. I do not mean to simply identify essentialism, overt or covert, in Anzaldúa's work. As Diana Fuss has noted, to discover essentialisms may be less useful than it is to inquire what motivates them and to examine their uses, "strategic" (in Gayatri Spivak's famous words) or otherwise.[41] While I am arguing that *Borderlands/La Frontera* may invite essentializations of *mestizaje* and/or liminality, I do not mean to suggest it is Anzaldúa's project to do this. On the contrary, *mestizaje* is a term Anzaldúa must privilege in order to articulate the politics of her own location, and which it is her explicit intent to reconstruct as a mobile configuration that opens out toward the future. Growing from a tradition of Chicano/a texts that address issues of historical and cultural hybridity and represent shifting positionalities, *mestiza* consciousness as a theoretical stance in Anzaldúa is not a unitary essence but the awareness and negotiation of multiple and sometimes contradictory subject-positions.[42] Like Chela Sandoval's "differential consciousness," it is a strategy for perception and action at least as much as it is the representation of an identity.[43] In this sense I concur with Norma Alarcón's assessment, that Anzaldúa's writing does not want to "remain at rest" in taxonomies of hybridity and syncretism but to "make a bid for new discourse formations bringing into view new subjects-in-process,"[44] and with Judith Raiskin's, that the synthesis Anzaldúa proposes through the figure of the *mestiza* is not designed to provide "unity or stasis" but to "embod[y] a continual confrontation of difference."[45]

To repeat, I am not arguing against the value of liminal models of the subject, and particularly not in the specific contexts of the US-Mexican border and Anzaldúa's project. Nor would I criticize every form of wholeness. I am advocating that criticism and theory not idealize multiplicity, nor remain at rest with the discovery and invocation of the liminal space. I am disagreeing with the more universalizing readings of *Borderlands/La Frontera*—readings that appropriate its metaphors for theoretical and political projects sympathetic to but not necessarily the same as Anzaldúa's. This critique of decontextualized readings of Anzaldúa, advanced early on by scholars like Yvonne Yarbro-Bejarano,[46] is not mainstream and is still needed; it is a critique of reading, not of Anzaldúa's writing, and it does not detract from the transformative project of the text. I would also suggest that the emphasis on plural identities, and the use of this text to bolster that emphasis, may obscure subaltern positions that do not exhibit hybridity or liminality as their most salient characteristic—or that are not available in English, or whose hybridization does not foreground elements from "First World" or metropolitan cultures.

To underscore these arguments, I would like to call attention to the tropes of hybridity and liminality in post-Independence Latin American cultural debates. Although Anzaldúa herself invites such a connection by her references to this context, my intention is not to claim that this is the "proper" or natural context for her work, which corresponds most specifically to Chicano/a culture. But Anzaldúa also extends her project to address the creation of radical American (and not just North American) identities. To do so, she draws on traditions whose roots lie further south, and it is worth excavating this layer of meaning in her text.

I also suspect this exercise may be useful in a more general way. While liminality and hybridity are relatively new terms in English-language studies, the Latin American tradition on which Anzaldúa partially draws is much older. As such, it has had a chance to reveal some of the impasses that inhere in the conceptualization and deployment of hybrid selves. Some of these impasses may be instructive to those of us working to construct counterhegemonic identities elsewhere. Like a number of Latin American authors, of a variety of ideological persuasions and subject-positions and at a variety of historical moments, Anzaldúa invokes mixed identities as salutary antidotes to ideologies of purity. But at the levels of race, ethnicity, and culture (although Anzaldúa's *mestizaje* refers to more than this), the discourse of hybridity has also long functioned in Latin America to maintain social divisions. Patricia J. Williams has noted that the recent and current US interest in mixed ethnicities risks replicating this problem:

> We must guard against replacing a two-story system of racism . . . with a multileveled caste system. We will end up only with something like what plagues parts of Latin America: whole skyscrapers of racial differentiation, with "white" still living in the penthouse, the "one drops" just below and those with buckets of black blood in the basement or out in the street.[47]

I raise the Latin American context to insist that we must think hybridity and liminality rigorously if we are to avoid falling into an old trap. I also wish to emphasize that this context is one of Anzaldúa's, who, tellingly enough, does not provide English versions of every Spanish section of her text. The open smuggling of this language—the much-denied other tongue of our hemisphere—into the US cultural scene is one of *Borderlands/La Frontera*'s most radical interventions, and it is worth throwing into relief some of the bridges south the text traces.

SUBALTERN REPRESENTATION

There are at least two overlapping but often conflicting discourses which shape the question of subaltern representation. One is the poststructuralist critique of the unitary subject as a construct which both denies and essential-izes difference. The other is the politics of identity, which asserts the neces-sity of positing a subject with voice and agency. The split between these two discourses creates a double bind: the oppressed subject and the intellectual who theorizes her are caught between choosing subjectivity within the terms of the dominant discourse or on the other hand, relinquishing the possibility of representation. Describing this double bind, Gayatri Spivak writes: "The radical intellectual in the West is either caught in a deliberate choice of sub-alternity, granting to the oppressed that very expressive subjectivity which s/he criticizes, or instead, a total unrepresentability."[48] Anzaldúa offers a way out of this impasse by positing an identity politics of the already divided/multiple subject, a subject between cultures, languages, and races. She theorizes this state of betweenness as a physical and psychic territory that she calls the borderlands. The inhabitants of the borderlands are defined by their divergence from hegemonic racial, cultural, and sexual identities: "*Los atravesados* live here: the squint-eyed, the perverse, the queer, the trouble-some, the mongrel, the mulatto, the half-breed, the half-dead; in short those who cross over, or go through the confines of the 'normal'."[49]

Anzaldúa describes the Chicana as "cradled in one culture, sandwiched between two cultures, straddling all three cultures and their value systems."[50] She herself has grown up "between two cultures, the Mexican (with a heavy Indian influence) and the Anglo (as a member of a colonized people in [their] own territory)."[51] Her text throws into relief the complex identifications that cross the Chicana subject, divided not only between Mexican and Anglo cul-ture but also between the expectations of gender inherent in both. As Carmen del Río explains,

[t]he Chicana's healthy distrust of Anglo culture and ideas has been used by the Chicano male to keep her in "her" place, indeed, to keep her silent and passive

when it comes to any criticism of the Chicano and his sexual oppression of
her, who very often applies . . . a double standard in judging the Chicana as a
vendida or worse, as a *malinchista*, a term which . . . implies treason to her own
culture and race.[52]

Since the *mestiza* can identify with neither a dominant culture nor a single,
unified minority group, the unitary subjectivity that poststructuralism critiques
is never available to her. Anzaldúa emphasizes the pain of speaking a "border
tongue,"[53] of feeling "orphaned" by her Native language and therefore culturally deficient.[54] The border, "this place of contradictions," is "not a comfortable territory to live in . . . Hatred, anger and exploitation are the prominent
features of this landscape."[55] But precisely because she is in so many senses
an outcast at the cross-section of cultures she inhabits, the Chicana is in a
position to draw on the strengths of several cultures and to use each of these
cultures to critique the other(s) from the point of view of an insider. Anzaldúa
writes that "the new *mestiza* copes by developing a tolerance for contradictions, a tolerance for ambiguity. She learns to be an Indian in Mexican culture,
to be Mexican from an Anglo point of view. She learns to juggle cultures. She
has a plural personality, she operates in a pluralistic mode . . . Not only does
she sustain contradictions, she turns the ambivalence into something else."[56]
   Lesbianism marks Anzaldúa's deviance from the heterosexual imperative
of Anglo, Mexican, and Chicano cultures,[57] as well as her identification with
liminal subjects of different cultural backgrounds: "Being the supreme cross-
ers of cultures, homosexuals have strong bonds with the queer white, Black,
Asian, Native American, Latino, and with the queer in Italy, Australia and the
rest of the planet. We come from all colors, all classes, all races, all time periods. Our role is to link people with each other."[58] This formulation appears
to essentialize the lesbian of color as a necessarily revolutionary class—a
question to which I return below. Anzaldúa, however, insists that life in the
borderlands is a practice, not an essence. Her *mestiza*

> puts history through a sieve, winnows out the lies, looks at the forces that we as
> a race, as women, have been a part of. *Luego bota lo que no vale* . . . This step
> is a conscious rupture with all the oppressive traditions of all cultures . . . She
> communicates that rupture, documents that struggle. She reinterprets history
> and, using new symbols, she shapes new myths . . . She surrenders all notions
> of safety, of the familiar. Deconstruct, construct.[59]

Finally, Anzaldúa's association of psychic unrest, writing, and the borderlands,[60] together with the heterogeneity of her implied audience and her
explicit invitations to non-Chicanas to meet her at the border,[61] suggests
that few of us escape the pain of the borderlands, and calls us to participate

actively in their work. The title of one poem, "To live in the Borderlands means *you*,"[62] insists we recognize the multiple communities to which we belong and examine the conflicts, as well as the connections among them. This poem ends, "To survive the Borderlands / you must live *sin fronteras* / become a crossroads."[63] Anzaldúa thus transforms the borderlands from a space in which she is caught among conflicting loyalties and overlapping oppressions into a space in which she remaps and revises her cultural identity.

The value of such remapping for less marginal subjects is highlighted in Minnie Bruce Pratt's autobiographical essay "Identity: Skin Blood Heart,"[64] which also transforms identity from essence into practice, or from "nature" into action. Pratt, a white woman of privileged class origins who has entered the sexual and racial borderlands, shows in this essay how the (childhood) "home" she was taught to associate with "safety, comfort, [and] familiarity"[65] revealed that the price of its protection was conformity and obedience. As Anzaldúa was limited by what she was denied, Pratt has been limited by what she was given. Pratt says,

> I had not admitted that the safety of much of my childhood was because Laura Cates, Black and a servant, was responsible for me; that I had . . . walks with my father because the woods were "ours" by systematic exploitation, instigated, at that time, by his White Citizens Council; that I was allowed one evening a month with woman friends because I was a wife who would come home at night . . . I had no understanding of the limits that I lived within, nor of how much my memory and my experience of a safe space was to be based on places secured by omission, exclusion, or violence, and on my submitting to the limits of that place.[66]

One of the gains she cites as a result of this realization is "a way of looking at the world that is more accurate, complex, multi-layered, multi-dimensioned, more truthful: to see the world of overlapping circles, like the movement on the millpond after a fish has jumped, instead of the courthouse square with me in the middle."[67] Pratt discusses her fear of losing an inherited or "natural" community, a fear she relates to "the fear of loss of self when we discover the connections between racism and anti-Semitism and our life as women."[68] Her essay reshapes identity in terms of rupture, struggle, or as Anzaldúa says, a process of "[putting] history through a sieve"[69] that enables her to replace her inherited community with a chosen one she builds as she reshapes her personal identity. So Pratt is able to cross barriers of class, race, and gender as she becomes aware of her conflicting loyalties and her specifically situated identity, while Anzaldúa transforms the borderlands she already inhabits, the social and psychic constraints of which she is already painfully aware, from a place of limitation into a multiple source of strength.

I have discussed and cited Pratt at length for two reasons. One of these is to underscore the ways in which people from more privileged social groups can and do enter the borderlands. Such a reshaping of identity is available to all of us and is not a responsibility only of those who suffer multiple oppression. The second, and for the purposes of my argument, most important reason, is to point out that while both authors narrate "borderlands" experiences and have constructed what we might call border identities, they do not necessarily meet at every crossroads. Pratt's development of "border" consciousness comes at a cost whose concrete features include the forced removal of her children as well as the loss of social and economic privilege. Yet, as she takes pains to make clear in her essay, the shifts she has made do not by themselves guarantee easy common ground or natural political community with other marginal or marginalized subjects. Pratt is someone who has *entered* the borderlands, having once occupied a position of privilege. In this her position differs from Anzaldúa's, for whom the borderlands have always been a primary condition of existence. Pratt's position differs again from that of those of us who enter the borderlands by choice (without the pressures that first propelled her there), and yet again from the position of those inhabitants of the border zone who do not hold a US passport. That is, all border identities are not necessarily similar, and once we enter the borderlands, there are still significant issues of power and of difference to be faced. The discovery and recognition of the borderlands as a site of the creation of a new, counterhegemonic subject is just that—the discovery of a site. Since it is only the discovery of a site, and since this site is plural and marked by divisions and gaps, the recognition and valorization of the borderlands is but one step in a political project, and not the final one.

The "borderlands" in Anzaldúa are at once a specific geographical location and the historical trajectory of a people in it, a space in which a new subjectivity is forged, a key characteristic of that subjectivity, and a more general model for the creation of counterhegemonic identities and subjectivities. In this last sense, the "borderlands" concept incorporates multiplicity as an alternative to the more traditional, Cartesian models which, even when used in resistance to oppression, replicate authoritarian structures of self. What the concept risks is the creation of new binaries (liminality versus centrality, hybridity vs. some form of purity) and the elision of inequalities and differences within the borderlands. These are the problems I wish to stress here by looking more closely at some implications of the model of subjectivity Anzaldúa creates in *Borderlands/La Frontera*.

As we think about the borderlands and their creative potential, it is important to remember that the historical US-Mexico border is still a space of pain and loss. The hybridization that takes place there in service to the global economy does not necessarily benefit, say, the factory worker who has gone there after being displaced from ancestral lands further south. It is also a site of struggles over meaning. Cultural theorist Néstor García Canclini notes that some Tijuana artists and writers criticized the Tijuana-San Diego journal *La Línea Quebrada/The Broken Line*, which worked to redefine identity and culture on the basis of the border experience, for what they see as its "euphemistic treatment of the contradictions and uprooting" that most closely describe the lives of many of the border's inhabitants. "They reject the celebration of migrations caused by poverty in the homeland and the United States," he writes.[70] Now the effects of free trade and transnational crime have driven many more migrants north, and current US and Mexican policy makes the borderlands yet harsher.

As we contemplate the possibilities for consciousness-raising, solidarity, and coalition-building "border" identities may offer, it is important to avoid what Caren Kaplan termed "theoretical tourism"—the glossing over of our centralities.[71] Yarbro-Bejarano makes this point when she asks, "if every reader who identifies with the border-crossing experience described by Anzaldúa's text sees her/himself as a 'New *mestiza*,' what is lost in terms of the erasure of difference and specificity?"[72] In addition, it is important to realize that consciousness-raising around racial and other forms of oppression among those in the dominant group(s) has limited value if not accompanied by a focus on institutional practice. Kimberly Christensen, for instance, points out that "the CR mode of knowledge production . . . often simply replicates rationalizations for inequality when used by oppressors to understand their own experiences."[73] She goes on to emphasize that "[r]acism is not primarily about 'how we feel about each other'" but about how wealth and power are distributed in society at large.[74] It is here, and not just at the level of private life, that members of dominant groups must assume responsibility for inequalities. Anzaldúa's invitation to enter the borderlands, in its strongest sense, means this.

DIFFERENCE AND WHOLENESS

As a figure of cross-cultural linkage, the liminal or "border" subject has become a paradigm for the politics of difference. Positing a subject-position based on the transgression of boundaries traditionally seen to shape identity enables critics to overcome some of the snarls in theorizing a speaking subaltern subject. It literalizes the call for a recognition of multiple oppression and of the heterogeneity of the oppressed subject. It theorizes the possibility of negotiating a cross-section of identities, so as to avoid the traps of Eurocentric "universalism" and of cultural nationalism. At the same time, it attempts to move away from politics based on essentialized identities (a politics which has been critiqued for being unable to contain differences, thus leading to the fragmentation of feminist and other counterhegemonic communities) and toward a politics which challenges the notion of stable, unitary identities. Chantal Mouffe, one of the better-known theorists of such a politics, says in an essay on the construction of a revolutionary subjectivity that "we are in fact always multiple and contradictory subjects, inhabitants of a diversity of communities (as many, really, as the social relations in which we participate and the subject-positions they define), constructed by a variety of discourses and precariously and temporarily sutured by the intersection of these subject-positions."[75] The "borderlands" would seem to be a clear instance of this model of the subject, and an ideal space for the creation of new forms of consciousness and solidarity.

But this liminal paradigm presents a problem: while, through its emphasis on conflict, discontinuity, and change, it initially throws into relief what Laclau and Mouffe call "the open, unsutured character of the social,"[76] it ultimately, through its emphasis on the pleasures and the possibilities of reconciliation the borderlands offer, risks glossing over the contradictions which inform this space. To return to the examples I have been discussing, a striking feature of Pratt's essay is her preoccupation with reclaiming a "home" or safe place (partly confused in her essay with political coalition) in which differences, including those of class and race, will no longer mean conflict. Anzaldúa evokes a similar resolution of differences by describing *mestizaje* as blending and homosexuality as a union of opposites. On lesbianism, she says, "I, like other queer people, am two in one body, both male and female. I am the embodiment of *hieros gamos*: the coming together of opposite qualities within."[77] On the political function of the new *mestiza*, she says, "the *mestizo* and the queer exist at this time and point on the evolutionary continuum for a purpose. We are a blending that proves that all blood is intricately woven together, and that we are spawned out of similar souls."[78]

At this moment in Anzaldúa the language of wholeness, of weaving, of similarity, replaces the language of fragmentation, of partiality, of multiplicity, and of contradiction. The heterogeneity that had given the liminal space its critical edge is ironed out. What had been presented as radical difference begins to look like liberal pluralism. Here it may be useful to consider a point raised, in different contexts, by John Beverley[79] and, once again, Chantal Mouffe.[80] Both remind us that political and cultural identity do not necessarily coincide. They emphasize that multiple though our identities may actually be, the logic of politics and of insurgency is still binary (one struggles for something, against something). I would add that to negotiate difference seriously even among comrades, conflict must be addressed directly and not simply contained in an ever-expanding whole.

If the first problem created by the glossing over of contradictions in the liminal subject as Anzaldúa formulates it is the reconciliation of opposites, a second one, closely related to the first, is a slippage back to the notion of wholeness. In both Pratt and Anzaldúa, the logic of fragmentation and unity supersedes the logic of difference(s).[81] In Pratt's model, we become (hyper-) aware of our own positionality and from here, make connections to other subject-positions as we come to perceive and understand relations of common oppression and of mutual domination and oppression. But though Pratt throughout her essay invokes what Laclau and Mouffe would call the "partial" and "provisional" fixity of subject-positions and their colligations, this lack of wholeness and permanence is most often, in this text, a source of alienation and pain whose imagined assuagement is a nostalgia for identity and unity: "For years, I have had a recurring dream: sleeping, I dream I am reconciled to a woman from whom I have been parted: my mother, the Black woman who raised me, my first woman lover, a Jewish woman friend; in the dream we embrace, with the sweetness that can come in a dream when all is made right."[82] When Anzaldúa speaks of uniting opposites, she reinstalls the binary oppositions, and by implication, the social hierarchies which her concept of liminality is designed to dismantle. By presenting liminality as the union of opposites, she brings self and other into contact without calling into question the oppositions that define these terms, nor destabilizing their construction as mutually exclusive. When she talks about identity and solidarity in terms of blending and weaving, she speaks as though each situated identity, each subject-position, were a fragment of a larger whole. To live in the borderlands is, initially, to live conflicts and contradictions:

To live in the Borderlands means knowing
that the *india* in you, betrayed for 500 years,
is no longer speaking to you,
that mexicanas call you *rajetas*,
that denying the Anglo inside you
is as bad as having denied the Indian
or Black.[83]

But the borderlands also promise the resolution of these contradictions in a new and improved, if not entirely even blending: "Yes, in a few years or centuries / la Raza will rise up, tongue intact / carrying the best of all the cultures."[84] These utopian evocations of future unity leapfrog over the questions of power and difference both writers have so painstakingly raised. I do not mean by this to deny the sustenance even an imagined home can offer, or the creative power of utopian visions, but to question the presentation of the liminal space as a sort of cure. It may be that this space is where questions of power and difference can be struggled over productively or negotiated in good faith. But the near sacralization of liminality here—an essentialization of both *mestizaje* as a historical project and of liminality as a theoretical and political concept—seems to substitute the work-space for the actual work. At this point liminality, though it may afford what in some versions of multiculturalism is called "diversity," functions to mask serious conflict, contradiction, and radical difference. This slippage back to wholeness is, as I suggested earlier, a negation of the partiality and multiplicity that the liminal model was designed to bring into view. Conceived of in this way, the liminal subject is converted into an essentialized identity.

MESTIZAJE

I have said that the essentialization of liminality is not Anzaldúa's problem alone, but a common one in theories of "minority" and postcolonial identity which base themselves on the idea of a liminal subject. Critiquing D. Emily Hicks's *Border Writing*, a book that appeared soon after the first publication of *Borderlands/La Frontera*, Neil Larsen suggested that "the project of a border writing (or border subject, border culture, etc.) must be seen as an ambiguous one, reflecting the configuration of the impasse [between Eurocentrism and cultural nationalism] itself."[85] If the question is how to endow subjects with voice and agency while avoiding essentialism and foundationalism, the "border" concept seems to work mainly as a theoretical holding pattern that is itself essentialized. As such, it is more a reflection or effect of the problem it is designed to solve than it is an actual solution. To elucidate the contradictions inherent in liminality as a theoretical construct I want to discuss briefly the Latin American discourse of *mestizaje*, on which Anzaldúa draws explicitly and of which many, though not all her commentators seem unaware. Anzaldúa invokes most explicitly the utopian dimension of this discourse. But the concept of *mestizaje* has a long and tangled history. In its modernist version, like the (also modern) discourses of nationalism and universalism, it has a repressive dimension as well. This is a context Anzaldúa avoids raising in her book, an omission or blind spot which invites the reader to an essentialization of *mestizaje* and liminality I doubt Anzaldúa intends. The romanticizing of *mestizaje*, the elision of its history in Anzaldúa's book, flaws her attempt to rework the term.

The *mestizo* is a colonial formation, and the mixture with the colonizer is the one that counts; historically speaking one can identify *mestizo-criollo* classes and *mestizo-criollo* cooperation, not opposition. Anzaldúa's *mestiza* is subaltern, but the *mestiza/o* is not necessarily subaltern in the texts from which she draws, and that she cites. Her text, insurgent for the United States, deploys a paradigm for the formation of national cultures widely used in Spanish America throughout the nineteenth and early twentieth centuries in the service of state projects almost diametrically opposed to her own. This is one reason why the text, as Debra Castillo has noted, does not resonate with left intellectuals and activists south of the US border the way it does in the United States, Europe, and the broader Anglosphere.[86] Furthermore, the text moves directly from pre-Columbian origins and the Conquest-era figure of Malinche or Malintzin, indigenous mother of *mestizo* children with Hernán Cortés, to modern and postmodern versions of *mestizaje* without addressing its complexities in the long colonial period. Anzaldúa's poetic choice is her own, but scholarship on the meanings and uses of *mestizaje* in her text should not ignore the existence of this history. It is worth knowing, for instance, that the term referred first to religious mixture and was always understood as cultural as well as biological. There were indigenous *mestizos* and multiple forms of hybridity from the beginning.[87] *Mestizo* culture could be creative and generative, but being *mestizo* could also mean deculturation *tout court*, without access to a new culture or transculturation.[88] Successful *mestizaje*, on the other hand, meant being part of the West and the *mestizo* class, and *mestizo* figures were not always counterhegemonic.[89]

Anzaldúa's *mestiza* is designed "with a heavy Indian influence," pulling to the indigenous side of the cultural mixture. Yet her references to pre-Columbian ancestral origins, and privileging of the deity Coatlicue, offer an idealized connection between Chicanos and pre-Columbian cultures that elides present-day indigeneity.[90] The cultures the text invokes are from central Mexico, not borderlands Mexico, which has its own Native cultures and gods; based on the model of cultural identity created during the Chicano nationalist movement of the 1960s and 1970s, Anzaldúa's border culture elides the Mexican side in the same way the US-based field of borderlands studies does.[91] This model, furthermore, replicates the statist policies of the postrevolutionary Mexico that draw on elements of ancient Aztec culture to promote the imagining of a national community that claims *mestizaje* while excluding the many living indigenous cultures—a point to which we shall return below.

A common response from scholars aware or made aware of these problems is to reiterate that the Chicano movement, in whose tradition Anzaldúa's work stands, has bent certain Mexican discourses and symbols to its own ends; that *Borderlands/La Frontera* is still a contestatory text; and that the author is a member and representative of not one but several oppressed groups in the United States. These somewhat defensive reactions miss the point, as it is not a question of discovering political errors in Anzaldúa but literary-historical ones in ourselves. That *Borderlands/La Frontera* addresses a US situation and speaks from that perspective; that its formulation corresponds to the

form theoretical debates on race, gender, and subalternity took at the time in
which it was composed; that the Latin American literary models on which it
draws are not necessarily, or not entirely subaltern; need not mean that there
is something "wrong" with Anzaldúa's text or her politics, but there may be
with taking her new *mestiza* as a model for a one-size-fits-all subaltern subject. Is the "border" subject necessarily a revolutionary one? Are borderlands,
by virtue of their layered, "fluid" culture, necessarily spaces of resistance?
What does it mean to set her work in a "transnational" frame while ignoring
the Latin American contexts it invokes? It is telling that a discussion like
Mariana Ortega's,[92] based in US and European theory, upholds hybrid and
transnationally inflected models of the subject, whereas one like Castillo and
Tabuenca's,[93] writing from the US-Mexico border including the Mexican
side, insist on more locally based nuance and history.

The ideology of *mestizaje* in modern Spanish America, especially as the
power of the United States grew from the nineteenth century forward, is in
important ways a critique of[94] Westernization and imperialism. Mexico has
a rich tradition of writing in this vein. Spanish intellectuals also participated
in the *mestizaje*-based critique of colonialism and imperialism;[95] they defined
Spain as *mestizo* and considered *mestizaje* a strength.[96] In the New World the
tradition of cultural self-definition in terms of hybridity functioned, at the
time of independence and afterward, for purposes of national consolidation,
legitimation, and the ensuring of governability.[97] This strategy has its roots in
romantic theories of national culture, according to which cultural specificity
and union were the bases of political autonomy and cohesion. The concept
of hybridity thus provided a model of cultural identity that could interpellate
former colonial subjects as citizens of the new nations. While this valorization of mixed identities, with its corollary of inclusivity, is significantly different from the United States' construction of national identity in terms of
"whiteness," it did not necessarily imply the dismantling of racial and other
hierarchies.[98] Indeed, concepts of hybridity and liminality often function in
Latin American cultural and political discourse to interpellate subjects into
a nation-state which, depending on their material position within it, may or
may not serve them well.[99]

I cannot survey the whole Latin American tradition on *mestizaje*/hybrid-
ity here, nor pursue all the interesting and productive parallels that could be
explored between liminality as it develops in the Chicano/a tradition and in
other modern and contemporary Latin American and Caribbean literature and
theory. I do want to point out that these traditions exist in Latin America, that
their vicissitudes may be instructive even to those whose interests lie in other
geographical and cultural areas. *Borderlands/La Frontera* picks up and works
with some of their threads, and those threads have histories. In addition,
discourses of hybridity and liminality can function as insurgent strategies

in some senses or circumstances and strategies of containment in others. I want to give some brief examples from the largely elite Latin American tradition upon which Anzaldúa draws (and it is important to remember that the discourse of *mestizaje* is an elite tradition) to illustrate this point, which I think her text obscures. The *mestizaje* tradition is, as we have already noted, reterritorialized and recontextualized in Chicano/a literature and theory, and means differently there. But Anzaldúa's text takes this meaning beyond the borders of Aztlán, and it is at that point that the ambiguities inherent in this model of liminality/hybridity resurface.[100]

My first example from the Latin American tradition is Simón Bolívar's insistence on mestizaje and hybridity in his speech before the Congress of Angostura (held in 1819, while the wars of independence were still in progress). The principal sense of Bolívar's project is anticolonial and democratizing. In his Angostura speech, he insists on *mestizaje* and hybridity as cardinal characteristics of Latin American culture. But in his quite authoritarian project of government and his well-known phrase "The blood of our citizens is diverse, let us mix it to unify it,"[101] remain the assumptions that the hybrid space must be shaped into a stable identity and the process of hybridization directed from above. This project was neither new nor anticolonial, as it echoed the 1503 instructions of Ferdinand and Isabel to Nicolás de Ovando, governor and captain-general of the Indies, encouraging mixed marriages as a means of imposing Christian culture,[102] and Ferdinand's 1514 decree giving civil status to mixed marriages made in church.[103] Three hundred years later there were *mestizos* in almost every class; to be *mestizo* meant to be Spanish-speaking and Westernized, not necessarily counterhegemonic. In his "Letter from Jamaica" (1815), Bolívar had been explicit: Latin Americans, understood as the *mestizo-criollo* class, were born here but with European rights; having thrown off the Spanish "usurper" of Native lands, they must now wrest control of it from its "legitimate owners."[104]

A slightly different example of hybridity in its hegemonic mode can be found in the sentimental novels of the middle nineteenth century that Doris Sommer has called "foundational fictions."[105] An important tool in the formation of national consciousness, these novels present idealized love stories between Indians and Europeans as the founding moments of unanimous national identities. Tellingly, the non-European protagonist most often dies or is otherwise eliminated by the time these novels end, having marked those they leave behind with a tinge of otherness which is now, however, a memory—a gentle, exotic glow that cannot spread. Vera Kutzinski offers a similar analysis of the *mulata*'s fetichization as symbol of a mixed-race Cuban nation.[106] For Kutzinski, the figure of the *mulata* functions in part to efface blackness and particularly black women as subjects in Cuban culture; the mulata's textual inscription and exaltation also works to elide the real conditions in which

actual, historical mulatas, and their darker mothers, have had to live. Julio
Ramos (1989) has noted this tendency toward a dominated inclusion of otherness even in a famous text from the late nineteenth century that is anticolonial
and antiracist in its manifest intent and widely considered to be so generally.[107]
The Cuban intellectual and revolutionary José Martí's "Our America" (1891) is
known for its valorization of Spanish America's African and Native American
roots and cultural and political redefinition of the former Spanish colonies. This
essay contrasts the new Spanish American nations with the officially monocultural United States and names them "our *mestizo* America."[108] Ramos points
out that the subaltern classes, although included in Martí's insurgent nation(s),
are also silent in his model.[109] Martí's speaking "we," although designed to
formulate a more democratic modernity than the one he observes in the United
States, still corresponds most clearly to elites of European descent.[110]

   In this tradition stands José Vasconcelos, Anzaldúa's (and the Chicano
movement of the 1960s and 1970s) main reference on *mestizaje*, whom I
discuss below. The texts to which I have referred, their contexts, and their
critical tradition are of course far more complex, and more sophisticated, than
I have been able to indicate here. My point for the purposes of the present
essay is that the hegemonic intellectual tradition that describes Latin America
in terms of interstitiality and hybridity attempts and purports to dismantle the
oppressive notions of racial and cultural purity inherited from colonialism,
but often does so by invoking a national or continental unity which glosses
over internal class, race, and gender oppression. Though such a stance can
be strategically necessary in context of resistance to neocolonialism in which
an author like Martí writes, this *mestizaje* in which "everyone" participates
is not without hierarchies. Nor does every member of the hybrid nation
experience hybridity in the same way, nor use it in ways that might bring the
nation together democratically. These liminal models of cultural identity can
serve the repressive dimension of nationalism as easily as its utopian one. In
their eagerness to valorize the *mestizo*, they also sometimes serve to further
marginalize the least privileged racial groups (e.g., indigenous populations)
and to weaken the cause of antiracism by denying its necessity. For instance,
when Martí says "There can be no racial hate, because there are no races,"[111]
he speaks in a utopian mode but does not acknowledge this. The problem
with statements like this one, which can function as denials even when initially uttered as aspirations or hopes, is that they may serve to disempower
those who have been oppressed as members of a particular social group from
resisting as such.

   The concept of border culture and the liminal model of the subject do
displace binary oppositions such as center and periphery or, in the case of
the American Southwest, Mexican and Anglo (just as in some parts of the

American South, the creole as a racial, social, and cultural category confounds the more common US binarism of black and white). But the border identity is nevertheless informed by these oppositions. As such, *mestizo*, hybrid, and other liminal identities are subversive only in a context where the traditional binarisms still hold sway. Once these have been dismantled, we must face configurations of power within the heterogeneous "border" space. My brief discussion of the hybridity/*mestizaje* tradition in Latin America is intended to provide some concrete examples of these problems. Once again, I wish to recast the concepts of hybridity, *mestizaje*, and liminality as possible starting points for the construction of a counterhegemonic subject, rather than taking them, as is often done, as counterhegemonic per se. This is particularly important given that in the twentieth century a number of Latin American scholars, including Antonio Cornejo Polar, Néstor García Canclini, Fernando Ortiz, and Angel Rama, did important work on cultural hybridity both in some of its concrete forms and as a concept.[112] This work, which critiques the more mainstream tradition into which Anzaldúa inscribes herself, was then critiqued by a new generation of scholars, including John Beverley, Mabel Moraña, and Alberto Moreiras, among a number of others. These scholars showed how concepts of *mestizaje*, hybridity, and liminality, which were deployed as ideologemes in the hegemonic projects I describe above, were then reworked to cast Latin America as a "border" space in which an alternative and more democratic modernity might be elaborated. It found in these theories impasses similar to those I am trying to underline in Anzaldúa.[113] Especially in this intellectual context, it is, to say the least, insufficient for critics to only point to liminality (hybridity, *mestizaje*, border culture) as antidotes to monoculturalism and the centered subject.

TALKING RACE

Anzaldúa invokes the *mestizaje* tradition in her title and refers specifically to the work of the Mexican writer, educator, and politician José Vasconcelos (1882–1959), whose best-known text is *La raza cósmica* (*The Cosmic Race*, 1925). This book celebrates the *mestizo* as harbinger of a mixed ("cosmic") race which will incorporate the positive characteristics of all previous peoples. Because it saw *mestizaje* and cultural hybridity as spiritual advances and not signs of decay, *La raza cósmica* was important in one of its original historical contexts, that of resistance to neocolonial domination, as it was again in the early days of the Chicano movement. As I have noted, such affirmations are subversive in the context of white supremacy, which depends on strict racial divisions and fears amalgamation. At least as important to Vasconcelos as this challenge to racial hierarchy is the idea that the creation of the "cosmic race" will signal the worldwide advent of a new, aesthetically and spiritually oriented age. As such, Vasconcelos's text takes part in a Hispanic modernist tradition which, as Iris Zavala puts it, posited "a third way out between European colonialism and North American imperialism,"[114] and created "a hegemony of cultural formalization founded in the logic of identity, while bringing into question modern forms of capitalist expansion."[115] In this sense, it can be (and has been) said that *La raza cósmica* is a philosophical essay and utopian projection rather than a program to be taken literally. It is nonetheless worth paying attention to the terms in which Vasconcelos casts his hopes, for the sake of what they reveal about the problems that inhere in them and thus, in the unexamined acceptance of the "hybridity" concept. We should note as well that Vasconcelos was head of the National University of Mexico and minister of Education during the presidency of Alvaro Obregón (1920–1924). In this postrevolutionary period, *mestizaje* was a state ideology wielded to strengthen citizens' adherence to the nation-state in a program that included the deculturation of indigenous peoples.[116] Vasconcelos developed his theories of *mestizaje* in this national context, where their meaning is explicitly hierarchical. Deployed in this way, *mestizaje* is a strategy of containment and not of transgression.[117]

Anzaldúa is careful to say that her ideas are a "takeoff" on Vasconcelos';[118] she is interested in him, she says, for his "inclusivity" (as opposed to white America's ideology of racial purity) and his defense of hybrid being as superior, rather than inferior.[119] So Anzaldúa's use of Vasconcelos is evocative rather than literal. Vasconcelos himself, however, strongly privileges the Caucasian element in his program for a "fifth universal race"[120] (7) whose creation, he says, is the "transcendental mission"[121] (7)—and, I point out, the justification—of what he considers to be the spiritual purpose of European, and in particular Iberian colonialism. Consider the attitude toward Native and African Americans expressed in this passage:

> North Americans have held very firmly to their resolution to maintain a pure stock, the reason being that they are faced with the Blacks, who are like the opposite pole . . . In the Ibero-American world, the problem does not present itself in such crude terms. We have very few Blacks, and a large part of them is already becoming a mulatto population. The Indian is a good bridge for racial mixing.[122]

To be fair to Vasconcelos, we must recognize that *La raza cósmica* in its happier moments is an attempt to formulate a program that looks like intercultural integration. In the following passage, for instance, the *mestizo* synthesis is articulated in part as a mobile configuration of differences.

This time, the race that will come out of the forgotten Atlantis will no longer be a race of a single color or of particular features. The future race will not be a fifth, or a sixth race, destined to prevail over its ancestors. What is going to emerge out there is the definitive race, the synthetical race, the integral race, made up of the genius and the blood of all peoples and, for that reason, more capable of true brotherhood and of a truly universal vision.[123]

Yet in his text as a whole, the subject-position with the greatest weight is male and Ibero-Caucasian, and the logic of fragmentation and unity supersedes the logic of difference(s).

The "cosmic" Ibero-American—exemplar of a master race?—may not have a specific phenotype, but the concept of racial hierarchy is preserved, and community is still thought of in terms of blood.

Vasconcelos's paradigm is here at best an oppositional stance to the US melting pot it so strongly resembles. Even if we justify it, as is possible in some of its contexts, as a form of "strategic" essentialism, its flaws are serious enough to call into question the implications of its use. It is my contention that Vasconcelos's model is not simply retrograde or unsophisticated, but rather a strikingly clear illustration of certain risks that inhere in more subtle liminal models as well. Some of these risks, as should be clear by now, are that hybridity and liminality as models for counterhegemonic identities fossilize all too easily into new unities, and that this privileging of hybridity and liminality as universalized theoretical concepts may gloss over the telling of specific histories and consciously formulated particularities. This is important because, despite Anzaldúa's invitation to meet her at the border, and despite the parallels a theorist like Jean-Luc Nancy draws between his own "mixed" history as a twentieth-century Frenchman and the Chicano experience, we are not all *mestizos* now.[124] Some choose to enter the borderlands, but others are irrevocably there. Everyone may be a fluctuating subject, but we did not all slip across the border last night, nor stand on a Los Angeles street corner this morning waiting to be picked up for a day's undocumented work. We have not all sewed in clandestine sweatshops, nor picked fruit at a few cents a box to pay the rent. And the borderlands, whatever else they may mean, also mean this.

The border paradigm does not include those who cannot pass, like the Tarascan fisherman Etienne Balibar met in Pátzcuaro,[125] or those whose racial and cultural mixtures do not include metropolitan elements. And the imagination of Aztlán invokes Native cultures and deities from central Mexico, as though the borderlands themselves had no Mexican side. At this point the "borderlands" are at once dislodged from local contexts and marked specifically as a US location—using a US-generated mythology and speaking from that home. In an extensive discussion of Vasconcelos's work and Anzaldúa's,

Juliet Hooker shows how myths of Latin American racial harmony have been used to posit a Latino racial exceptionalism in the United States. She notes that these claims are also used to enable conservative Latino racial projects that "depict Latinos as an alternative to the US racial order, and to African Americans in particular."[126]

Rubén Medina has also traced out connections and disjunctions between *mestizaje* as formulated by Vasconcelos and Anzaldúa, in the context of Latin American discourse on the topic since the colonial period and contemporary theory on the hybrid subject. Using the material Vasconcelos deploys to theorize *mestizaje* and propose a model for national culture, Anzaldúa, speaking as a *mestiza* subject, models an aspirational culture outside nation, often articulated at the level of inner life. In a section on *mestizaje* as "self-fashioning" in Anzaldúa, he poses an important question: how possible is it, really, to untangle elements of a national culture to design one's own?[127] The tension between giving voice to the oppressed and forming a new, solidary but liberated subject seems unresolved. Yet this is the most fundamental of the chasms Anzaldúa tries to bridge.

BEYOND HYBRIDITY

In the search for nonhomogenizing, nonauthoritarian ways to build coalitions, the mere invocation of mestizaje and other liminal identities and spaces, as against essentialized identities, is insufficient: we must go on to ask ourselves what happens once we recognize that liminality in fact, to a greater or lesser extent, characterizes the spaces we inhabit. Indeed, theories of heterogeneity, when they fossilize into new unities, maybe doing this to compensate for their inability to sustain an examination of power relations within liminal spaces and contradictions within so-called hybrid identities.

Theories of heterogeneity develop partially out of the desire to overcome the limitations of a politics based on essentialized identities. But they themselves substantially risk idealizing the liminal subject, and in this way come to constitute the creation of a new, unitary subject. In this essay I have tried to show how theories of heterogeneity, which appear to undermine the self/other paradigm by positing a nonunitary subjectivity, bring the two terms into contact (the "new *mestiza*" is a bridge between unities) but do not necessarily call the oppositions which define selfness and otherness into question or undermine their construction as mutually exclusive. An example of this is Anzaldúa's figuration of the "new *mestiza*" as a bridge between unities (e.g., Mexico, "white America," male, female). Her text wants to corrode these unities and call into question the neatness of their separation and hierarchization. But when it conceives the "borderlands" in terms of oppositions and their reconciliation, it reinstalls dualistic thought and the hierarchies that dualisms force us to replicate.

I have added to this that the language used to describe heterogeneity, in Anzaldúa's text and elsewhere, often reveals the slippage between a theory which affirms multiplicity and a theory which creates a new hegemony, a new, unitary subject, and thence, perhaps, a recurrence of the myth of cultural "purity." I have criticized also the idealization of the "borderlands," which may just as easily be a space of deracinated incoherence as of celebratory heterogeneity. Because they can mean loss without gain, the borderlands, though they offer opportunities to rethink and reshape identities, cannot be construed as a space of free play. Anyone who has inhabited an actual border zone can attest to the difference one's papers and one's looks make there.

Another problem deriving from what I have called the "slippage back to wholeness" in Anzaldúa's text is that her use of the Chicana lesbian as supreme example of both multiple oppression and "border" identities may in fact reinstall racial and sexual hierarchies—albeit inverted ones. The "new *mestiza*" in *Borderlands/La Frontera* occupies a combination of the most abject subject-positions this text imagines, and because of her position between worlds, she becomes, in the logic of this text, an ideal agent of social change. But as we know, the presentation of any single constellation of subject-positions as the "most" abject or the "most" liminal easily functions to obscure other subaltern positions. For instance, the "new *mestiza*," marginalized though she may be, speaks English and holds a US passport. In these aspects of her social positioning she is privileged in relation to, say, the undocumented Mayan worker who also crosses the border, but who knows no English and speaks Yucatec Maya better than they do Spanish. A further implication of the reinstallation of hierarchies in Anzaldúa's text and in some other theories of hybridity is that it may assign the heaviest tasks of social change to those most marginalized, those most discriminated against. In Anzaldúa's context, that subject is the multiply oppressed *mestiza*. In contexts where the liminal or hybrid subject is a not a figure of multiple oppression but one of conciliation, the assignation of primary revolutionary work to them actually functions to obscure subaltern representation.

Whether "border" identities are necessarily radical ones is another pertinent question here. Though Anzaldúa's book is based on the notion of radicalizing experience, it does not address the failure of experience to provide radical consciousness. For example, when Anzaldúa asserts a type of natural bond between the gay and the mestiza, she denies the existence of racism in the gay community. Where does the gay white Republican fall on the [r]evolutionary continuum? How do we account for the assimilationist politics of Chicano writer Richard Rodríguez—a contemporary of Anzaldúa's—or explain intraminority racisms? Why is solidarity so hard to attain?[128]

The problem here may be that Anzaldúa's text bears witness in one direction but theorizes in another. Liminality, which is poetically evocative of a historical situation in Anzaldúa's text, functions differently when the same text proposes it as a theoretical model. At that point, liminality begins to conceal the contradictions it was initially invoked to expose and celebrate. Liminality and hybridity, initially transgressive, are shaded into figures of conciliation that obscure conflict and difference. It is here that *Borderlands/ La Frontera* invites universalizing readings, idealizations of mestizaje and hybridity, and emulations of the "new *mestiza*" by more privileged subjects who might better spend our time doing concrete political work. It is when Anzaldúa emphasizes a liminality or *mestizaje* which does not smooth over a multiplicity of differences, and a solidarity that does not rely on "natural" connections, that she best shows how we might, in Toni Cade Bambara's words, "fearlessly work towards potent meshings."[129]

Such meshings are most effectively made when specific histories and local knowledge are not glossed over. How to conjugate local knowledge and a postnational universalism that might contest the increasing marginalization of already marginal subjects in the current global order is perhaps the most important question in left theory today. In *Borderlands/La Frontera*, Anzaldúa addresses this question by bringing into view a Chicano/a history and a lesbian subjectivity within it. She then reveals how these stories are connected with those of a dominant culture that tries not to see how closely its own history is imbricated with that of its others. She shows how, particularly along the US-Mexico border, those others are in fact barely foreign. Mexican and indigenous difference challenges "American" unity. And it does not attack from the outside but corrode from within. That this corrosion may be a good thing for the mythical body it attacks is one of Anzaldúa's more important theses. I am more interested in her text when it works this medicine of corrosion than when it speaks a language of easy inclusivity. I am interested in the corrosion of centralities—including that of the "new *mestiza*," to the extent that she may suffer fetichization in theory—because I suspect such corrosion is a necessary precondition for coalition-building.

If the exposition in *Borderlands/La Frontera*'s of liminality and multiple differences slips sometimes toward a wholeness that is problematic because it may obscure subaltern positions on the one hand, and on the other enable more privileged subjects to identify all too easily with the "borderlands," one level at which it does not do this is the level of language. As Anzaldúa tells us and a number of her commentators emphasize, the bilingualism of this text confounds both English- and Spanish-language purity. Unevenly divided between the several idioms in which it is written, *Borderlands/La Frontera* shifts tongues unpredictably.[130] Although she provides English versions for some of the Spanish-language sections and explanatory footnotes for others,

Anzaldúa never implies an easy translatability of tongues, and some sections are not translated at all. This is to say that this text offers no single, easily accessible common language. Its various tongues cut against each other, running both together and apart. In this way it presents a serious challenge to the monocultural reader, and it interdicts any facile access to the borderlands. Through their languages, these borderlands show layer upon layer of history to those who follow their tangled paths, or in Anzaldúa's metaphor, their forking tongues. This intertwining of differences does not take recourse in myths of commonality, imperial-humanist, or otherwise. Nor does it allow assertions of difference that avoid addressing what there is of a common history. Anzaldúa's linguistic thickets also engage the reader in a way that blocks the easy pluralism which, as Joan Wallach Scott puts it, "is seen as a condition of human existence rather than as the effect of difference that constitutes hierarchies."[131] Rather, the use of language(s) in *Borderlands/La Frontera* works to show a historical interconnectedness among them, and to reveal the ways in which difference and conflict structure that history.

This linguistic challenge—which José David Saldívar also discusses in some detail[132]—is the aspect of her text that meets the strongest resistance from monocultural readers, although other kinds of readers are exhilarated with the legitimation of linguistic *mestizaje* (Castillo 2006: 265).[133] The evocation of the pain *of the colonial experience* is another aspect of the text that meets strong resistance, and the third is the political nature of Anzaldúa's lesbianism or more precisely, her rejection of what Adrienne Rich called "compulsory heterosexuality."[134] It appears to me, accordingly, that these are the points at which *Borderlands/La Frontera* is a radical intervention. The topics of border-crossing, personal transformation, breaking from home, and writing seem to get the most play, both among general readers of liberal bent and critics seeking a general model for the decolonized, or decolonizing subject. The actual US-Mexico borderlands are still a place of difficulty and conflict. Turning inward from the fields, the guards, and now the detention camps, the psychic borderlands in which Anzaldúa writes are a fertile spiritual space. But the "borderlands" as theoretical concept seems to leave the material borderlands behind.

Castillo notes that this point has been raised before by Chicano intellectuals like Pablo Vila and Benjamín Alire Sáenz and the Mexican scholar María Socorro Tabuenca, but that the "dominant-culture academic establishment" has maintained its fascination with the project of reimagining the United States, or the nation-state in general, as transnational borderlands, ignoring these more complex readings of Anzaldúa's text. Respectful recognition of these criticisms such as those found in Mariana Ortega's philosophical work *In-Between* still grounds Anzaldúa's work in the United States Southwest and in European philosophy,[135] which are, perhaps, its actual locations. Again, this is not a problem with Anzaldúa herself as much as it is with the attempts to hold her work up not as speech from a place but as a general model for a contestatory subject—transnational, intersectional, decolonial, subaltern. Similarly, *mestizaje* in Spanish America, as should be clear by now, "is a nation-building concept, not a resistant one . . . that often resolves to racialist usages."[136] It also draws on racialist theories, and it coexists with and supports racist practices.

That is, *mestizaje* and *mestizo* culture are not always antidotes to racism or cross-cultural alliances for liberation. Although *mestizaje* in daily life can be heterogeneous and inclusive, not homogenizing and hierarchical,[137] it can also intertwine with discrimination in such a way as to fragment, rather than unite communities, and to reproduce hierarchies and social distance.[138] This is true even though terms like *métissage* have other meanings in other places.[139] I would add and emphasize that the literary construction of a national subject with indigenous roots, modern-democratic feeling, and transnational potential has been an elite, not a subaltern project in Latin America for over two hundred years. This subject is a product of colonialism, and it could be argued that it was crafted after formal decolonization to anchor the modern/colonial world system in place, not to dismantle it. In addition, Anzaldúa and her commentators seem far more interested in borders between the "Third World" and the First than they do in borders outside metropolitan space; the same can be said for their emphasis on cultural and racial mixtures that include a large "First World" component. This is, of course, because the *mestizo* is a colonial formation; *mestizaje* as mixture is fraught because of the power differential and colonial history it implies. But when the *mestizo/a* is essentialized as an insurgent class, actual *mestizo* histories are obscured; the universalized borderlands become the terrain of a familiar, now generic Other in global metropolitan space. Those with access to this space may invoke intersectionality or "new *mestizaje*," but darker others—differently intersectional and transnational—disappear from view. And as Olguín points out,[140] so does the fact that not every *mestizo* position is an insurgent one.

Such disappearance, of course, is not what Anzaldúa wanted. The fundamental problems she tackles—how to build coalitions across social boundaries, how to enable subaltern representation, and how (paradoxically enough) to dismantle the cultural and political structures that produce subalternity—are still with us, and she has given us valuable tools for this work. But is "borderland" always a useful metaphor? When I go in to advocate for ICE detainees tomorrow (my political work of late), it will not be at the border; it will be deep inside the US prison system, in an out-of-the-way town in rural Louisiana. The facility—for these prisons are privatized—is owned and operated by a transnational corporation but I, and the prisoners I visit, will be bound to nations by the documents we have and lack. We will be in my country, and we will reach across national boundaries and class lines. We will do it as *mestizos* or not, *nepantleras* or not.

The issue here may be, as Emiko Saldívar puts it for the Mexican case, that multiculturalism and interculturality—revisions of hegemonic *mestizaje*—all emphasize cultural recognition and rights over political rights and the recognition of racial injustice.[141] To echo Rubén Medina, one may design a "border" identity of one's own, outside discourse and daily life, but how possible is it to disentangle that identity from the elements with which it was made?[142] It is also that transnationalism, like *mestizaje*, can be deployed in multiple ways. Much work on Anzaldúa locates her in US-based debates and her affinities worldwide, and cites Latin American theorists of subalternity and decoloniality, but sidelines a more serious look at Anzaldúa's own interaction with, and insertion in the Mexican and broader Latin American fields. At this point the question of what we mean when we use terms like transnationalism and intersectionality, not to mention comparative studies or America, must still be asked.

NOTES

1. Gloria Anzaldúa, *Borderlands/La Frontera: The New Mestiza* (San Francisco: Spinsters/Aunt Lute, 1987).

2. An early version of this essay was coauthored with Lisa Walker and presented at the forty-seventh International Conference of Americanists (New Orleans, 1991). I am grateful for Lisa's insights, which still mark the text.

3. Cherríe Moraga and Gloria Anzaldúa, eds., *This Bridge Called My Back: Writings by Radical Women of Color* (New York: Kitchen Table/Women of Color Press, 1983).

4. Sonia Saldívar-Hull, "Introduction to the Second Edition," in Gloria Anzaldúa, *Borderlands/La Frontera: The New Mestiza*, 2nd ed. (San Francisco: Aunt Lute Books, 1999), 1–15.

5. Sonia Saldívar-Hull, *Feminism on the Border: Chicana Gender Politics and Literature* (Berkeley: University of California Press, 2000).

6. Octavio Paz, *El laberinto de la soledad* (Mexico: Ediciones Cuadernos Americanos, 1950).

7. AnaLouise Keating, "Re-envisioning Coyolxauhqui, Decolonizing Reality: Anzaldúa's Twenty-First-Century Imperative," in Gloria Anzaldúa, *Light in the Dark/Luz en lo Oscuro: Rewriting Identity, Spirituality, Reality*, edited by AnaLouise Keating (Durham: Duke University Press, 2015), ix–xxxvii.

8. Clara Román-Odio, *Sacred Iconographies in Chicana Cultural Productions* (New York: Palgrave, 2013), 51.

9. See Walter Mignolo, *Local Histories, Global Designs: Coloniality, Subalternity, and Border Thinking* (Princeton, Princeton University Press, 2000).

10. Frances Negrón-Muntaner, "Bridging Islands: Gloria Anzaldúa and the Caribbean," *PMLA* 121, no. 1 (January 2006): 272–78.

11. Paola Bacchetta, "Transnational Borderlands. Gloria Anzaldúa's Epistemologies of Resistance and Lesbians 'of color' in France," in Norma Cantú and Christina L. Gutiérrez (eds.), *Güeras y Prietas: Celebrating Twenty Years of Borderlands/La Frontera* (San Antonio: Adelante Project, 2009), 77–92.

12. Maria Antònia Oliver-Rotger, "Gloria Anzaldúa's Borderless Theory in Spain," *Signs: Journal of Women in Culture and Society* 37, no. 1 (Autumn 2011): 5–10.

13. Tereza Kynčlová, "Prospects of Anzaldúan Thought for a Czech Future," *Signs: Journal of Women in Culture and Society* 37, no. 1 (Autumn 2011): 23–29; Ewa Majewska, "La Mestiza from Ukraine? Border Crossing with Gloria Anzaldúa," *Signs: Journal of Women in Culture and Society* 37, no. 1 (Autumn 2011): 34–41; and Grażyna Zygadło, "Where the Third World Grates Against the First: Teaching Gloria Anzaldúa from a Polish Perspective," *Signs: Journal of Women in Culture and Society* 37, no. 1 (Autumn 2011): 29–34.

14. Anna Guttman, *The Nation of India in Contemporary Indian Literature* (New York: Palgrave, 2007), 68–69.

15. Smadar Lavie, "Where is the Mizrahi-Palestinian Border Zone? Interrogating Feminist Transnationalism through the Bounds of the Lived," *Social Semiotics* 21, no. 1 (2011): 67–83.

16. Nepantla is a Nahuatl term meaning "in the middle" or "in between," famously cited by the Dominican friar Diego Durán in 1579 and used throughout the colonial period to mean being between religions and cultural worlds. Anzaldúa uses the term in reference to Chicano culture. In *Borderlands/La Frontera* it means torn or uprooted, but also indicates a psychic or spiritual "borderlands," a space of transformation. This is the sense she develops for *nepantla* in her later work. See nuanced discussion by Viviana Díaz Balsera, "Voicing Mesoamerican Identities on the Roads of Empire," in *To Be Indio in Colonial Spanish America*, edited by Mónica Díaz (Albuquerque: University of New Mexico Press, 2017), 169–90, and history of the term's use in Mexico, including in Rosario Castellanos (clearly one of Anzaldúa's sources), by Lourdes Parra Lazcano in "Rosario Castellanos entre México e Israel," *Bulletin of Hispanic Studies* 95, no. 7 (2018): 784–86. See also Victor Turner's concept of the "liminal" space and the transformative power of "liminal" beings in *The Ritual Process: Structure and Anti-Structure* (London: Penguin, 1969), and the critique of Anzaldúa's use of *nepantla* in Marcos de R. Antuna, "What We Talk about When We Talk about *Nepantla*: Anzaldúa and the Queer Fruit of Aztec Philosophy," *Journal of Latinos and Education* 17, no. 2 (2018): 159–63.

17. Walter Mignolo, *The Darker Side of the Renaissance: Literacy, Territoriality, and Colonization* (Ann Arbor: U of Michigan P, 1995), xiii.

18. Mignolo, *Local Histories, Global Designs*, 3.

19. See Rafael Pérez-Torres, *Mestizaje: Critical Uses of Race in Chicano Culture* (Minneapolis, University of Minnesota Press, 2005), 3–50, on Anzaldúa's contexts in Chicano cultural expression and the reflections on race and culture her work has inspired, and Mariana Ortega, *In-Between: Latina Feminist Phenomenology,*

Multiplicity, and Self (Albany: SUNY Press, 2016), 17–86, on intersubjectivity and selfhood in Anzaldúa.

20. In Castillo and Tabuenca, *Border Women: Writing from La Frontera* (Minneapolis: University of Minnesota Press, 2002); Debra A. Castillo and María Socorro Tabuenca Córdoba point out that Anzaldúa's borderlands are specifically the US borderlands, eliding the border culture of the other side. Castillo's "Anzaldúa and Transnational American Studies" (PMLA 121, no. 1 [January 2006]: 260–65) expands upon this point, noting that Anzaldúa's *mestizaje* is contestatory in the United States but not in Spanish America, where the embrace of Spanish and the Indianizing stance are conservative positions. In *In-Between*, Ortega responds to the comment that Anzaldúa narrates from a US perspective by pointing out that she lacks privilege and is still marginalized within the United States (29–35). This response, again, is based on US debates.

21. Anzaldúa, *Borderlands/La Frontera*, 3.

22. Rodrigo Lazo and Jesse Alemán (eds.), *The Latino Nineteenth Century* (New York: New York University Press, 2016).

23. Kirsten Silva Greusz, *Ambassadors of Culture: The Transamerican Origins of Latino Writing* (Princeton: Princeton University Press, 2002); "The Gulf of Mexico System and the 'Latinness' of New Orleans," *American Literary History* 18, no. 4 (Fall 2006): 468–95; "Alien Speech, Incorporated: On the Cultural History of Spanish in the U.S.," *American Literary History* 25, no. 1 (Spring 2013): 18–32; "What Was Latino Literature?" *PMLA* 127, no. 2 (March 2012): 335–41; "Mexican/American: The Making of Borderlands Print Culture," *US Popular Print Culture, 1860–1920*, edited by Christine Bold (Oxford: Oxford University Press, 2011), 457–76; "Transamerican New Orleans: From the Spanish Period to Post-Katrina," *Cambridge History of Latino/a Literature*, eds. John Morán González and Laura Lomas (Cambridge: Cambridge University Press, 2018), 176–89.

24. See Mariana Alessandri and Alexander Stehn, "Gloria Anzaldúa's Mexican Genealogy: From *Pelados* and *Pachucos* to New Mestizas," *Genealogy* 4, no. 1 (2020): 12, https://doi.org/10.3390/genealogy4010012.

25. Tace Hedrick, "Queering the Cosmic Race: Esotericism, Mestizaje and Sexuality in the Work of Gabriela Mistral and Gloria Anzaldúa," *Aztlán: A Journal of Chicano Studies* 2 (Fall 2009): 67–98.

26. Gilda Luongo, "Amasijo. 'En la tierra de en medio' o Nepantla en la poesía de Rosario Castellanos," *Revista Nomadías* 22 (December 2016): 50.

27. Lazcano, "Rosario Castellanos entre México e Israel."

28. Josefina Saldaña-Portillo, *The Revolutionary Imagination in the Americas and the Age of Development* (Durham: Duke UP, 2003).

29. Sheila Marie Contreras, *Blood Lines: Myth, Indigenism, and Chicana/o Literature* (Austin: University of Texas Press), 2008.

30. B. V. Olguín, "Caballeros and Indians: Mexican-American Whiteness, Hegemonic Mestizaje, and Ambivalent Indigeneity in Proto-Chicana/o Autobiographical Discourse, 1858–2008," *MELUS: Multi-Ethnic Literature of the United States* 38, no. 1 (2013): 30–49.

31. Olguín, "Caballeros and Indians," 32.

32. Luis Leal, "El corrido de Joaquin Murrieta: origen y difusión," *Mexican History/Estudios Mexicanos* 11, no. 1 (Winter 1995): 1–23.

33. Robert Irwin, "Toward a Border Gnosis of the Borderlands: Joaquín Murrieta and Nineteenth Century U.S.-Mexico Border Culture," *Nepantla: Views from the South* 2–3 (2001): 516–19.

34. Anzaldúa, *Borderlands/La Frontera*, 3. Translation mine.

35. Anzaldúa, *Borderlands/La Frontera*, 3.

36. José David Saldívar, "Unsettling Race, Coloniality and Caste: Anzaldúa's *Borderlands/La Frontera*, Martinez's *Parrot in the Oven*, and Roy's *The God of Small Things*," in *Globalization and the Decolonial Option*, edited by Walter Mignolo and Arturo Escobar (London: Routledge, 2004), 216.

37. See Chela Sandoval, "U.S. Third World Feminism: The Theory and Method of Oppositional Consciousness in the Postmodern World," *Genders* 10 (Spring, 1991), on the distinction between oppositional identities which reproduce the dominant social order and the counterhegemonic "tactical subjectivity" she calls "differential consciousness" (14), and her development of this concept in Sandoval, *Methodology of the Oppressed* (Minneapolis: University of Minnesota Press, 2000), 41–66. By "oppositional identities," I mean identities which oppose the "norm" and therefore risk strengthening the power of the norm as such, as well as reinstalling such binary oppositions as black/white, male/female, inside/outside.

38. Linda Gordon, "On Difference," *Genders* 10 (Spring 1991): 91.

39. Alberto Moreiras, *The Exhaustion of Difference: The Politics of Latin American Cultural Studies* (Durham: Duke UP, 2001), 190.

40. Nancy K. Miller, "Changing the Subject: Authorship, Writing, and the Reader," *Feminist Studies/Critical Studies*, edited by Teresa de Lauretis (Bloomington: Indiana UP, 1986), 106.

41. Diana Fuss, *Essentially Speaking: Feminism, Nature, and Difference* (New York: Routledge, 1989).

42. Angie Chabram-Denersersian, "I Throw Punches for My Race, but I Don't Want to Be a Man: Writing Us—Chica-nos (Girl, Us)/Chicanas—into the Movement Script," in *Cultural Studies*, edited by Lawrence Grossberg, Cary Nelson, and Paula Triechler (New York: Routledge, 1992), 81–95.

43. Yvonne Yarbro-Bejarano notes, however, that the terms "border" and "*mestiza*" invite decontextualized, universalizing readings in a way that Sandoval's "oppositional" and "differential" do not. See Yarbro-Bejarano, "Gloria Anzaldúa's *Borderlands/La Frontera*: Cultural Studies, 'Difference,' and the Non-Unitary Subject," *Cultural Critique* 28 (Autumn 1994): 7–9.

44. Norma Alarcón, "Conjugating Subjects: The Heteroglossia of Essence and Resistance," in *An Other Tongue*, edited by Alfred Arteaga (Durham: Duke University Press, 1994), 136–37.

45. Judith Raiskin, "Inverts and Hybrids: Lesbian Reworkings of Sexual and Racial Identities," in *The Lesbian Postmodern*, edited by Laura Doan (New York: Columbia University Press, 1994), 162–63.

46. See Yarbro-Bejarano, "Gloria Anzaldúa's *Borderlands/La Frontera*."

47. Patricia J. Williams, "Big Words, Small Divisions," *The Nation* 265, no. 6 (August 25/September 1, 1997): 9.

48. Gayatri Chakravorty Spivak, "Subaltern Studies: Deconstructing Historiography. Historiography," In *Other Worlds: Essays in Cultural Politics*, edited by Gayatri Spivak (New York: Methuen, 1987), 209.

49. Anzaldúa, *Borderlands/La Frontera*, 3.

50. Anzaldúa, *Borderlands/La Frontera*, 78.

51. Anzaldúa, *Borderlands/La Frontera*, Preface.

52. Carmen M. del Río, "Chicana Poets: Re-visions from the Margin," *Revista canadiense de estudios hispánicos* XIV, no. 3 (1990): 432–33.

53. Anzaldúa, *Borderlands/La Frontera*, 55.

54. Anzaldúa, *Borderlands/La Frontera*, 58.

55. Anzaldúa, *Borderlands/La Frontera*, Preface.

56. Anzaldúa, *Borderlands/La Frontera*, 79.

57. Anzaldúa, *Borderlands/La Frontera*, 18–20.

58. Anzaldúa, *Borderlands/La Frontera*, 84.

59. Anzaldúa, *Borderlands/La Frontera*, 82.

60. Anzaldúa, *Borderlands/La Frontera*, 72, 73.

61. Anzaldúa, *Borderlands/La Frontera*, Preface.

62. Anzaldúa, *Borderlands/La Frontera*, 194, emphasis added.

63. Anzaldúa, *Borderlands/La Frontera*, 195.

64. Minnie Bruce Pratt, "Identity: Skin Blood Heart," in *Yours in Struggle: Three Feminist Perspectives on Anti-Semitism and Racism*, edited by Elly Bulkin et al. (Brooklyn: Long Haul Press, 1984), 1–63.

65. Pratt, "Identity: Skin Blood Heart," 16.

66. Pratt, "Identity: Skin Blood Heart," 25–26.

67. Pratt, "Identity: Skin Blood Heart," 17.

68. Pratt, "Identity: Skin Blood Heart," 50.

69. Pratt, "Identity: Skin Blood Heart," 82.

70. Néstor García Canclini, "Cultural Reconversion," in *On Edge: The Crisis of Contemporary Latin American* Culture, edited by George Yúdice, Jean Franco, and Juan Flores (Minneapolis: University of Minnesota Press, 1992), 42.

71. Caren Kaplan, "Deterritorializations: The Rewriting of Home and Exile in Western Feminist Discourse," in *The Nature and Context of Minority Discourse*, edited by Abdul JanMohamed and David Lloyd (New York: Oxford UP, 1990), 357–68.

72. Yarbro-Bejarano, "Gloria Anzaldúa's *Borderlands/La Frontera*," 8.

73. Kimberly Christensen, "'With Whom Do You Believe Your Lot Is Cast?' White Feminists and Racism," *Signs* 22, no. 3 (Spring 1997): 619.

74. Christensen, "With Whom Do You Believe," 621.

75. Chantal Mouffe, "Radical Democracy: Modern or Postmodern?" in *Universal Abandon: The Politics of Postmodernism*, edited by Andrew Ross (Minneapolis: University of Minnesota Press, 1988), 44.

76. Ernesto Laclau and Chantal Mouffe, *Hegemony and Socialist Strategy* (London: Verso, 1985), 192.

77. Anzaldúa, *Borderlands/La Frontera*, 19.

78. Anzaldúa, *Borderlands/La Frontera*, 85.

79. John Beverley, "Does the Project of the Left Have a Future?" *Boundary 2* 24, no. 1 (1997): 35–57.

80. Chantal Mouffe, "Democratic Politics and the Question of Identity," in *The Identity in Question*, edited by John Rajchmann (New York: Routledge, 1995), 33–45.

81. "Difference" is a loaded term which needs further explanation. In this sentence I am using it to signify the imagining of identities that are neither unified nor fragments of a supposed unity.

82. Pratt, "Identity: Skin Blood Heart," 57.

83. Anzaldúa, *Borderlands/La Frontera*, 195.

84. Anzaldúa, *Borderlands/La Frontera*, 203.

85. Neil Larsen, "Foreword," in *Border Writing: The Multidimensional Text*, edited by D. Emily Hicks (Minneapolis: University of Minnesota Press, 1991), xx.

86. See Castillo, "Anzaldúa and Transnational American Studies."

87. Marisol de la Cadena, "Are *Mestizos* Hybrids? The Conceptual Politics of Andean Identities," *Journal of Latin American Studies* 37, no. 2 (2005): 259–84.

88. Claudio Lomnitz-Adler, *Exits from the Labyrinth: Culture and Ideology in the Mexican National Space* (Berkeley: University of California Press, 1992), 39.

89. Jorge Klor de Alva, "The Postcolonization of the (Latin) American Experience: A Reconsideration of 'Colonialism,' 'Postcolonialism,' and 'Mestizaje,'" in *After Colonialism: Imperial Histories and Postcolonial Displacements*, edited by Gyan Prakash (Princeton: Princeton UP, 1995), 241–75.

90. See Yarbro-Bejarano, "Gloria Anzaldúa's *Borderlands/La Frontera*," and Contreras, *Blood Lines*.

91. See Irwin, "Toward a Border Gnosis."

92. Ortega, *In-Between*.

93. Castillo and Tabuenca, *Border Women*.

94. Lomnitz-Adler, *Exits from the Labyrinth*, 2, 261–81.

95. Iris Zavala, *Colonialism and Culture: Hispanic Modernisms and the Social Imaginary* (Bloomington: Indiana University Press, 1992).

96. Joshua Goode, *Impurity of Blood: Defining Race in Spain, 1870–1930* (Baton Rouge: Louisiana State University Press, 2009).

97. Leslie Bary, "The Search for Cultural Identity," in *Problems in Modern Latin American History*, edited by John C. Chasteen and Joseph Tulchin (Wilmington: Scholarly Resources, 1994), 169–70.

98. See Lomnitz-Adler, *Exits from the Labyrinth*, 30–34, and Richard Graham (ed.), *The Idea of Race in Latin America, 1870–1940* (Austin: University of Texas Press, 1990).

99. Useful discussions of the *mestizo* as hegemonic category include John Kraniauskas, "Hybridity in a Transnational Frame: Latin-Americanist and Postcolonial Perspectives on Cultural Studies," *Nepantla: Views from the South* 1, no. 1 (2000): 111–37; Moreiras, *The Exhaustion of Difference*, 184–207, and Gonzalo Portocarrero, *Racismo y mestizaje y otros ensayos* (Lima: Fondo Editorial del Congreso del Perú,

2007). On the *mestizaje*-based critique of colonialism and imperialism by Hispanic authors since the late nineteenth century, see Zavala, *Colonialism and Culture*.

100. Unlike Judith Raiskin and some later critics who on this point speak to Anzaldúa's intentions more than to the way her text actually works, I do not think *Borderlands/La Frontera*'s postmodern reworking of nineteenth-century racial classifications frees itself of their contradictions. See Raiskin, "Inverts and Hybrids," 162.

101. Simón Bolívar, "Discurso ante el Congreso de Angostura," in *Simón Bolívar: Escritos fundamentales* (Caracas: Monte Avila, 1982), 137 (translation mine).

102. Laura Catelli, "'Y de esta manera quedaron todos los hombres sin mujeres': Mestizaje como estrategia de colonización en la Española (1501–1503)," *Revista de crítica literaria latinoamericana* 74 (2011): 232.

103. Gonzalo Conrado Cabrera Quintero, *La creación del imaginario del indio en la literatura mexicana del siglo XIX* (Puebla: Benemérita Universidad Autónoma de Puebla, Dirección General de Fomento Editorial, 2005), 44.

104. Simón Bolívar, "The Jamaica Letter: Response from a South American to a Gentleman of this Island," in *El Libertador: Writings of Simón Bolívar*, edited by David Bushnell (New York: Oxford UP, 2003), 18.

105. Doris Sommer, *Foundational Fictions: The National Romances of Latin America* (Berkeley: University of California Press, 1991).

106. Vera Kutzinski, *Sugar's Secrets: Race and the Erotics of Cuban Nationalism* (Charlottesville: University Press of Virginia, 1993).

107. See Julio Ramos, *Desencuentros de la modernidad en América Latina* (Mexico City: Fondo de Cultura Económica, 1989), José David Saldívar, *The Dialectics of Our America: Genealogy, Cultural Critique, and Literary History* (Durham: Duke University Press, 1991), 123–48, and Roberto Fernández Retamar, *Caliban and Other Essays*, translated by Edward Baker (Minneapolis: University of Minnesota Press, 1989.

108. José Martí, "Our America," in *The America of José Martí*, translated by Juan de Onís (New York: Noonday Press, 1953), 138–51.

109. Ramos, *Desencuentros de la modernidad*, 239.

110. As in this passage, where it is clear who directs the multiracial nation: "The Indian circled about us in silent wonder . . . The runaway negro poured out the music of his heart . . . alone and unknown among the rivers and wild beasts . . . . The stroke of genius would have been to couple the headband and tunic with the charity of heart and daring of the founding father; to rescue the Indian; to make a place for the able Negro. . . ." Martí, "Our America," 146.

111. Martí, "Our America," 150.

112. Sylvia Spitta's *Between Two Waters: Narratives of Transculturation in Latin America* (College Station: Texas A&M University Press, 2005) is a good, extended discussion of this work.

113. See John Beverley, *Subalternity and Representation: Arguments in Cultural Theory* (Durham: Duke University Press, 1999); Moreiras, *The Exhaustion of Difference*, and Eric Lott's discussion of the politics of "diversity" in the United States in "The New Cosmopolitanism: Whose America?" *Transition* 72 (Winter 1996): 108–35.

114. Zavala, *Colonialism and Culture*, 9.

115. Zavala, *Colonialism and Culture*, 5.

116. See Lomnitz-Adler, *Exits from the Labyrinth*, 281, and Saldaña-Portillo, *The Revolutionary Imagination*.

117. See Juliet Hooker, *Theorizing Race in the Americas: Douglass, Sarmiento, DuBois, and Vasconcelos* (New York: Oxford University Press, 2017), 155–94; Joshua Lund, *The Mestizo State: Reading Race in Modern Mexico* (Minneapolis: University of Minnesota Press, 2012), ix–xx; and Marilyn G. Miller, *Rise and Fall of the Cosmic Race: The Cult of Mestizaje in Latin America* (Austin: University of Texas Press, 2004), 27–44, 141–56.

118. Anzaldúa, *Borderlands/La Frontera*, 91.

119. Anzaldúa, *Borderlands/La Frontera*, 77.

120. Anzaldúa, *Borderlands/La Frontera*, 7.

121. Anzaldúa, *Borderlands/La Frontera*, 7.

122. José Vasconcelos, *La raza cósmica/The Cosmic Race*, translated by Didier Jaén (Los Angeles: Centro de Publicaciones, Department of Chicano Studies, California State University at Los Angeles, 1979), 24.

123. Vasconcelos, *La raza cósmica*, 18.

124. Jean-Luc Nancy, "Cut Throat Sun," In *An Other Tongue*, edited by Alfred Arteaga (Durham: Duke UP, 1994), 113–23.

125. Castillo and Tabuenca, *Border Women*, 1–3.

126. Hooker, *Theorizing Race in the Americas*, 193.

127. Rubén Medina, "El mestizaje a través de la frontera: Vasconcelos y Anzaldúa," *Mexican Studies/Estudios Mexicanos* 25, no. 1 (Winter 2009): 129.

128. See also Joan Wallach Scott, "Multiculturalism and the Politics of Identity" in *The Identity in Question*, edited by John Rajchmann (New York: Routledge, 1995), 9–10, on the notion of radicalizing experience. Scott writes that in "much current usage of 'experience,' references to structure and history are implied but not made explicit; instead, personal testimony . . . replaces analysis" (10). It is this individualizing conception of politics I see in Anzaldúa's formulations, though not in her intentions.

129. Toni Cade Bambara, "Foreword," in *This Bridge Called My Back: Writings by Radical Women of Color*, edited by Cherríe Moraga and Gloria Anzaldúa (New York: Kitchen Table/Women of Color Press, 1983), vii.

130. The exact number of languages embedded in the text is interestingly unclear. Anzaldúa herself lists eight (*Borderlands/La Frontera*, 55). Mignolo refers to three "linguistic memories" in her text—one of which is Nahuatl, the pre-Columbian language of Mexico to whose traditions Anzaldúa refers, although she does not claim Nahuatl as a language she speaks. Several commentators refer to the triad of English, Spanish, and Chicano Spanish, which condenses Anzaldúa's eight categories into three. I refer here to only two for the sake of brevity, but an in-depth study of linguistic heterogeneity in this text would be useful for reasons that go beyond the challenge to "standard" or hegemonic languages and the revindication of a Chicano/a linguistic space. See Walter Mignolo, "Linguistic Maps, Literary Geographies, and Cultural Landscapes: Languages, Languaging, and (Trans)nationalism," *Modern Language Quarterly* 57, no. 2 (June 1996): 189.

131. Scott, "Multiculturalism and the Politics of Identity," 5.
132. Saldívar, "Unsettling Race, Coloniality and Caste," 206–07.
133. See Castillo, "Anzaldúa and Transnational American Studies," 265. The fact that English translations are not provided for the parts of the book written in Spanish is a basic feature of the text, and the discomfiture this can cause is key to the reading experience it offers.
134. Adrienne Rich, "Compulsory Heterosexuality and Lesbian Existence," *Signs: Journal of Women in Culture and Society* 5, no. 4 (Winter 1980): 631–60.
135. Ortega, *In-Between*.
136. Castillo, "Anzaldúa and Transnational American Studies," 263.
137. See Peter Wade, "Rethinking Mestizaje: Ideology and Lived Experience," *Journal of Latin American Studies* 37, no. 2 (May 2005): 239–57.
138. See Gonzalo Portocarrero, *Racismo y mestizaje y otros ensayos* (Lima: Fondo Editorial del Congreso del Perú, 2007).
139. See Édouard Glissant, *Le discours antillais* (Paris: Seuil, 1981); and Serge Gruzinski, *La pensée métisse* (Paris: Fayard, 1999).
140. Olguín, "Caballeros and Indians."
141. Emiko Saldívar, "Uses and Abuses of Culture: Mestizaje in the Age of Multiculturalism," *Cultural Studies* 32, no. 3 (2018): 48–59.
142. Medina, "El mestizaje," 119–20, 123.

BIBLIOGRAPHY

Alarcón, Norma. "Conjugating Subjects: The Heteroglossia of Essence and Resistance." *An Other Tongue*, edited by Alfred Arteaga, 125–38. Durham: Duke University Press, 1994.

Alessandri, Mariana; Stehn, Alexander. "Gloria Anzaldúa's Mexican Genealogy: From *Pelados* and *Pachucos* to New Mestizas." Genealogy 4, no. 1 (2020): 12. https://doi.org/10.3390/genealogy4010012

Antuna, Marcos de R. "What We Talk about When We Talk about *Nepantla*: Anzaldúa and the Queer Fruit of Aztec Philosophy." *Journal of Latinos and Education* 17, no. 2 (2018): 159–63.

Anzaldúa, Gloria. *Borderlands/La Frontera: The New Mestiza*. San Francisco: Spinsters/Aunt Lute, 1987.

Anzaldúa, Gloria, and Sonia Saldívar Hull. "Introduction to the Second Edition." In *Borderlands/La Frontera: The New Mestiza*, 1–15. San Francisco: Aunt Lute Books, 1999.

Anzaldúa, Gloria, and AnaLouise Keating. "Re-Envisioning Coyolxauhqui, Decolonizing Reality: Anzaldúa's Twenty-First-Century Imperative." In *Light in the Dark/Luz En Lo Oscuro*, ix-xxxvii. Durham, NC: Duke UP, 2015.

Anzaldúa, Gloria, and Cherríe Moraga, eds. *This Bridge Called My Back: Writings by Radical Women of Color*. New York: Kitchen Table: Women of Color Press, 1983.

Bacchetta, Paola. "Transnational Borderlands. Gloria Anzaldúa's Epistemologies of Resistance and Lesbians 'of color' in France." In *Güeras y Prietas: Celebrating*

Twenty Years of Borderlands/La Frontera, edited by Norma Cantú and Christina L. Gutiérrez, 77–92. San Antonio: Adelante Project, 2009.

Bambara, Toni Cade. "Foreword." In *This Bridge Called My Back: Writings by Radical Women of Color*, edited by Cherríe Moraga and Gloria Anzaldúa, vi–viii. New York: Kitchen Table/Women of Color Press, 1983.

Bary, Leslie. "The Search for Cultural Identity." In *Problems in Modern Latin American History*, edited by John C. Chasteen and Joseph Tulchin, 168–98. Wilmington, DE: Scholarly Resources, 1994.

Benítez-Rojo, Antonio. *The Repeating Island: The Caribbean and the Postmodern Perspective*. Trans. James E. Maraniss. Durham and London: Duke UP, 1992.

Beverley, John. *Subalternity and Representation: Arguments in Cultural Theory*. Durham: Duke University Press, 1999.

Bolívar, Simón. "Discurso ante el Congreso de Angostura." In *Simón Bolívar: Escritos fundamentales*, 112–45. Caracas. Monte Avila, 1982.

———. "The Jamaica Letter: Response from a South American to a Gentleman of this Island." In *El Libertador: Writings of Simón Bolívar*, edited by David Bushnell, 12–30. New York: Oxford UP, 2003.

Cabrera Quintero, Conrado Gilberto. *La creación del imaginario del indio en la literatura mexicana del siglo XIX*. Puebla: Benemérita Universidad Autónoma de Puebla, Dirección General de Fomento Editorial, 2005.

Castillo, Debra A. "Anzaldúa and Transnational American Studies." *PMLA* 121, no. 1 (January 2006): 260–65.

Castillo, Debra A., and María Socorro Tabuenca Córdoba. *Border Women*. Minneapolis: University of Minnesota Press, 2002.

Catelli, Laura. "'Y de esta manera quedaron todos los hombres sin mujeres': Mestizaje como estrategia de colonización en la Española (1501–1503)." *Revista de crítica literaria latinoamericana* 74 (2011): 217–38.

Chabram-Dernersesian, Angie. "I Throw Punches for My Race, but I Don't Want to Be a Man: Writing Us—Chica-nos (Girl, Us)/Chicanas—into the Movement Script." *Cultural Studies*, edited by Lawrence Grossberg, Cary Nelson, and Paula Triechler, 81–95. New York: Routledge, 1992.

Christensen, Kimberly. "'With Whom Do You Believe Your Lot Is Cast?' White Feminists and Racism." *Signs* 22, no. 3 (Spring 1997): 617–48.

Contreras, Sheila Marie. *Blood Lines: Myth, Indigenism, and Chicana/o Literature*. Austin: University of Texas P, 2008.

de la Cadena, Marisol. "Are *Mestizos* Hybrids? The Conceptual Politics of Andean Identities." *Journal of Latin American Studies* 37, no. 2 (2005): 259–84.

del Río, Carmen M. "Chicana Poets: Re-visions from the Margin." *Revista canadiense de estudios hispánicos* XIV, no. 3 (1990): 431–45.

Díaz Balsera, Viviana. "Voicing Mesoamerican Identities on the Roads of Empire." In *To Be Indio in Colonial Spanish America*, edited by Mónica Díaz, 169–90. Albuquerque: University of New Mexico P, 2017.

Fernández Retamar, Roberto. *Caliban and Other Essays*. Trans. Edward Baker. Minneapolis: University of Minnesota Press, 1989.

Fuss, Diana. *Essentially Speaking: Feminism, Nature, and Difference.* New York: Routledge, 1989.

García Canclini, Néstor. *Culturas híbridas: estrategias para entrar y salir de la modernidad.* Mexico: Grijalbo, 1989.

———. "Cultural Reconversion." Translated by Holly Staver. In *On Edge: The Crisis of Contemporary Latin American* Culture, edited by Ed. George Yúdice, Jean Franco, and Juan Flores, 29–43. Minneapolis: U of Minnesota P, 1992.

Glissant, Édouard. *Le discours antillais.* Paris: Seuil, 1981.

Goode, Joshua. *Impurity of Blood: Defining Race in Spain, 1870–1930.* Baton Rouge: Louisiana State University Press, 2009.

Gordon, Linda. "On Difference." *Genders* 10 (Spring 1991): 91–111.

Graham, Richard, ed. *The Idea of Race in Latin America, 1870–1940.* Austin: University of Texas Press, 1990.

Gruesz, Kirsten Silva. *Ambassadors of Culture: The Transamerican Origins of Latino Writing.* Princeton: Princeton University Press, 2002.

———. "The Gulf of Mexico System and the 'Latinness' of New Orleans." *American Literary History* 18, no. 4 (Fall 2006): 468–95.

———. "Mexican/American: The Making of Borderlands Print Culture." In *US Popular Print Culture, 1860–1920,* edited by Christine Bold, 457–76. Oxford: Oxford University Press, 2011.

———. "What Was Latino Literature?" *PMLA* 127, no. 2 (March 2012): 335–41.

———. "Alien Speech, Incorporated: On the Cultural History of Spanish in the U.S." *American Literary History* 25, no. 1 (Spring 2013): 18–32.

———. "Transamerican New Orleans: From the Spanish Period to Post-Katrina." In *Cambridge History of Latino/a Literature,* edited by John Morán González and Laura Lomas, 176–89. Cambridge: Cambridge UP, 2018.

Glissant, Édouard. *Le discours antillais.* Paris: Seuil, 1981.

Gruzinski, Serge. *La pensée métisse.* Paris: Fayard, 1999.

Guttman, Anna. *The Nation of India in Contemporary Indian Literature.* New York: Palgrave, 2007.

Hedrick, Tace. "Queering the Cosmic Race: Esotericism, Mestizaje and Sexuality in the Work of Gabriela Mistral and Gloria Anzaldúa." *Aztlán: A Journal of Chicano Studies* 2 (Fall 2009): 67–98.

Hicks, D. Emily, and Neil Larsen. Foreword. In *Border Writing: The Multidimensional Text,* xi–xxi. Minneapolis: U of Minnesota P, 1992.

Hooker, Juliet. *Theorizing Race in the Americas: Douglass, Sarmiento, DuBois, and Vasconcelos.* New York: Oxford UP, 2017.

Irwin, Robert. "Toward a Border Gnosis of the Borderlands: Joaquín Murrieta and Nineteenth Century U.S.-Mexico Border Culture." *Nepantla: Views from the South* 2–3 (2001): 509–37.

Jaén, Didier. "Introduction." In José Vasconcelos, *La raza cósmica / The Cosmic Race,* translated by Didier Jaén, xi–xxxiv. Los Angeles: Centro de Publicaciones, California State University at Los Angeles, 1979.

Kaplan, Caren. "Deterritorializations: The Rewriting of Home and Exile in Western Feminist Discourse." In *The Nature and Context of Minority Discourse,* edited by Abdul JanMohamed and David Lloyd, 357–68. New York: Oxford University Press, 1990.

Klor de Alva, Jorge. "The Postcolonization of the (Latin) American Experience: A Reconsideration of 'Colonialism,' 'Postcolonialism,' and 'Mestizaje.'" In *After Colonialism: Imperial Histories and Postcolonial Displacements*, edited by Gyan Prakash, 241–75. Princeton: Princeton University Press, 1995.

Kraniauskas, John. "Hybridity in a Transnational Frame: Latin-Americanist and Postcolonial Perspectives on Cultural Studies." *Nepantla: Views from the South* 1, no. 1 (2000): 111–37.

Kutzinski, Vera. *Sugar's Secrets: Race and the Erotics of Cuban Nationalism.* Charlottesville: University Press of Virginia, 1993.

Kynčlová, Tereza. "Prospects of Anzaldúan Thought for a Czech Future." *Signs: Journal of Women in Culture and Society* 37, no. 1 (Autumn 2011): 23–29.

Laclau, Ernesto, and Moutte, Chantal. *Hegemony and Socialist Strategy.* London: Verso, 1985.

Lavie, Smadar. "Where is the Mizrahi-Palestinian Border Zone? Interrogating Feminist Transnationalism through the Bounds of the Lived." *Social Semiotics* 21, no. 1 (2011): 67–83.

Lazo, Rodrigo, and Jesse Aleman, eds. *The Latino Nineteenth Century.* New York: New York UP, 2016.

Leal, Luis. "El corrido de Joaquin Murrieta: origen y difusión." *Mexican History/ Estudios Mexicanos* 11, no. 1 (Winter 1995): 1–23.

Lomnitz-Adler, Claudio. *Exits from the Labyrinth: Culture and Ideology in the Mexican National Space.* Berkeley: University of California Press, 1992.

Lott, Eric. "The New Cosmopolitanism: Whose America?" *Transition* 72 (Winter 1996): 108–35.

Lund, Joshua. *The Mestizo State: Reading Race in Modern Mexico.* Minneapolis: U of Minnesota P, 2012.

Luongo, Gilda. "Amasijo. 'En la tierra de en medio' o Nepantla en la poesía de Rosario Castellanos." *Revista Nomadías* 22 (December 2016): 59–80.

Mackey, Eva. "Postmodernism and Cultural Politics in a Multicultural Nation: Contests over Truth in the Into the Heart of Africa Controversy." *Public Culture* 7, no. 2 (Winter 1995): 403–31.

Majewska, Ewa. "La Mestiza from Ukraine? Border Crossing with Gloria Anzaldúa." *Signs: Journal of Women in Culture and Society* 37, no. 1 (Autumn 2011): 34–41.

Martí, José, and Federico de Onís. "Our America." In *The America of José Martí: Selected Writings of José Marti, Translated from the Spanish by Juan de Onís. With an Introduction by Federico de Onís*, 138–51. New York: Noonday Press, 1953.

Medina, Rubén. "El mestizaje a través de la frontera: Vasconcelos y Anzaldúa." *Mexican Studies/Estudios Mexicanos* 25, no. 1 (Winter 2009): 101–24.

Mignolo, Walter. *The Darker Side of the Renaissance: Literacy, Territoriality, and Colonization.* Ann Arbor: University of Michigan Press, 1995.

———. "Linguistic Maps, Literary Geographies, and Cultural Landscapes: Languages, Languaging, and (Trans)nationalism." *Modern Language Quarterly* 57, no. 2 (June 1996): 181–96.

————. *Local Histories, Global Designs: Coloniality, Subalternity, and Border Thinking*. Princeton: Princeton UP, 2000.

Miller, Marilyn G. *Rise and Fall of the Cosmic Race: The Cult of Mestizaje in Latin America*. Austin: U of Texas P, 2004.

Miller, Nancy K. "Changing the Subject: Authorship, Writing, and the Reader." *Feminist Studies/Critical Studies*, edited by Teresa de Lauretis, 102–20. Bloomington: Indiana UP, 1986.

Moraña, Mabel. "El boom del subalterno." *Cuadernos americanos* 67, no. 1 (Jan.–Feb. 1998): 214–22.

Moreiras, Alberto. *The Exhaustion of Difference: The Politics of Latin American Cultural Studies*. Durham: Duke UP, 2001.

Mouffe, Chantal. "Radical Democracy: Modern or Postmodern?" In *Universal Abandon: The Politics of Postmodernism*, edited by Andrew Ross, 31–45. Minneapolis: U of Minnesota P, 1988.

————. "Democratic Politics and the Question of Identity." In *The Identity in Question*, edited by John Rajchmann, 33–45. New York: Routledge, 1995.

Nancy, Jean-Luc. "Cut Throat Sun." In *An Other Tongue*, edited by Alfred Arteaga, 113–23. Durham: Duke UP, 1994.

Negrón-Muntaner, Frances. "Bridging Islands: Gloria Anzaldúa and the Caribbean." *PMLA* 121, no. 1 (January 2006): 272–78.

Olguín, B. V. "Caballeros and Indians: Mexican-American Whiteness, Hegemonic Mestizaje, and Ambivalent Indigeneity in Proto-Chicana/o Autobiographical Discourse, 1858–2008." *MELUS: Multi-Ethnic Literature of the United States* 38, no. 1 (2013): 30–49.

Oliver-Rotger, Maria Antònia. "Gloria Anzaldúa's Borderless Theory in Spain." *Signs: Journal of Women in Culture and Society* 37, no. 1 (Autumn 2011): 5–10.

Ortega, Mariana. *In-Between: Latina Feminist Phenomenology, Multiplicity and the Self*. Albany: SUNY Press, 2016.

Ortiz, Fernando. *Contrapunteo cubano del tabaco y el azúcar*. Caracas: Ayacucho, 1978.

Parra Lazcano, Lourdes. "Rosario Castellanos entre México e Israel." *Bulletin of Hispanic Studies* 95, no. 7 (2018): 784–86.

Paz, Octavio. *El laberinto de la soledad*. México: Cuadernos Americanos, 1950.

Pérez Firmat, Gustavo. *The Cuban Condition*. London and New York: Cambridge UP, 1989.

Pérez-Torres, Rafael. *Mestizaje: Critical Uses of Race in Chicano Culture*. Minneapolis: U of Minnesota P, 2005.

Piedra, José. "Literary Whiteness and the Afro-Hispanic Difference." *New Literary History* 18, no. 2 (1987): 303–32.

Portocarrero, Gonzalo. *Racismo y mestizaje y otros ensayos*. Lima: Fondo Editorial del Congreso del Perú, 2007.

Pratt, Minnie Bruce. "Identity: Skin Blood Heart." In *Yours in Struggle: Three Feminist Perspectives on Anti-Semitism and Racism*, edited by Elly Bulkin et al., 1–63. Brooklyn: Long Haul Press, 1984.

Raiskin, Judith. "Inverts and Hybrids: Lesbian Reworkings of Sexual and Racial Identities." In *The Lesbian Postmodern*, edited by Laura Doan, 156–72. New York: Columbia UP, 1994.

Ramos, Julio. *Desencuentros de la modernidad en América Latina*. Mexico City: Fondo de Cultura Económica, 1989.

Ribeiro, Darcy. "Etnicidad, indigenismo, y campesinado. Futuras guerras étnicas en América Latina." In *La diversidad prohibida*, edited by Susana B. C. Devalle. México: Colegio de México, 1989.

Rich, Adrienne. "Compulsory Heterosexuality and Lesbian Existence." *Signs: Journal of Women in Culture and Society* 5, no. 4 (Winter 1980): 631–60.

Román-Odio, Clara. *Sacred Iconographies in Chicana Cultural Productions*. New York: Palgrave, 2013.

Saldaña-Portillo, Josefina. *The Revolutionary Imagination in the Americas and the Age of Development*. Durham: Duke UP, 2003.

Saldívar, Emiko. "Uses and Abuses of Culture: Mestizaje in the Age of Multiculturalism." *Cultural Studies* 32, no. 3 (2018): 48–59.

Saldívar, José David. *The Dialectics of Our America: Genealogy, Cultural Critique, and Literary History*. Durham: Duke UP, 1991.

———. "Unsettling Race, Coloniality and Caste: Anzaldúa's *Borderlands/La Frontera*, Martinez's *Parrot in the Oven*, and Roy's *The God of Small Things*." In *Globalization and the Decolonial Option*, edited by Walter Mignolo and Arturo Escobar, 193–221. London: Routledge, 2004.

Saldívar-Hull, Sonia. "Introduction to the Second Edition." In *Borderlands/La Frontera: The New Mestiza*, edited by Gloria Anzaldúa, 1–15. San Francisco: Aunt Lute Books, 1999.

———. *Feminism on the Border: Chicana Gender Politics and Literature*. Berkeley: U of California P, 2000.

Sandoval, Chela. "U.S. Third World Feminism: The Theory and Method of Oppositional Consciousness in the Postmodern World." *Genders* 10 (Spring 1991): 1–24.

———. *Methodology of the Oppressed*. Minneapolis: U of Minnesota P, 2000.

Scott, Joan Wallach. "Multiculturalism and the Politics of Identity." In *The Identity in Question*, edited by John Rajchmann, 3–12. New York: Routledge, 1995.

Sommer, Doris. *Foundational Fictions: The National Romances of Latin America*. Berkeley: U of California P, 1991.

Spitta, Sylvia. *Between Two Waters: Narratives of Transculturation in Latin America*. College Station: Texas A&M UP, 2005.

Spivak, Gayatri Chakravorty. "Subaltern Studies: Deconstructing Historiography. Historiography." In *Other Worlds: Essays in Cultural Politics*, edited by Gayatri Spivak, 197–221. New York: Methuen, 1987.

Turner, Victor. *The Ritual Process: Structure and Anti-Structure*. London: Penguin, 1969.

Vasconcelos, José. *La raza cósmica/The Cosmic Race*. Translated by Didier Jaén. Los Angeles: Centro de Publicaciones, Department of Chicano Studies, California State University at Los Angeles, 1979.

Wade, Peter. "Rethinking mestizaje: Ideology and Lived Experience." *Journal of Latin American Studies* 37, no. 2 (May 2005): 239–57.

Williams, Patricia J. "Big Words, Small Divisions." *The Nation* 265, no. 6 (August 25/September 1 1997): 9.

Yarbro-Bejarano, Yvonne. "Gloria Anzaldúa's *Borderlands/La Frontera*: Cultural Studies, 'Difference,' and the Non-Unitary Subject." *Cultural Critique* (Fall 1994): 5–28.

Zavala, Iris. *Colonialism and Culture: Hispanic Modernisms and the Social Imaginary*. Bloomington: Indiana University Press, 1992.

Zygadło, Grażyna. "Where the Third World Grates Against the First: Teaching Gloria Anzaldúa from a Polish Perspective." *Signs: Journal of Women in Culture and Society* 37 (Autumn 2011): 29–34.

Chapter 2

Tuning In

Intimacy and Networks in Diamela Eltit's Fuerzas especiales

Sowmya Ramanathan

INHERITED INEQUALITIES

In October of 2019, massive public demonstrations erupted in Santiago, Chile, over a 3.75% hike in public transportation fares. At the center of the protests were Chilean students who organized a widespread evasion of fares in protest of one of Latin America's most expensive "public" transportation systems, the TransSantiago. In reality, though the protests were precipitated by the fare increase, they immediately pivoted to calling out a broader set of issues brought on by political and economic policies that have produced profound social inequalities in Chile, including the privatization of water and electricity, the chipping away at pensions (AFPs) for the elderly, the impunity given to the wealthy and corrupt government officials and businesspeople, and the violent policing of poor neighborhoods. Protestors identified the 1980 Constitution, written and drafted by Augusto Pinochet's military government, as the origin of many of these issues. Ratified seven years after the 1973 coup d'état, this document provided impunity to the military as it carried out a systematic and violent elimination of its opposition and paved the way for the country's "economic miracle," based on privatization, deregulation, and unbounded economic liberalism, which marginalized an overwhelmingly large fraction of the population. Securing the date for a plebiscite, if accomplished, is one accomplishment in a long list of proposed social and civil reforms to draft a new Constitution and reduce the vast inequalities produced and sustained during the country's seventeen-year dictatorship and transition to democracy.

A prominent voice in Chilean literary and cultural circles is that of writer, intellectual, and activist, Diamela Eltit. Beginning in the 1970s, Eltit was recognized as a cultural figure whose work was central to disrupting the traditional foundations of literature and aesthetics, while also critiquing repressive state politics and the advancement of neoliberal capitalism in Chile and Latin America more broadly. In 2018, she was awarded the National Prize for Literature by Chile's Ministerio de las Culturas, las Artes y el Patrimonio (Ministry of Cultures, Arts, and Heritage), making her the fifth woman in Chilean literary history to be honored within this prize. A year later, in the midst of the protests, Eltit told interviewer Roberto Ibáñez that despite being in New York and far away, she has experienced a sense of proximity unimaginable in the past, facilitated by messaging platforms, social networks, and access to Chilean television. With respect to her own work, she states, "For decades I have written about inequality and indifference toward the peripheries."[1] She comments that the current *estallido social* (social outcry) is the result of a history of worsening inequalities, producing an enormous collective frustration that has accumulated over time.

Eltit's penultimate novel, the focus of this chapter, is set on an apocalyptic stage in which contemporary networks of information sharing, surveillance, and technological connectivity are implicated in sustaining deep, structural inequalities produced by the neoliberal project in Chile. In *Fuerzas especiales*, published in 2013, Eltit explores the lives of the inhabitants of a *bloque de vivienda social* (a social housing block) as they navigate the daily rhythms of a highly policed and technologized existence on the peripheries of Santiago. The novel narrates the inhabitants' attempts to survive constant police brutality and subsist in a highly speculative economy by performing sex work via webcam. From the material and social reality of the peripheral *bloque*, *Fuerzas especiales* challenges the rhetoric and ideology of the Chilean government from the Transition period to the present. The novel invites us to wonder about who could truly experience the national-scale reconciliation process and by what means collective healing can be achieved, while avoiding the erasure of and complicity with past violence. Furthermore, the novel suggests an interrogation of the neoliberal capitalist paradigm of "good life" and exposes the categorical exclusions of marginal subjects from an ideological framework based on practices of consumption and networked connectivity. In this chapter, I analyze the emergence of collectivity in *Fuerzas especiales*, based on the affective frictions and relationships that are generated in the characters' efforts to subvert, challenge, and defy normative constraints and repressive systems of discipline from the *bloque*. It is my claim that Eltit's framing of affective relations in the *bloque* presents a notion of a "relationship" that stands in stark contrast to the atomized, technologically mediated paradigm of the network and instead, offers a promising reimagination of the frictions and potential that constitutes social collectivity.

THE UNDERSIDES OF GLOBAL CAPITALISM: LIFE FROM THE *BLOQUE*

Fuerzas especiales is narrated from the perspective of an unnamed female protagonist, living on the peripheries of Santiago where she and the other characters experience a truly devastating underside of neoliberal order that touches all aspects of life. The *bloque*, home to the novel's characters, is described in a typically Chilean lexicality and geography, and likely refers to the public housing projects built by the Chilean government beginning in the early 1950s. During this period, Presidents Carlos Ibáñez and Jorge Alessandri initiated the first state housing projects as a solution to a growing number of *poblaciones callampa* ("camps" or "tent cities") emerging on the peripheries. With President Salvador Allende's election in 1970, social housing was declared an unalienable right and the government passed the Plan de Emergencia 1971 (Emergency Plan 1971) in order to construct 90,000 housing units within that same year.[2] While these ambitious plans could not be fully realized, the *bloques de vivienda social* were seen as part of the state's fundamental responsibility to provide for its citizens, a philosophy which would radically change after the coup d'état in 1973. Under Pinochet's rule, the responsibility for constructing housing was transferred into the hands of private developers and the parameters for basic living needs, such as the minimum size of an apartment, were drastically altered to maximize profit rather than standard of living.[3] The military was itself involved in many of these projects, leading to a higher rate of violence and policing of poor neighborhoods. Eltit notes that one lasting consequence of dictatorship is the dissolution of public housing as a form of state protection and security, affirming that these poorer neighborhoods are, to this day, subject to constant policing: "How long has the district of La Legua been intervened in by the police? Another example is the death of the mapuche youth, Matías Catrileo, whom they killed from behind. This is the symptom of a law that borders on state crime."[4]

In *Sociophobia*, Spanish sociologist César Rendueles considers the global rise of slums and shantytowns as the often-ignored underside of the capitalist city: "Hypergraded urban zones, or megaslums, are the colonial problem of the twenty-first century; like the Victorian holocaust, they are the product of economic liberalism. Shantytowns are the other face of casino capitalism, the levees that dam the human remainders of an increasingly speculative and technologized economy."[5] Looking at the *bloque* in *Fuerzas especiales*, the erosion of state protection is clear: the once social housing project has become a shantytown or squat, in which the inhabitants enjoy no social or legal protections; in addition, the characters are generally unemployed or restricted to the informal or illegal economies, working as street vendors or sex workers. They are also intensely aware that their highly policed reality is not unique to the *bloque*. As the protagonist states: "But that happens in all the corners of the earth . . . where the detectives and policemen of the world attack each other for the scraps they recover from the incomes in the *bloques*, in the *villas*, in the projects,[6] and in the agglomeration of the *favelas*."[7] The inhabitants of the *bloque* are part of a growing population of what Rendueles has called the "fragile subjects" of postmodernity,[8] and their knowledge of their interconnectedness within this contemporary reality sheds light on the fact of increasingly large populations subjected to precarious living and labor conditions globally.

Rendueles studies the effects of cyberutopianism—the unquestioning celebration of cyber-space and the internet as a horizontal and egalitarian ideal—on contemporary social relationships, and he is particularly astute in coining the term "sociophobia" to refer to a kind of contemporary individualism that rejects traditional forms of social ties as outmoded, old-fashioned, or reactionary. He argues, "postmodernity has sped the destruction of traditional social ties, throwing the continuity of employment, interpersonal relationships, and political loyalties up in the air."[9] In their destructive tendencies, the processes of postmodernity that Rendueles mentions produce evermore fragile subjects, who cling to a subjectivity stitched together by atomized and individualized experiences, redefining traditional forms of relationship. In *Fuerzas especiales*, this is evident in the portrayal of the "family" as a formation that teeters on the brink of disappearance, which we observe in the novel's first chapter in which the protagonist narrates the numerous losses her family has suffered. She recounts that her two brothers are now incarcerated, while her sister remains at home, battling depression after the state removed her two young children from her custody. Furthermore, it is not only the protagonist's family that experiences the reality of family separation. The fellow residents of the *bloque*, el Cojo Pancho, who sells *fricas* on the street, la Guatona Pepa, a fellow worker in the cyber-café, along with the protagonist's two friends, el Omar y el Lucho, have all lost family members, a fact which is emphasized several times in the repetition of the phrase: "the family I have left"[10] or "the women of the family that remain."[11] The impact of precarious labor conditions and an unsafe, insecure daily reality reverberates through the social reality of the novel, profoundly shaping the characters' consolidation of subjecthood and social relationships.

NETWORKED SUBJECTS AND
DISEMBODIED CONNECTIVITY

Eltit illuminates the increasingly complex role of the internet and contemporary image-space in the mediation of social life within this violent and disaggregated reality. This mediation has direct and dire consequences for the characters and subjects living on the fringes of society, for while an internet presence is inherently tied to their ability to be "subjects," these technologies have profoundly alienating and disaggregating effects. As workers in the cyber-café, many of the characters earn just enough money to temporarily abate their hunger until the next day. They sit in front of a webcam and provide services in virtual space to buyers from all over the world. While this work provides the protagonist with the material subsistence in everyday life, she describes an alienating relationship with the computer screen: "Now it's time to forget the stairs and the problems in my family. I have to forget myself in order to give myself up, in body and soul, to the transparency that radiates from the computer screen."[12] Alienated from her body, family, and the *bloque*, she immerses herself in a universe of images and waits for her 30-minute session to end. She embraces the distractions provided by the internet, perusing Russian clothing sites as a way of forgetting the labor she is performing. She also reads articles that teach her that pain is purely mental and instruct her to focus on particular images to shift her attention away. As a point of access to mainstream consumer culture and a form of entry into the market, the cyber-café is a tether to subjecthood, providing both the possibility of self-optimization and economic subsistence.

Furthermore, for the characters of the *bloque*, images of themselves that circulate through information networks confer on them normative and legible subjecthoods within the global economy. For instance, the protagonist describes the 48 hours immediately following the state's seizure of her nephews, expressing the powerful effects that news coverage and outrage expressed on social networks has on the family. She states, "Over a year has passed since the images of the children overflowed in the papers, newscasts, and erupted in the frayed routes of the (social) networks."[13] The images are replayed infinitely through the media, "on infinite replay"[14] that the protagonist recalls from memory a year later. She remembers wanting nothing more than for the panic to abate, but notes that the proliferation of images provides her with a confirmation of her own existence: "A public event that freed me from questioning the veracity of my existence."[15] This media recognition confers an individualism and subjecthood onto the children—"The children existed for one part of the word, and my sister existed as well, and finally, throughout 48 hours, all of our lives acquired a deserved significance"[16]—and by extension, the family is immediately significant and recognized: "In the midst of powerful sparks, information detailed with deliberate cruelty erased our insignificance and asymmetries."[17] The confirmation of each character's existence as a subject is tied to their presence in this virtual image-space, a record of this instant of normative legibility.

Be that as it may, even as technology captures and affirms the subjectivities of these characters, they simultaneously see it as a kind of burial or afterlife in a virtual world. This is evident when the protagonist tries to photograph her father. One day, he gets dressed and leaves the *bloque*. His ribs are broken, his clothing is torn and beaten, and she is plagued with fear about how he will protect himself from the dangers outside. As he leaves, the protagonist reaches for her cell phone: "I took out my cell phone to try to save the last image of my father. I wanted to upload the image to (social) networks and show his wiry, but existent figure."[18] Her comments frame the internet as a simulacrum of a burial place for his emaciated body, cementing his image in digital space and securing for him a bodyless afterlife.

Perhaps this scene represents a moment in which digital and information networks emerge as truly egalitarian spaces with the potential to allow their users to live, work, and consume in ways that are somewhat free of the restrictions of space, geography, class, or politics. Rendueles writes that this was the early promise of a digital utopia. In particular, he calls attention to the belief that digital or cyber-space "offers an alternative grounded in what one imagines are the new forms of sociality: a growing network of contacts among fragile subjects, dense but tenuous nodes connected with the help of elaborate technological tools."[19] However, he dedicates the entirety of *Sociophobia* to debunking the digital utopian myth and demonstrating its complicity in a larger postmodern, neoliberal capitalist model of commercializing experience, work, and life: "The Internet . . . is not a sophisticated laboratory in which delicate strains of communities of the future are being developed but is instead a run-down zoo housing the decrepit forms of age-old problems that still haunt us, though we prefer not to see them."[20] His writings suggest that a deeper understanding of the internet and technology is necessary: one that is willing to interrogate the underlying and sustained inequalities at its center.

In *Fuerzas especiales*, contemporary technologies and networks project "symmetry" onto the inhabitants of the *bloque*; through images that circulate through the internet and the media, a socially and economically ostracized population is rid of its constitutive asymmetry (its inequality) and achieves a moment, however brief, of normative legibility. Why, then, does the protagonist imagine a burial?

Perhaps we can consider the idea of *symmetry* in conjunction with Byung-Chul Han's analysis of a *smooth* or *pure* aesthetic of neoliberalism. Han argues that neoliberalism's technologies and networks erase the dynamic complexity from life, so as to make information fit into smooth and transparent information streams:

> Pure is transparency, and things become transparent then they fit into the smooth streams of information and data. Data have something pornographic and obscene about them. They have no inside, no flip sides; they are not ambiguous. In this, they differ from language which does not permit things to come into perfectly clear focus. Data and information deliver themselves to total visibility and they make everything visible.[21]

As imperatives in information processing, both smoothness and symmetry strip subjects of interiority, making them codified and easily legible. In a similar vein, German filmmaker Hito Steyerl analyzes surveillance technologies in *Duty Free Art: Art in the Age of Planetary Civil War* and demonstrates the ways in which dynamic information is flattened, codified, and used in the process of racial profiling.[22] Han and Steyerl coincide in their beliefs that both visual and information technologies, in the effort to systematize diverse and complex social phenomena and organize them into simplified data points, turn the complexity of everyday life into static code, abstraction, and exteriority.

In *Fuerzas especiales*, the family's subjecthood and legibility depends on a symmetry that erases the frictions of their existence, and therefore simultaneously functions as a digital burial. In fact, code and abstraction have tangible, material impacts on the characters' lives beyond this singular event covered in the newspapers, as evident when the protagonist's reveals that she and *compadres*, el Lucho and el Omar, were all born on the same day, of the same month, of the same year. The protagonist reflects on this coincidence: "The shocking coincidence of the numbers that we carry scares us, because we think of a combination that could involve bad arts of some sect or the deliberate actions of a transnational organization or a state agenda through which the police can locate us in the center of their archives."[23] It is important to highlight the diversity of the contemporary "technologies" that fall prey to this flattening logic. For the inhabitants of the *bloque*, these mechanisms are not solely those of the surveillance state and a deregulated global economy, but also of transnational organizations and diverse cultural practices. In this sense, *Fuerzas especiales* frames artistic and literary registers as technologies that are coimplicated in mediating subjecthood and legibility, producing a host of images that also circulate contemporaneously in these high-speed networks.

STAGING PERFORMATIVITY

In an interview with performance studies scholar Diana Taylor, Eltit discussed the importance of theater at different moments of her career, remembering her work during the 1970s and 1980s with the art collective, Colectivo de Acciones de Arte. With a group of artists including Lotty Rosenfeld, Raúl Zurita, Fernando Balcells, and Juan Castillo, Eltit staged art-actions in the city of Santiago that were intended to disrupt the dynamics of social space and the daily rhythms of life during the dictatorship. Much later, thinking in conjunction with Taylor's work, she comments on her broadened understanding of performance:

> I broadened my understanding of performance to think of it as an activity that can accompany life itself, in all its dimensions—even life practices could be thought of as "performatic" because life practices are inserted in protocols and rituals—in familial, personal, or work rituals, and so on. And I think that it is there, in that protocol, where we could also talk about a performatic life, or of performatic lives unified to the multiplicity of the "I's" that we carry, that is, each "I" of the multiple "I's" that make up our identities, always ongoing, always difficult, complex and multiple.[24]

Performatic life surfaces the frictions that constitute subjectivity, capturing the multiplicity of individual "I" that discourse and discipline attempt to tame. An individual's effort to follow familiar, personal, and social codes gives rise to a notion of life that is fundamentally unstable: contradictory, ongoing, and difficult.

As Eltit's narrative moves between different forms of technological, artistic, and psychological mediation, she mobilizes a dance between static images or codes and the dynamic scenes of this everyday, performatic life. For *Fuerzas especiales* is a novel filled with images—mental, printed, and digital photographs—that add textures to the unfolding of perception, identity, and subjectivity. In one instance, while walking home from the cybercafé, the protagonist is overcome by the mental image of her sister's hair—"I am invaded with the image of her hair, black, thick and surprising"[25]—which immediately causes her to replay a series of family conflicts in her mind. She describes the violent nature of an encounter between her mother and sister over the latter's hair, is deemed unattractive by her mother's standards: "The beatings, her hair, hardened by her blood's density, the street, the silence between us, the irritation I provoked in both of them as I became a dispassionate witness."[26] Paradoxically, after this heated conflict, the protagonist remembers that her mother and sister ended the altercation in deep embrace, at which point, the protagonist reaches for her cell phone to photograph the moment. She states, "I focused them both in a medium-shot, hugging. Because that is how they are, affectionate, attractive, encapsulated, alike. It is an immaterial similarity that goes far beyond a simple organic coincidence, because they have nothing in common."[27] Between the mental image of her sister's hair and the final photograph of the embrace, Eltit's narrative unearths a medial space in which performativities collide and ambivalent, affective experiences surface.

Beyond the photographic frame, this *scene* is a site of ongoing frictions that add contextual and affective textures to this family conflict. Returning to the scene of her father's abandonment, we can recall that the protagonist's original intention is to capture her father's image, but she is unable to do so when faced with a situation that competes for her attention: "My intention was to hold onto my father, to capture him in my cell phone, but at the same time, I could not disregard the scene between my mother and sister."[28] She wishes to "capture" her father, recruiting the photograph to encapsulate this affective reality within a single frame that will ultimately circulate endlessly in visual networks. The scene, however, which competes for her limited attention, becomes the stage for the messiness of actual human relationships that resist superficial codification and elude the facile translation into the neat photograph captured by the cell phone.

Furthermore, the protagonist is aware that the image's status as proof or evidence of the moment is impossible without considering its emergence from the scene. This is evident in her concerted visual experiments after leaving her mother and sister to wander toward the cyber-café and await her father's return. Drunk, she leans against a lamp post and looks back at her *bloque*: "Then, supported by the pillar, I raised my head and tried to look at our story, the fourth story, as though I did not know it. My idea was to perform a visual experiment through a forced distance."[29] She purposefully alters her visual perception, imposing a distance which allows her to see the figure of her father descending the stairway, unharmed. In her altered state of perception, she receives a wave of mental images of the family's reencounter and predicts the impending scene: "It was not difficult to comprehend the scene of reencounter. I was able to foretell the yelling, the insults, the blows and my father's dismay at finding his box of wine empty, my mother's explanations and my sister's inconclusive babbling."[30] While she seems convinced of the accuracy of her images, she suggests that they are insufficient until she can return to the scene to involve herself directly: "I returned to verify my images. I ran to our *bloque*. I rapidly climbed the stairs. I entered, full of violence, and I joined in."[31] The image is not a disconnected, disembodied, or abstract piece of code. Instead, the protagonist maintains its relation to a context of emergence, establishing these moving, affective, and performative scenes as central to the process of generating meaning and shaping how the characters know, act, and relate.

Staging the dynamic scenes of life necessitates attention to convulsive social encounters: from the sister's media scandal, to the father's disappearance, to the heated mother-daughter arguments that occur frequently in the novel. However, though conflict and pain are predominant affective manifestations within social encounters in *Fuerzas especiales*, Eltit maintains affect's innate ambivalence, affirming its transformative possibility or potential. In a conversation with Omar, the protagonist discusses her fears of working in the cyber-café. This long and intimate conversation, in which the two describe their daily panic and pain, ends in a conflict between the two. After the argument, the protagonist reflects on Omar's behavior: "Despite everything, he does not convert his pain into a resource, nor much less in an excuse, but instead he explains it to me to impose a challenge between us that may truly enable us to understand. His fear and my own."[32] The pain at the center of their relationship is not a utilitarian good (a resource) or a discursive trick (excuse). Instead, it maintains a dynamic complexity in the form of a "challenge" that allows both the protagonist and Omar to reach a great understanding of their context. Affective friction is a condition of possibility, permitting insight and connection that resists superficial similarity or symmetry between the two characters.

Once socially coded, relationships, kinships, and partnerships in *Fuerzas especiales* are the primary channels of affective relations between social actors. These novel's dynamics scenes give us a glimpse of how affect reverberates through the social space, shaping the explicit relationships that are formed between the characters. As Zygmunt Bauman notes, "in our world of rampant 'individualization' relationships are mixed blessings. They vacillate between sweet dream and nightmare, and there is no telling when one turns to the other . . . In a liquid modern setting of life, relationships are perhaps the most common, acute, deeply felt and troublesome incarnations of ambivalence."[33] In her representation of relations in the *bloque*, Eltit illuminates the underlying and sinuous connections between characters, whose world is constituted by these convulsive, affective dynamics that resist discursively codifying and romanticizing relationships. Affect's volatility, instead, challenges the notion of atomized and compartmentalized experience and dismantles the notion of an autonomous and self-sufficient individual upon which neoliberal capitalism desperately depends.

THE FACT OF RELATIONALITY: AFFECT, SOUND, AND VIBRATIONAL ONTOLOGY

It is of great interest to me that the epigraph to *Fuerzas especiales* is a quotation by Cuban writer, Severo Sarduy, that reads, "Soy una Juana de Arco electrónica, actual" (I am Joan of Arc, electronic, current). As Anke Birkenmaier notes, despite the fact that Sarduy composed six radio-plays published in *Para la voz* in 1985, he wrote much more on literature and visual arts. Incidentally, this epigraph comes from his only essay on sound and for Sarduy, voice and sound were integral to his conception of literature. He believed his literary and poetic texts to be embodied transmissions of the voices in his surrounding reality and their communication to the reader in poetic form. In "Soy una Juana de Arco electrónica, actual," he writes:

> Like the holy warrior [Joan of Arc] I hear voices. They don't order me any sacrifice or oblation of my body or person. But I *only* write for these voices. The text—and not only a radiophonic text; all of them, even a poem—never presents itself to me in an abstract, unembodied way, if I may say so, reduced to its nakedness or conceptuality. I never think of an argument or content matter that words, later on, would have to render and carve laboriously. Everything is already "said" from the beginning, there is no beginning but in *listening*.[34]

The radiophonic quality of his work—from poetry and novels to radio-plays—emerges from listening to distinct voices and sounds that make up reality. He understands a "text's" origin in orality, voice, and sound, the material supports of writing itself.

Eltit's reference to the Cuban writer at the start of the novel not only under-scores her connections to the postmodern and neo-baroque literary traditions, but also leads me to consider the radiophonic qualities present in her own work. Through her own writing, Eltit registers and communicates *el habla popular chileno*, which she values for the crises or ruptures it generates in the dominant "laws" of language. These crises are apparent in conversations and dialogues within *Fuerzas especiales*, such as "and you, *what're you doin'* in the street, don't you *realize we're* hungry. There were 230 W71 bombs. Don't you *realize* that we're waiting for you to *make* us food. There were 1,000 W79 bombs. Or maybe you don't *understand* that your mother is sick, shak-ing, more lost than ever."[35] In the original Spanish, these italicized verbs are conjugated in the Chilean *voseo*, an informal and spoken register of Chilean Spanish. In addition to these linguistic specificities, *Fuerzas especiales* is full of local references: the characters live in the *bloque*; their names are typi-cally Chilean ("La Guatona Pepa"); and Eltit even refers to the structures of surveillance and policing with the colloquial lexicon, *los pacos* and *los tiras*, signaling the uniformed police (Carabineros de Chile) and the private detec-tives of the Policía de Investigaciones (Investigations Police of Chile, PDI). In a Sarduy-like fashion, Eltit registers a range of Chilean voices that speak through a similarly radiophonic text.

Sarduy's interest in radio leads me back to the fundamentally social ques-tion raised by César Rendueles's work on the emergence of contemporary networks. As Rendueles points out, the radio was one of the first technologi-cal devices that created a vast network of voices, disseminated widely, which consequently produced a mass of listeners. In a cyberutopian view, one could envision the radio as an emerging form of collectivity, a medium for connecting disparate voices through vibrational contact of sound and listening. In the foreword to Rendueles's *Sociophobia*, Roberto Simanowski contextualizes the debate on cyberutopianism by going back to Bertolt Brecht's writings on radio. He notes that the German theatrical practitioner believed that "the task of turning radio from an 'apparatus of distribution' into 'the finest possible communications apparatus in life' was impossible to achieve under the existing social order, but it could be possible in another one, which it was therefore necessary to propagate."[36] Simanowski underscores Brecht's criticism of early broadcasters, who imitated the old theatrical and print media, "addressing the masses from the 'stage' of the ether" rather than working toward the emancipation of the individual through the radio as the "locus of political information and discussion [that] should sharpen society's critical awareness."[37] Simanowski notes that for Brecht, early deregulatory tendencies in radio attempted to produce and "maintain *without consequences* the most harmless entertainment possible."[38] The evolution of radio did not, for Brecht, Theodor Adorno, and Rendueles, promote a transition to increased egalitarianism or enlightened individualism. As a technological network, in its unwillingness to regulate information, the radio was embedded within and reproduced unequal social relationships, while perpetuating the illusion of increasing global connectedness.

Rendueles's work on cyberutopianism builds upon this discussion; from radio, it traces a history of how technology is at the center of reproducing the processes of speculation and disaggregation of social bonds. His work dialogues with that of Bauman, who writes about the implications of a change in thinking that turns away from considering "relations" and toward a model of sociality organized by "networks":

> Unlike "relations," "kinships," "partnerships" and similar notions that make salient the mutual engagement while excluding or passing over in silence its opposite, the disengagement, the "network" stands for a matrix of simultaneously connecting and disconnecting; networks are unimaginable without both activities being simultaneously enabled. In a network, connecting and disconnecting are equally legitimate choices, enjoy the same status and carry the same importance.[39]

In Bauman's view, where previous forms of sociality—relationships, kinships, and partnerships—necessitated a mutual engagement from two or more actors, the idea of the network erases the element of mutuality. "In a network," Bauman writes, "connections are entered on demand, and can be broken at will."[40] To be part of a network, then, upholds a sense of individualism that relieves users of relationships based on mutuality and permits the disconnection and disengagement on a whim.

Eltit's citation of Sarduy connects *Fuerzas especiales* to the Cuban writer's idea of sound as a profoundly social force rooted in speaking and listening. Like affect, sound is relational and rescues mutuality without collapsing diverse entities into sameness or symmetry. Following Baruch Spinoza, Brian Massumi understands affect as open-endedly social: "A *prepersonal* intensity corresponding to the passage from one experiential state of the body to another and implying an augmentation or diminution in that body's capacity to act. L'affection (Spinoza's affection) is each such state considered as an encounter between the affected body and a second, affecting, body."[41] Affect is an intensity that exists within and between bodies that impact one another. Steve Goodman builds on this notion and frames affect as a vibrational ontology that connects one body to another: "If affect describes the ability of one entity to change another from a distance, then the mode of affection will be understood as vibrational." As Brandon LaBelle notes, sound is also a fundamentally relational force: "Sound is intrinsically and unignorably relational: it emanates, propagates, communicates, vibrates, and agitates; it leaves a body and enters others; it binds and unhinges, harmonizes and traumatizes; it sends the body moving, the mind dreaming, the air oscillating. It seemingly eludes definition, while having profound effect."[42] As underscored by Massumi, Goodman, and LaBelle, these vibratory relations are rooted in embodied experience that resonates between and within bodies, inevitably connecting them. In Goodman's words, "all entities are potential media that can feel or whose vibrations can be felt by other entities . . . This is a realism, albeit a weird, agitated and nervous one."[43] Though it is not my aim to tease apart the specific differences between affective and sonic vibrations, I do wish to stress a fundamental commonality: as vibrational ontologies, both affect and sound rescue the underlying mutuality of relations that are rooted within the body.

In *Fuerzas especiales*, sound is a vibrational force that functions like affect in mediating connections and relationships between bodies and characters. For example, at the end of the novel, when the cell phone towers are at the brink of failure, la Guatona Pepa tries obsessively to get in contact with her family members who live elsewhere: "She feels that even if she could photographically remember some of her family scenes, they no longer belong to her and they are distant or outright alien, because since the material disappearance of the family, only she exists and it is her daily movements that she must remember to get her through the next day."[44] While the photograph is an insufficient capture of the broader and more complex scenes of family encounter, through the cell phone, la Guatona Pepa takes comfort in voice: "For that reason, the only thing that exists is the intensity of sound through the telephone that connects her to a voice without a body, or a body with the hint of a voice, as though some form of a bodyless world were there to sustain her."[45] She accesses voice as a sonorous intensity not unlike the intensities transmitted in the scenes of her family, from which she is now estranged. While sometimes mediated by contemporary technologies, such as the cell phone, these vibratory relations and intensities are rooted in mutual relations that are produced by sensory and affective experience, inherently embodied, unlike the abstract relationships modeled by networked connectivity.

The sonorous materiality of daily life for the inhabitants of the *bloque* is present in these cell phone calls, but also in a range of sounds including video-chats, police sirens, gunshots, tears and crying, dogs barking, and music. One day a week, the inhabitants come together in a frenetic dancing, which provides them with their only moment of respite from the daily rhythms of police sirens, gunshots, and dogs barking: "Now I hear the volume of the music that rises, along with Saturday's laughter and tears, and for a few hours the police disappear and leave the *bloque* orphaned from the howling sirens."[46] The protagonist and her friend, el Omar, are aware that this heterogenous, vibrational force is essential to their connection to existence. As the protagonist states, "I know that Omar is determined to give his corner a new life. He invites, pushes, demands, and yells at me, because still, there exists a music for us, since we are both addicted to the most successful and resounding rhythm: the *bloque-fusion* that descends the stairs and touches every single step."[47] The *bloque-fusion* disrupts dominant rhythms and social order and is a relational force that moves through the *bloque*, touching each building and corner, leading the protagonist to deem it the most full and resounding rhythm.

The vibrational forces in *Fuerzas especiales* constitute forms of collective affinity, but also organize a rationality in the *bloque*, whereby members reorganize ways of doing, being, and knowing and reconfigure traditional relationships of power. In N*eoliberalism from Below*, Verónica Gago adopts Foucault's notion of "governmentality" to expand the understanding of neoliberalism as a "set of skills, technologies and practices [that deploy] a new type of rationality."[48] These networked systems of survival are embodied by a collective whistling, led by the *bloque*'s experts who have studied police surveillance and activity: "Who whistles? The *bloque*'s experts . . . the whistling is completely human, it comes from lungs of the specialists who analyze the police's activity when we are invaded."[49] The whistling constitutes a form of expertise, mastery or knowledge, that is essential in protecting the *bloque*'s inhabitants from repressive social forces. More importantly, however, in contrast to the police's abstract systems of data and surveillance, the whistling is "completely human," an embodied, vibrational force that emanates from the lungs of these experts. This force, as Gago argues, resists the idea of neoliberalism articulated from above, from the macropolitical or purely abstract level, and shows "the proliferation of forms of life that reorganize notions of freedom, calculation, and obedience, projecting a new collective affectivity and rationality."[50] In contrast to a disembodied, superficial connectivity, the vibrational and sonorous forces in the *bloque* constitute the textures of collective affinity based on relationality, or the mutuality of affective and vibrational connections.

"THE CARE WE OFFER": INTIMATE NETWORKS AND VIBRATIONAL CONNECTIVITY

In *The Cultural Politics of Emotion*, feminist scholar Sara Ahmed demonstrates how official powers utilize a rhetoric based on emotion to discipline affective experience, often neutralizing contradictory experiences in moments when the state is pressed to reassert its authority. While Ahmed's case study deals with the Australian government's attempt at reconciliation with aboriginal tribes, in the context of postdictatorship Chile, Eltit's embrace of affective volatility and ambivalence presents an ethical challenge toward the neutralizing politics of Transition government that urged "consensus" at all costs.

As cultural critic Nelly Richard argues in *Cultural Residues*, the consensus model "neutralized different counterpoints, antagonistic and polemical stances . . . by means of an institutional pluralism that forced diversity to become noncontradictory."[51] This rhetoric of consensus piggybacked onto the illusion of the Chilean "miracle" celebrated by Milton Friedman, and painted Chile as a developing nation "saved" from the dangers of socialism that threatened the country decades before by the miraculous forces of democracy and the market (Grandin 22). As many scholars have argued— from Nelly Richard, to Francine Masiello, to Diamela Eltit—these political and market-based ideological programs obfuscated the complex experience of the Chilean Transition, erasing the intimate frictions that characterized the moment in favor of reconciliation as an abstract, top-down project. As the neoliberal project took hold, Lauren Berlant's *Cruel Optimism* examines its ideological promise of the "good life," and recognizes how the optimism deployed by subjects in an effort to reproduce this ideal leads to a suppression of the less favorable manifestations of performative life, such as "dread, anxiety, hunger, curiosity, the whole gamut."[52] *Fuerzas especiales* asks us to consider the structural biases or inequalities inherent in these projects, as well as the ongoing frictions that are produced as subjects negotiate discursive and disciplinary constraints, construct their personal, biographical narratives and consolidate relationships.

In late November and early December of 2019, the *Feria Internacional del Libro de Guadalajara* (Guadalajara International Book Fair) convened writers, artists, and cultural critics in the largest annual publishing gathering in Latin America. Present in the many discussions that took place were Chilean writers and feminists, who discussed the significance of the recent protests. Among them were Alejandra Costamaga, a writer and journalist, and Andrea Jeftanovic, who form part of the Organización de Escritoras Chilenas (Organization of Chilean Women Writers), a group founded in 2009 and responsible for distributing, investigating, and forming networks between women writers in Chile. Costamaga spoke about the significance of this particular moment in Latin America more broadly and addressed the connections between state violence, neoliberal crisis, and popular uprisings in Chile, Nicaragua, Venezuela, Colombia, Bolivia, and Ecuador. From her specific competency as a writer and creator, she remarked that this moment represents an opportunity to critically reflect on "the link between art and politics. Always a problematic relationship, but one that is important to continue to explore."[53] Jeftanovic, feminist novelist and writer noted the presence of a polyphonic chorus on Santiago's streets: "We maintain that this has to do with an awakening, with a shift in paradigm and with a form of coral writing that exists on the streets."[54]

Eltit's novel lays the groundwork for giving a form to this coral writing, constituted by affective and vibrational connections as irreconcilable and ambivalent textures of experience at the core of an interdependent social reality. Vibratory connections pose a form of thinking about relations beyond disembodied and networked connectivity, embracing the volatility of social life while resisting the unidimensional valorization of *all* relationships. Consequently, interdependence, constituted by this affective ambivalence, manifests in relationships and collectivities as an ongoing and contradictory process, rather than a fixed ideal. Against the backdrop of the current social protests and mediated interconnectivities in Chile, attention to vibratory and affective relations encourages us to consider how local practices of organization pose an ethical and political challenge to the neutralizing and disaggregating disciplinary paradigms of the present. In *Fuerzas especiales*, the dynamic dance between conflict *and* cohesion illuminates the textures of a collectivity that not only reorganizes power relations, but also permits us to think beyond the power-resistance dyad to reframe solidarity and coalition-building as ongoing and challenging processes tied to a specific context of emergence. As Rendueles notes, "if we see ourselves as fragile beings that depend on one another, we must think of cooperation as a human trait as essential as rational thought, perhaps even more so. Our lives are unthinkable without the care we offer one another."[55]

NOTES

1. "Hace décadas que escribo sobre la desigualdad y la indiferencia hacia las periferias." Diamela Eltit, "Diamela Eltit: 'La revuelta social no puede ser adjudicada a la delincuencia, eso es cómodo e inexacto.'" Interview with Roberto Ibáñez. *Culto, La Tercera,* October 25, 2019.

2. César Rendueles, *Sociophobia: Political Change in the Digital Utopia,* trans. Heather Cleary (New York: Columbia University Press, 2019), 83, Kindle.

3. In the case of Chile, the origins of neoliberalism came from the collaboration between the Chicago School of Economics and the Universidad Católica in the 1950s, which was later followed up by overarching economic reforms under the dictatorship and Transition governments. Guadalupe Salazar refers to the effects of Pinochet's economic reforms in the early 1980s as an "economic genocide" and Chilean sociologist Patricio Navia estimates that later, during Transition, the government largely upheld these policies and the Chilean public sector accounted for only 20% of the national economy.

4. "¿Cuánto tiempo lleva intervenida por la policía la población La Legua? Otro ejemplo es la muerte del joven mapuche Matías Catrileo, a él lo mataron por la espalda. Esto es el síntoma de una ley que está al límite de un crimen estatal.", Diamela Eltit in "'Fuerzas Especiales', nueva novela de Diamela Eltit," Interview with Carolina Rojas N. Accessed April 1, 2020. https://www.mcnallyjackson.com/event/spanish-book-lab-fuerzas-especiales-de-diamela-eltit.

5. Rendueles, *Sociophobia*, 6

6. The original quotation in Spanish contains the world "proyect," whose spelling conveys the oral pronunciation of the work "projects," or public housing units located in the United States.

7. "Pero eso pasa en todos los contornos de la tierra . . . donde los tiras y los pacos del mundo se atacan con todo por las minucias que recogen de los saldos en los bloques, en las villas, en los proyect y en la aglomeración de las favelas." Diamela Eltit, *Fuerzas especiales* (Santiago: Planeta Chilena, 2013), 51–52.

8. Rendueles, *Sociophobia,* 23.

9. Rendueles, *Sociophobia,* 26.

10. "la familia que me queda." Eltit, *Fuerzas especiales*, 49.

11. "las mujeres de la familia que vamos quedando." Eltit, *Fuerzas especiales*, 118.

12. "Ya es hora de olvidarme de las escaleras y de los problemas que tiene la familia. Tengo que olvidarme de mí misma para entregarme en cuerpo y alma a la transparencia que irradia la pantalla." Eltit, *Fuerzas especiales*, 40.

13. "Más de un año ya desde que las imágenes de los niños desbordaron los periódicos, los noticieros e irrumpieron en la crispada ruta de las redes." Eltit, *Fuerzas especiales*, 17.

14. "en una cita infinita." Eltit, *Fuerzas especiales*, 19.

15. "Un hecho público que ya no me obligaba a preguntarme por la veracidad de mi existencia." Eltit, *Fuerzas especiales*, 18.

16. "Los niños existían ante una parte del mundo y existía también mi hermana y, por fin, a lo largo de cuarenta y ocho horas la vida de todos nosotros adquiría un merecido relieve." Eltit, *Fuerzas especiales*, 18.

17. "En medio de poderosos chispazos, las informaciones detalladas con una deliberada crueldad, borraban nuestra insignificancia y las asimetrías." Eltit, *Fuerzas especiales*, 19.

18. "Yo saqué mi celular para conseguir resguardar la última imagen de mi padre. Quería subir esa imagen a las redes y mostrar su figura enjuta pero consistente. Deseaba enterrar su salida en el cementerio visual de las redes." Eltit, *Fuerzas especiales*, 55.

19. Rendueles, *Sociophobia*, 23.

20. Rendueles, *Sociophobia*, 26.

21. Byung-Chul Han, *Saving Beauty* (Cambridge UK: Polity Press, 2017), 8.

22. Hito Steyerl, *Duty Free Art* (New York: Verso, 2017). Please see chapter 5, "A Sea of Data: Apophenia and Pattern (Mis-)Recognition."

23. "La asombrosa coincidencia en los números que cargamos nos asusta porque pensamos en una conjunción que podría implicar las malas artes de alguna secta o los deliberados procedimientos de una organización transnacional o una jugada estatal de los pacos para ubicarnos en el centro de sus archivos." Eltit, *Fuerzas especiales*, 68.

24. Diamela Eltit, "What is Performance Studies?," Interview with Diana Taylor, Hemispheric Institute: Digital Video Library, December 15, 2015, Accessed April 1, 2020, http://hidbl.nyu.edu/video/003674813.html

25. "solo me invade la imagen de su pelo negro, grueso y sorprendente." Eltit, *Fuerzas especiales,* 31.

26. "Los golpes, su pelo endurecido por la densidad de la sangre, la calle, el silencio entre nosotras, la molestia que yo les provocaba cuando me convertía en una desapasionada testigo." Eltit, *Fuerzas especiales,* 31.

27. "Las enfocaba en un plano medio a las dos abrazadas. Porque así son ellas, afectuosas, atractivas, encapsuladas, parecidas. Es una semejanza inmaterial que va mucho más allá de la simple coincidencia orgánica, porque ambas no tienen nada en común." Eltit, *Fuerzas especiales,* 32.

28. "Mi intención era retener a mi padre, capturarlo en mi celular, pero a la vez no podía desatender la escena entre mi madre y mi hermana." Eltit, *Fuerzas especiales,* 55.

29. "Entonces, apoyada en el poste, levanté la cabeza y quise mirar nuestro piso, el cuarto, como si no lo conociera. Mi idea era hacer un experimento visual a partir de una forzada distancia." Eltit, *Fuerzas especiales,* 58.

30. "No fue difícil comprender la escena del reencuentro. Pude presagiar los gritos, los insultos, los golpes y el desconsuelo de mi papá ante su caja de vino vacía, las explicaciones de mi madre y los balbuceos inconclusos de mi hermana." Eltit, *Fuerzas especiales,* 58.

31. "Me devolví para comprobar mis imágenes. Corrí hasta nuestro bloque. Subí velozmente las escaleras. Entré con toda violencia y me sumé." Eltit, *Fuerzas especiales,* 58.

32. "A pesar de todo, no convierte su dolor en un recurso ni menos en coartada, sino más bien me lo explica para imponer entre nosotros un desafío que realmente nos permita comprender. Su miedo y el mío." Eltit, *Fuerzas especiales,* 86.

33. Zygmunt Bauman, *Liquid Love: On the Frailty of Human Bonds* (Cambridge/ Malden: Polity Press, 2003), viii.

34. "Como la santa guerrera, oigo voces. No me ordenan ningún sacrificio, ninguna oblación de mi cuerpo, de mi persona. Sólo que no escribo más que para esas voces. El texto—y no sólo un texto radiofónico; todos, hasta un poema—nunca se me presenta en abstracto, desencarnado, si así puede decirse, reducido a su desnudez o a su conceptualidad. Nunca pienso en un argumento o en un contenido preciso que las palabras, más tarde, se encargarían de consignar laboriosamente, de cincelar. Todo ya está 'dicho' desde el comienzo, no hay más comienzo que el de la escucha" (S. Sarduy Obra completa I, 30), Severo Sarduy quoted and translated by Birkenmaier.

35. "Y tú, qué andai haciendo en la calle, que no te dai cuenta de que tenimos hambre. Había doscientas treinta bombas W71. O no te dai cuenta que te estamos esperando pa que hagai la comida. Había mil bombas W79. O acaso no entendís que tu mamá está enferma, tiritando, más perdida que nunca." Eltit, *Fuerzas especiales,* 28.

36. Roberto Simanowski, "Culture Industry 2.0, or the End of Digital Utopias in the Era of Participation Culture," in *Sociophobia: Political Change in the Digital Utopia*, Insurrections: Critical Studies in Religion, Politics, and Culture (New York: Columbia University Press, 2017), v.

37. (viii) Bertolt Brecht quoted by Simonowski.

38. Simanowski, *Sociophobia: Political Change in the Digital Utopia,* viii.

39. Simanowski, *Sociophobia: Political,* xi–xii.

40. Simanowski, *Sociophobia: Political,* xii.

41. Simanowski, *Sociophobia: Political,* xvi.

42. Brandon LaBelle, "Auditory Relations," in *The Sound Studies Reader,* ed. Jonathan Sterne (New York: Routledge, 2012), 68.

43. Steve Goodman, "The Ontology of Vibrational Force," in *The Sound Studies Reader,* ed. Jonathan Sterne (New York: Routledge, 2012), 71–2.

44. "She feels that even if she could remember, in a photographic register, some of her family scenes, they no longer belong to her and they are distant or directly unconnected, because since the material disappearance of the family, only she exists and it is her daily movements that get her through the next day." Eltit, *Fuerzas especiales,* 132.

45. "Por eso sólo existe intensidad en el sonido del teléfono que la conecta con una voz sin cuerpo o con el cuerpo de los matices de la voz como si una forma de mundo sin cuerpo estuviera allí para sostenerla." Eltit, *Fuerzas especiales,* 132.

46. "Ahora escucho el volumen de la música que sube junto con las risas y las lágrimas de los sábados y durante unas horas la policía desaparece y deja los bloques huérfanos del ulular de las balizas." Eltit, *Fuerzas especiales,* 43.

47. "sé que el Omar está decidido a darle una nueva vida a su esquina. Me invita, me impulsa y me demanda y me grita porque existe todavía una música para nosotros pues los dos somos adictos al ritmo más exitoso y más rotundo: la fusión bloque que

baja por las escaleras y retoca cada uno de los escalones." Eltit, *Fuerzas especiales,* 44.

48. Verónica Gago, *Neoliberalism from Below: Popular Pragmatics and Baroque Economies,* Radical Américas (Durham: Duke UP, 2017), loc 103 of 6397.

49. "Quiénes silban? Los expertos del bloque . . . Los silbidos son completamente humanos, vienen de los pulmones de los especialistas en analizar las acciones de la policía cuando nos invaden." Eltit, *Fuerzas especiales,* 67.

50. Gago, *Neoliberalism from Below,* loc 174 of 6397.

51. Nelly Richard, *Cultural Residues: Chile in Transition* (Minneapolis: University of Minnesota Press, 2004), 38.

52. Lauren Berlant, *Cruel Optimism* (Durham: Duke UP, 2011), 2.

53. "el vínculo entre arte y política. Una relación siempre problemática que vale la pena seguir escarbando." Alejandra Costamanga, "Autoras chilenas relatan los cambios del país en Feria de Guadalajara." Interview with Camila Sánchez. *Mujer Dinamo,* December 5, 2019. Accessed April 1, 2020. https://mujer.eldinamo .cl/libros/2019/12/05/autoras-chilenas-relatan-los-cambios-en-chile-en-feria-de-gua dalajara/

54. "Rescatamos que esto tiene que ver con un despertar, con un cambio de paradigma y con una forma de *escritura coral* que está en las calles." Andrea Jeftanovic, Interview with Camila Sánchez.

55. Rendueles, *Sociophobia,* 121.

BIBLIOGRAPHY

Ahmed, Sara. *The Cultural Politics of Emotion.* 2nd ed. Edinburgh: Edinburgh UP, 2014.

Bauman, Zygmunt. *Liquid Love: On the Frailty of Human Bonds.* Cambridge/ Malden: Polity, 2003.

Berlant, Lauren Gail. *Cruel Optimism.* Durham: Duke UP, 2011.

Birkenmaier, Anke. 'Soy una Sor Juana de Arco electrónica: Severo Sarduy's Radio Play: 'Dolores Rondón.'" *La Habana Elegante* 57, November 2015. Accessed April 1, 2020. http://www.habanaelegante.com/November_2015/Invitation_Birke nmaier.html.

Bresnahan, Rosalind. "Introduction: Chile since 1990 the Contradictions of Neoliberal Democratization." *Latin American Perspectives* 30, no. 5 (2003): 3–15.

Costamaga, Alejandra and Andrea Jeftanovic. "Autoras chilenas relatan los cambios del país en Feria de Guadalajara." Interview with Camila Sánchez. *Mujer Dinamo,* December 5, 2019. Accessed May 2, 2020. https://mujer.eldinamo.cl/libros/2019 /12/05/autoras-chilenas-relatan-los-cambios-en-chile-en-feria-de-guadalajara.

Deleuze, Gilles, and Felix Guattari. *A Thousand Plateaus: Capitalism and Schizophrenia.* Translated by Brian Massumi. 2 edition. Minneapolis: U of Minnesota P, 1987.

Eltit, Diamela. *Fuerzas especiales.* 1. ed. Santiago: Planeta Chilena, 2013.

———— "Diamela Eltit: "La revuelta social no puede ser adjudicada a la delincuencia, eso es cómodo e inexacto." Interview with Roberto Ibáñez. *Culto*, La Tercera, October 25, 2019.

———— "'Fuerzas Especiales', nueva novela de Diamela Eltit." Interview with Carolina Rojas N. McNally Jackson, n.d., Accessed April 1, 2020. https://www.mcnallyjackson.com/event/spanish-book-lab-fuerzas-especiales-de-diamela-eltit

———— "What is performance studies?" Interview with Diana Taylor. Hemispheric Institute: Digital Video Library, December 15, 2015. Accessed April 1, 2020. http://hidbl.nyu.edu/video/003674813.html

Gago, Verónica. *Neoliberalism from below: Popular Pragmatics and Baroque Economies*. Durham: Duke UP, 2017. http://dx.doi.org/10.1215/9780822372738

Goodman, Steve. "The Ontology of Vibrational Force." In *The Sound Studies Reader*, edited by Jonathan Sterne, 70–72. New York: Routledge, 2012.

Grandin, Greg. "The Instruction of Great Catastrophe: Truth Commissions, National History, and State Formation in Argentina, Chile, and Guatemala." *American Historical Review* 110, no. 1 (2005): 46–67.

Greene, Margarita and Pablo C. Fuentes. "Rehabilitación de bloques de vivienda básica: Construcción de casa, comunidad y barrio." In *Camino al Bicentenario, Doce propuestas para Chile*, edited by Vicerrectoría de Comunicaciones y Asuntos Públicos, 81–107. Pontificia Universidad Católica de Chile: Santiago, 2006.

Han, Byung-Chul. *Saving Beauty*. Cambridge, UK: Polity Press, 2017.

Heiss, Claudia, and Patricio Navia. "You Win Some, You Lose Some: Constitutional Reforms in Chile's Transition to Democracy." *Latin American Politics and Society* 49, no. 3 (2007): 163–90.

LaBelle, Brandon. "Auditory Relations." In *The Sound Studies Reader*, edited by Jonathan Sterne, 468–74. New York: Routledge, 2012.

Mani, Lata. *Integral Nature of Things: Critical Reflections on the Present*. London/New York: Routledge, 2013.

Rendueles, César. *Sociophobia: Political Change in the Digital Utopia*. Translated by Heather Cleary. New York: Columbia UP, 2017. Kindle.

Richard, Nelly. *Cultural Residues: Chile in Transition*. Minneapolis: U of Minnesota P, 2004. Kindle.

Salazar, Guadalupe. "The Politics of Street Children in Chile." In *Lost in the Long Transition: Struggles for Social Justice in Neoliberal Chile*, edited by William L. Alexander, 169–84. Lanham: Lexington Books, 2009.

Steyerl, Hito. *Duty Free Art*. New York: Verso, 2017. Kindle.

Zuboff, Shoshana. *The Age of Surveillance Capitalism: The Fight for a Human Future at the New Frontier of Power*. New York: Public Affairs, 2019.

Chapter 3

Transculturation and the Body

Edwidge Danticat and Judith Ortiz Cofer

Raysa E. Amador

In reconstructing and representing transnational experiences within the space of fiction, Edwidge Danticat and Judith Ortiz Cofer articulate individual differences with regard to their ethnic and cultural heritage. The writers present the local and global inequalities that reflect their transnational experience as both authors produce literature that moves from the confines of a conventionally national repertoire to a representation of their own experience. Danticat and Ortiz Cofer construct a space where identity is formulated by weaving history and fiction to create an imaginary context that is informed by a connection to multiple national, cultural, and historical issues. Their cultural voices ask for a renewed debate on national identity and the role of the fictional space they create in the articulation of different kinds of identity. These writers treat the woman's experience as homogeneous to examine how multiple systems of discrimination overlap in what Grabe and Else-Quest called transnational intersectionality. Grabe and Else-Quest argue that

> transnational intersectionality places importance on the intersection among gender, ethnicity, sexuality, economic exploitation, and other social hierarchies . . . Thus, because understanding gender oppression at the intersection of other imbalances of power is increasingly imperative in a globalizing world, transnational feminist actors can and do make use of international data to advance local causes.[1]

Danticat and Ortiz Cofer call into question the very essence of difference and identity, providing occasions for a self-narrative of culturally marginalized people and integrating memory into this constructed identity. Their characters' representation relies on their migration experiences, finding difficulty in speaking of any given national identity since they are negotiating constantly between the place where they live and their place of origin. In the process, Edwidge Danticat and Judith Ortiz Cofer reconnect and rearrange the narrative discussing their own experience as immigrants in order to transform it into a stable construction of identity. The fictional transnational identity can certainly be defined by the metaphor of the 'ajiaco,' as it was used by Fernando Ortiz, in which some elements come together while others preserve their distinct qualities.[2] These narratives emerge from a multihistoric and political experience and seek to construct a more inclusive and diverse identity.

Interestingly enough, these novelists write in English, placing their fiction in the web of exile, immigration to the United States, and a reconstruction of the self that the transculturation process entails, as they find themselves located between two worlds, two languages, and two ways of understating the world. The characters are neither here nor there but in a new hybrid space, articulating how migration redefines gender and national identities by reconstructing the contested spaces of the body, of the land and sea. Focusing on the relationships of power, the writers subvert the migration experience by placing their fictional characters in a moment of flux between the "here" and the "there"; formatting and leading into a narrative that is marked by the transnational paradigm. Concurring with Ferreira Pinto-Bailey's discussion on identity, Danticat and Ortiz Cofer "rewrite the 'major narrative' of the nation through 'minor narratives' or the microhistory of previously invisible segments of their society through the life stories of everyday individuals whose experiences may seem irrelevant in the large scale of national history."[3]

Danticat and Ortiz Cofer tell tales of migration, exile, assimilation, and integrity of self, announcing new embodiments of the self that are based on their own physical experience and also on a communal experience. I concur with Roger Célestin, Elaine DalMolin, and Isabelle de Courtivron regarding fiction in the belief that these authors "use their writing mostly to express a feeling of loss with regard to their country of origin while also partaking of a new type of freedom as women living in the West. For them the challenge is to retain or rebuild their sense of female identity outside any form of acceptable home."[4] Dandicat's and Ortiz Cofer's' preoccupation with identity points to their efforts to make connections to history and multiple national and historical issues, in order to present an identity in flux that informs the transnational experience. I would like to stress, however, that while the writings emerge through a common historical process, this does not mean that the writing cannot be reduced to commonalities, but, rather, that it invites the reader to recognize and explore the differences that constitute a transnational reality.

Danticat's and Ortiz Cofer's works generate dialogues and testimonies that serve as agents for transformation. They focus their attention on the past, which also serves to create a sense of community. Their characters negotiate between the demands of a new geographical space, in this case the United States, and their recollections of their own fragmented and lost history. In the transnational fictional space, the individuals in the stories negotiate the transition through traces left by the body in the form of a diary, recipes, letters, language, and relationships. The characters resist a fixed identity rooted in a nation and in history and opt to relate to the cross-cultural experiences of other Haitians and Puerto Ricans.

The art of remembering is an attempted restoration of what was lost at the moment of displacement, bringing integrity to the past in order to go forward, thus suggesting that "memory is always a function of the imaginary and from it [we find] its condition to reconcile and conform to a community amongst those who share it."[5] These writers treat the act of writing as an act of representation and presentation that has been fashioned within a cultural and communal memory. Danticat and Ortiz reconnect and rearrange their narrative by "carefully positioning . . . elements—such as imagery, language, metaphor, theme, and narrative mode [which] is not only aesthetically satisfying but useful in terms of the kinds of personal and political statement it makes about female belonging within the fictional and historical as well as social and national communities."[6] The writers studied here create a transnational fictional space where both personal and collective identities produce a body of literature in the United States that constitutes a cultural production that allows them to recollect and restitute their past in order to go forward. The stories allow the writers to promote a debate about the processes of acculturation, resistance, rejection, loss, language, culture, traditions, and history, opting for a transculturation process that seeks a new representation of the personal and the collective.

Danticat and Ortiz Cofer have produced a vibrant and energetic discourse that clearly calls for a process of building a transnational imaginary. Both writers create "a fictional space . . . that rewrites national histories and problematizes rooted identities through their works' characterization."[7] The writers inscribe the characters' bodies with multiple identities at work, at school, at home, and on the streets as they dwell in two cultures. Thus, the characters evolve through switching from one culture to the other and, in the process, revealing a transcultural version of the self in different societies. The fictional space becomes a "transnational paradigm that . . . explores the effects of cultures founded on ideas of relation and affiliation rather than on rooted-socio-cultural legitimacy and ethno-political authority."[8] The characters' representation that Danticat and Ortiz Cofer articulate dismantles the dominant stereotypical image of women, simultaneously revising, rearticulating, and negotiating their experience of dispersion as the writers formulate an identity. At the core of this process, the characters struggle to constitute themselves by dealing with power relations and discursive formations. The characters are situated in a given geographical space that allows for the shaping of a unique identity. By celebrating the physical and verbal strengths of the characters, these artists undermine the traditional discourse on gender by representing the female body as an agent with a cultural history. In Danticat's short story, "Children of the Sea" the female character in Haiti writes in her journal that "manman says that banyan trees are holy, and sometimes if we call the gods from beneath them, they will hear our voices clearer."[9] In Ortiz Cofer's short story "Bad Habits," the main character, Rita, spends her summer with her grandparents in Puerto Rico as a punishment for her behavior in New Jersey. Upon her return, Rita explains her transformation as follows: "I'd had one of the best summers of my life with Angela, and I was really getting to know my grandparents—the Ghostbusting magnificent duo."[10] By then Rita had learned to determine when people were bothered by something. These characters engage in the process of self-knowledge through which the writers make us aware of the relationship between their subject-character body and the cultural body, in relation to the body politic. As Pultz confirms, "representations of the body reflect not only obvious issues of personal identity, sexuality, gender, and sexual orientation but also issues of power, ideology, and politics."[11]

The works of Danticat and Ortiz Cofer can be seen as a transnational creative space where "the politics of identity manifests itself with the greatest resonance, it functions as a model of and for the urgency of social action."[12] These female artists of the diaspora have produced a body of literature in the United States that can be read as a memorial to family and collective histories attesting to the power of female connections, especially familial relationships between grandmothers, mothers, aunts, female friends, daughters, and others. The power of female character connections demonstrates the triumph over tensions brought about by the essential power of collective womanhood. By elaborating on these female connections, the artists recreate a forum for the exploration of the self and the body in which the dialogue serves as a site of encounter between different generations of women as speaking subjects, structuring the configuration of the text and the reading of that text. As Nancy Mair states, "writing my past as a body enacts that circle game, I invite you through my openings because I have been schooled in hospitality."[13] I concur with Mair in that through the act of writing those past moments, the writer invites us to be part of a private world whose locus is the body.

Edwidge Danticat was born in Port-au-Prince in Haiti under the dictatorship of Duvalier. Her father André was a cab driver who moved to New York when she was two years old. Danticat's mother, Rose, a textile worker, joined him two years later, leaving Edwidge behind to be raised by an aunt. At the age of twelve, Edwidge joined her parents in the United States. In her short story collection *Krik? Krak?*, written in English, the author raises awareness about the people that she knew while she was growing up. They were poor people who struggled, suffered, and overcame amazing obstacles. She refers to herself as "a weaver of tales," for her stories, as much of the literature of the diaspora, are full of memory, of loss and assimilation and resistance. She compartmentalizes the spaces of the house, the kitchen and her body where the writing activity becomes a possibility for the young narrator. In the kitchen, she learns that it

> was their whispers that pushed [her], their murmurs over pots sizzling in your head. A thousand women urging you to speak through the blunt tip of your pencil. Kitchen poets, [she] calls them. Ghosts like burnished branches on a flame tree. These women, they asked for your voice so they could tell [her] mother in [her] place that yes, women like you do speak, even if they speak in a tongue that is hard to understand. Even if it's patois, dialect, Creole.[14]

The title of the book, as stated in the epigraph, confronts us with a way of telling stories as when an "old granny smokes her pipe, surrounded by the village children. . . We tell the stories so that the young ones will know what came before them. They ask Krik? We say Krak! Our stories are kept in our hearts."[15] Danticat invokes stories that keep Haitians connected. The reader is invited actively to participate in the Krik-Krak ritual. In Haiti, this is a wordplay that identifies relationships between women. For many of the characters who reside in the United States, the reenactment of the tradition is an opportunity to reconnect with their identity as Haitians. In the epilogue, when the narrator's mother asks to name the women of her past, she states: "Those nine hundred and ninety-nine women who were boiling in [her] blood, and since [she] had written them down and memorized them, the names would come rolling off your tongue. And this was your testament to the way that these women lived and died and lived again."[16]

In the epilogue, the narrator acknowledges those who came before her. The young woman asks, "are there women who both cook and write? Kitchen poets, they call them. They slip phrases into their stew and wrap meaning around their pork before frying it. They make narrative dumplings and stuff their daughter's mouth so they say nothing more."[17] It is in the space of the kitchen and on the body of the daughter that the inscription of the memories takes place. The young woman then realizes that it is in these moments where and when she writes that she finds solace in her "only notebook made out of discarded fish wrappers, [and] panty-hose cardboards."[18] Danticat highlights what it means for her to write, and she further refers to the braiding of her hair, transforming it into a metaphor of writing: "When you write, it's like braiding your hair. Taking a handful of coarse unruly strands and attempt to bring them unity . . . Like the diverse women in your family. Those whose fables and metaphors, whose similes, and soliloquies, whose diction and *je ne sais quoi* daily lip into your survival soup, by way of their fingers."[19] This act of locating and enacting subjectivity through the body and its signs characterizes the work of Danticat and offers a different perspective about Haitian history. It is a female voice that will disrupt a history with a unified national objective in order to bring multiple perspectives of that history. Danticat, and also Ortiz Cofer, "interweave fiction and history in the creation of an imaginary space that promotes fluidity in the process of identity and in our representations of the past and future."[20]

In Danticat's works, the author honors "the voices of others."[21] Most importantly, "she gives a voice to the people who appear in news photos of Haiti."[22] The stories presented are those of letters between a girl and a boy who will die at sea; of a woman in the prison of Port-au-Prince, the capital of Haiti, because she is accused of having wings; the life of a couple, Guy and Lili, and their son, trying to make ends meet under very difficult economic conditions; a young woman of twenty-five who works as a prostitute at night and her son; a woman unable to have children, who becomes a servant in Port-au-Prince, finds a dead baby wrapped in a pink blanket, and tries to take care of her; a grandmother and a fourteen-year-old who after a coup rent a room to a Haitian American journalist who helps the young girl become her own person; a young Haitian girl who poses for a French artist and who learns about painting and art; a story of an immigrant mother and her Americanized daughter who follows her mother secretly through Manhattan, and a story of a mother from Haiti living in New York and her two daughters. Caroline, the younger daughter, is to be married to a non-Haitian; such an act disturbs the mother. The story deals with the sacrifice of immigrant families and how immigration changes traditions. In the "Epilogue: Women Like Us," the narrator insists that the repeated appearances of the images of a daughter who in turn looks like her mother who looks like her grandmother, as well as the constant use of the bodily metaphor of "braiding your hair" for the writing process brings forward the fact that it is with her mother that the narrator first "heard the echoes of the tongue [she] now speak[s]"[23] and then is able to transmute them into writing. This bodily presence, in association with the issue of writing the memories, is how Danticat individualizes the nation within a transnational fictional space. In the texts of Danticat and Ortiz Cofer, the characters "struggle with identities rooted in nation and history, but find stability in learning how to relate cross-culturally to the experience of other Haitians and [Puerto Ricans]."[24]

The narrator's subjective gaze gives a precise and limited vision of the body in her search for meaning as when the narrator of "Caroline's Wedding," Gracina, expresses the need of not only remembering but holding onto the mother's body as she replies to her when the latter asks her to destroy the marriage proposal letter when she dies: "I will want to hold on to things when you die. I will want to hold on to you."[25] The urgency of the body marked by pain is what prompted Caroline and Gracina's father to swallow his mother's hair beads in order to keep "a piece of her inside of him."[26] As a storyteller, Danticat gives us a vision of the world that is fragmented and focused on the body and on the violence toward the body that transforms it into pain, into absence. As Adjarian states regarding Caribbean writers, "born as they are at specific time and specific places, these bodies not only serve as records of the violent historical processes that cultural dominants have forgotten but also as glosses for the geographical landscapes they inhabit."[27]

History becomes the source of bedtime stories that were only understood by the young people when they were fully grown and "they [the stories] became [their] sole inheritance."[28] In Danticat's own words,

what makes the newly arrived immigrant writing so strong is that it embodies the immediate meeting of two worlds. It is full of grief in some cases, grief for a very recent loss of a homeland. It is full of anger sometimes, full of laughter too. But the emotions are still very raw, very strong. The wounds are still deep. The jokes are still remembered in their entirety. The memories are still not too fragmented, so that makes for strong writing.[29]

The implication of Danticat's writing metaphor points also to the specificity of a geographical location, Haiti, and the new home, the United States.

The female writers I study in this chapter are reproducers of historical narrations that go beyond the particular to include the transnational experience. By addressing the body, Danticat's writing provides an open venue where the voices of the past are heard in connection to those of the present, resonating in very powerful voices of resistance. As Adjarian concludes, "Danticat . . . [is] therefore not only literary rebel, but a discursive one as well. Like the women who inhabit [her] fiction, [she] uses literature as a mean to end the strange hold of both history and the men who made it."[30] It is important to indicate that the short stories provide the readers with a glimpse of what people had to endure. It is through literature that we can rescue those memories, and as Lucia M. Suárez states in *Tears of Hispaniola*, "if memory can be stolen from the masses, by powerful leaders, it can be returned to the people through literature."[31] As Danticat revisits her past, she records those memories empowering her experience and that of many Haitians following the long tradition of many Haitian writers whose work has been associated with activism. As Wucker points out, "Marie Chauvet . . . inspired Danticat for her bravery . . . Danticat's work also clearly draws on the influence of Jacques Stephen Alexis."[32] As Danticat writes about violence against the body, she presents a clear example of how the narrative genre gives power to those who have been left out.

Judith Ortiz Cofer, in her collection of short stories *An Island Like You: Stories of El Barrio*, sets out to write the experiences of adolescents in two worlds. The title itself calls the attention to the "Island/la Isla" as the location mediated by cultural issues, pointing to a social definition of the place of origin. The island makes clear reference to Puerto Rico but, in the collection, refers to a building in El Barrio that is central to the narrative. The island serves to reconnect and rearrange all the characters that inhabit it, becoming the focal point in the stories. Despite their differences, all the narrators, six girls and one boy, share a common experience that defines and connects them. In the introductory poem "Day in the Barrio," Ortiz Cofer focuses on her own body as she writes of herself in connection to the others by saying "you watch the people below, / each one an island like you."[33] Ortiz Cofer makes reference to "an island like you," elaborating on what Chadwick calls the "constructedness of nature itself."[34] Her body becomes an active agent that looks at others while writing about them and with them. This verse in the poem foretells the content of the collection. For, as Ortiz Cofer has stated, "poetry is what connects [her] to [her] memory, to [her] imagination, to [her] subconscious life, and to [her] original language."[35] This connection acts as a source of her writing, pointing to the need for inclusiveness while acknowledging the influences of the people in her life, her grandmother, mother, and female friends.

In her short story "Bad Influences," the protagonist, Rita, comes to terms with her maternal grandparents, especially her grandmother, after spending her summer vacations in Puerto Rico. Through the thoughts of Rita, a young fifteen-year-old, the reader discovers that "[Rita] didn't want her (her mother) to think it all had been a vacation . . . [she] had one of the best summers of [her] life with Angela" and her grandparents.[36] She spends time with her grandparents and recognizes that she has come to know them. The connection points to the way in which identity is elaborated by the recording of experiences that the narrator recalls. Ortiz Cofer uses memory and writing as tools to provide evidence of the character's physical experiences. Rita concludes that she had learned much from her grandparents; she was even "taking medium lessons from them."[37] The other young female character, Angela, is a rich girl in Puerto Rico who suffers from anorexia. She was cured by a ritual of cleanliness administered by Rita's grandfather in order to chase away the bad influences in her house. Rita was creating a stronger relationship with her grandmother, Mama Ana, and her mother. The writing of the character, in this case, Rita, evolves in a discourse that is female-centered from the grandmother–mother bodily experiences. By writing Rita, Ortiz Cofer recaptures the past and, most of all, a personal history. In this respect, Cofer's writing points to a locus in which the actions are generated by the female character's experience. It is from the female body, as a source, that a powerful alternative discourse emerges in order to represent the world.

The stories like "Arturo's Flight," "White Balloons," and "Beauty Lessons" also depict the essence of living in El Barrio. El Barrio becomes the island, the center from which the characters evolve. In "Bad Influences," Rita's life fluctuates between el Barrio and Puerto Rico, between Mama and Papa and the grandparents. In addition to the writing of the body, Ortiz Cofer challenges the reader with the use of two languages, by proposing the reality of two worlds/bodies and two cultures. Arturo, during a visit to his grandfather, comes to the realization that he needs to "keep fighting to make his dream come true."[38] Language becomes a way of representing the development and evolution of the characters. Ortiz Cofer "views both Puerto Rico and the United States as 'transnational' home space by resisting the ideological imperative of dichotomies and by refusing imposed social strictures of monolingual identity."[39] By reading in English and Spanish, the reader is experiencing some of what it means to live in-between the two cultures.

This technique also allows for the inclusion of personal narratives and acts as a crucial element, reminding the reader of the essence of the story told. The reader discovers the meaning of the terms "mama," "abuelo," "hijo" in the context of the story allowing for a fluidity of meaning that lets the author and the reader switch from one world to the other. Physicality is explored in the story "The One Who Watches" where one of the narrators, Doris, tells the reader that "[she] keeps it greased down, and [she is] short and plain."[40] Appearances are defining and recognizable traits for Doris. She feels that they set her apart from others. Doris describes herself as an observer, while Yolanda is "the star." Doris tells herself that "[she] just stand[s] to the side and watch[es] everything . . . [She is] not flashy as Yolanda. [She is] practically invisible . . . Not ugly, not beautiful. Just nothing."[41] At the end of the story and after Yolanda's shoplifting experience, Doris comes to the realization that she does not need anyone to figure out who she is. Doris regrets having gone with Yolanda to the store. She finally realizes that "[she] needs to start trying to figure out who [she] is and where [she] wants to go before [she] can help anyone else." It is that at this point that she sees her mother as a source of support, letting "her take care of [her] for a little while."[42] Once more Ortiz Cofer recurs to the familial bonds as a form of security. It is with the mother or grandmother in El Barrio or in Puerto Rico that the narrator can find support and connection.

"Don Jose de la Mancha" is another story about family where the narrator comes to terms with the fact that her mother needs to continue her life after the father's death. It is through the mother's meeting of Don Jose that the young woman starts to feel "love, happiness . . . it feels good."[43] The comfort zone that a mother and daughter can feel is expressed in the last section of the story, a love that is eternal. In "Abuela Invents the Cero," Ortiz Cofer calls to mind the meaning of the Spanish phrase "es un cero a la izquierda (a zero to the left, meaning a nobody)," to portray the relationship between the grand-daughter (Constancia) and the grandmother. The mother reminds her daughter, Constancia, that "if it wasn't for this old woman whose existence you don't seem to value, you and I would not be here."[44] In "A Job for Valentin," the young female protagonist comes to understand the life of a disabled man, Valentin, who through the act of saving her and Pablito from drowning, gains the respect of the young protagonist, as she learns that it does not matter how you look or are. Anita, after a brief love affair with Frank, in "Home to El Barrio," feels reassured in "el building" of "el barrio," her home, a physical space that embraces the body.

The stories also introduce new subjects connected to the body. In the story "White Balloons," the protagonist called Doris is rescued by her mother singing "Las Mañanitas" after organizing a birthday party for Ricky, who has died of AIDS and whom no one in El Barrio wanted to relate to. In this short story, Ortiz Cofer elaborates on the experience of the Puerto Ricans in diaspora in relation to the reality of the twentieth-century AIDS epidemic. Doris feels, through her mother's tight grip, the flow of energy and courage she needs in order to continue the in-memoriam birthday party for Ricky, who was different from others. As she held her mother's hand, she felt the energy and the courage to sing. Ricky's sick body is marginalized because of his illness. The way Doris relates to her community shifts into a transnational experience through the manner in which they react to the AIDS epidemics. At the end, Doris's bodily presence brings everyone together on the building's roof "like a family posing for a picture after a celebration."[45]

Danticat and Ortiz Cofer present in their stories the local and global inequalities that reflect their transnational experience. The short stories elaborate in the experience of Puerto Ricans and Haitians in order to create a space where the characters undergo a particular experience. The protagonists in the stories "claim voices through acts of writing that connect the private lives to public histories."[46] In these stories, the characters survive because of their body connectedness as mother/grandmother/sister/aunt/daughters. They can have their stories told because other significant characters will tell and retell their stories. The writing of memories represents a triumph over forget-fulness and builds a foundation for the (re)construction of cultural identity across time and space, simultaneously searching for memories of the past in order to discover what we can learn from the past as well as from a universe of real and imaginary possibilities. In this chapter, I am proposing a dialogue that would address the "small fragments of truth" springing from these ex-centered voices.

NOTES

1. Else-Quest and Grabe, "The Role of Transnational Feminism in Psychology," *Psychology of Women Quarterly* 36 (2012): 160.

2. Ortiz, Fernando, *Los factores humanos de la cubanidad* (La Habana: Molina y Cía., 1940), 12.

3. Judith Ortiz Cofer, *An Island Like You. Stories of the Barrio* (New York: Penguin Books, 1996), 204.

4. Roger Celestine, Elaine DalMolin and Isabelle de Courtivron, *Beyond French Feminism. Debates on Women, Politics, and Culture in France, 1981–2001* (New York: Palgrave Macmillan, 2003), 11.

5. Guillermina Wallas, *Entre dos Américas: narrativas de Latinas en los 90's* (Lanham.: U of America P, 2000), 1.

6. Maude M. Adjarian, *Allegories of Desire: Body, Nation, and Empire in Modern Caribbean Literature by Women* (Westport: Greenwood Press), 4.

7. Erik R. Kerby, "Negotiating in the Transnational Imaginary of Julia Alvarez's and Edwidge Danticat's Literature" (PhD diss., Brigham Young University, 2008), n.p.

8. Kerby, "Negotiating in the Transnational Imaginary," n.p.

9. Edwidge Danticat, *Krik? Krak!* (New York: Random House, 1996), 28.

10. Ortiz Cofer, *An Island Like You*, 25.

11. John Pultz, *The Body and the Lens: Photography 1983 to the Present* (New York: Harry N. Adams, 1995), 7.

12. Alberto Sandocal-Sánchez and Nancy Sternbach, *Stages of Life. Transcultural Performance and Identity in the U.S. Latina Theater* (Arizona: U of Arizona P, 2001), 2.

13. Sidonie Smith and Julia Watson, *Reading Autobiography: A Guide for Interpreting Life Narrative* (Minnesota: University of Minnesota Press, 2010), 473.

14. Danticat, *Krik? Krak!*, 222.

15. Danticat, *Krik? Krak!*, n.p.

16. Danticat, *Krik? Krak!*, 224.

17. Danticat, *Krik? Krak!*, 220.

18. Danticat, *Krik? Krak!*, 220.

19. Danticat, *Krik? Krak!*, 220.

20. Kerby, "Negotiating in the Transnational Imaginary," 3.

21. Michelle Wucker, "Edwidge: A Voice for the Voiceless," *America Magazine* 52, no. 3 (May/June 2000): 40.

22. Wucker, "Edwidge," 42.

23. Danticat, *Krik? Krak!*, 224.

24. Kerby, "Negotiating in the Transnational Imaginary," 8.

25. Danticat, *Krik? Krak!*, 213.

26. Danticat, *Krik? Krak!*, 179.

27. Adjarian, *Allegories of Desire*, 4.

28. Danticat, *Krik? Krak!*, 180.

29. Wucker, "Edwidge," 45.

30. Adjarian, *Allegories of Desire*, 114.

31. Lucía M. Suárez, *The Tears of Hispanionla: Haitian and Dominican Diaspora Memory* (Florida: University Press of Florida, 2006), n.p.

32. Wucker, "Edwidge," 45.

33. Ortiz Cofer, *An Island Like You*, ix.

34. Celestine, Dalmolin and Courtivron, *Beyond* 147.

35. Harold Augenbraum and Margarite Fernandez Olmos, *The Latino Reader: An American Literary Tradition from 1542 to the Present* (Boston: Houghton Mifflin, 1997), 49.

36. Ortiz Cofer, *An Island Like You*, 25.

37. Ortiz Cofer, *An Island Like You*, 25.

38. Ortiz Cofer, *An Island Like You*, 71.

39. Faymonville, "New Transnational Identities in Judith Ortiz Cofer's Autobiographical Fiction," *MELUS* 26, no. 2 (2001): 154.

40. Ortiz Cofer, *An Island Like You*, 74.

41. Ortiz Cofer, *An Island Like You*, 74.

42. Ortiz Cofer, *An Island Like You*, 80.

43. Ortiz Cofer, *An Island Like You*, 106.

44. Ortiz Cofer, *An Island Like You*, 111.

45. Ortiz Cofer, *An Island Like You*, 165.

46. Susan Strehle, *Transnational Women Women's Fiction: Unsettling Home and Homeland* (New York: Palgrave MacMillan, 2008), 186.

BIBLIOGRAPHY

Adjarian, Maude M. *Allegories of Desire: Body, Nation, and Empire in Modern Caribbean Literature by Women*. Westport: Greenwood P, 2004.

Augenbraum, Harold and Margarite Fernandez-Olmos. *The Latino Reader: An American Literary Tradition from 1542 to the Present*. Boston: Houghton Mifflin, 1997.

Célestin, Roger, Eliane Dal Molin, and Isabelle de Courtivron, eds. *Beyond French Feminism. Debates on Women, Politics, and Culture in France, 1981–2001*. New York: Palgrave Macmillan, 2003.

Collins, Lynn H., Sayaka Machizawa, and Joy K. Rice, eds. *Transnational Psychology of Women: Expanding International and Intersectional Approaches*. Washington: American Psychological Association, 2019.

Cusset, Catherine. "The Nieces of Margarite: Novels by Women at the Turn of the Twentieth Century." In *Beyond French Feminism. Debates on Women, Politics, and Culture in France, 1981–2001*, edited by Roger Célestin, Eliane Dal Molin, and Isabelle de Courtivron, 155–60. New York: Palgrave Macmillan, 2003.

Danticat, Edwidge. *Krik? Krak!*. New York: Random House, 1996.

Else-Quest, Nicole M., and Shelly Grabe. "The Role of Transnational Feminism in Psychology: Contemporary Visions." *Psychology of Women Quarterly* 36 (2012): 158–61.

Faist, Thomas and Eyüp Özveren. *Transnational Social Spaces: Agents, Networks and Institutions*. London & New York: Routledge, 2004.

Faymonville, Carmen. "New Transnational Identities in Judith Ortiz Cofer's Autobiographical Fiction." *MELUS* 26, no. 2 (2001): 129–58.

Fernandez, Leela. *Transnational Feminism in the United States*. New York: NYU Press, 2013.

Ferreira Pinto-Bailey, Cristina. "Women, Memory, Nation: Writing Identities in Three Latin American Novels." *A Quarterly Journal of Modern Literatures* 68, no. 4 (2014): 203–17.

Hai, Ambreen. "Motherhood and Domestic Servitude in Transnational Women's Fiction: Thrity Umrigar's *The Space Between Us* and Mona Simpson's *My Hollywood.*" *Contemporary Literature* 57, no. 4 (2016): 501–40.

Jones, Ann Rosalind. *Renaissance Clothing and the Material of Memory*. Cambridge: Cambridge UP, 2001.

Kerby, Erik R. "Negotiating Identity in the Transnational Imaginary of Julia Alvarez's and Edwidge Danticat's Literature." PhD diss., Brigham Young University, 2008

Nazmeen, Sohela and Maheen Sultan. *Voicing Demands: Feminist Activism in Transitional Contexts*. London: Zed Books, 2014.

Ortiz, Fernando. *Los factores humanos de la cubanidad*. La Habana: Molina y Cía., 1940.

Ortiz Cofer, Judith. *An Island Like You. Stories of the Barrio*. New York: Penguin Books, 1996.

Padilla, Yajaira M. *Changing Women, Changing Nation: Female Agency, Nationhood, and Identity in Trans-Salvadoran Narratives*. New York: State U of New York P, 2012.

Pultz, John. *The Body and the Lens: Photography 1983 to the Present*. New York: Harry N. Adams, 1995.

Rodriguez, Ana Patricia. "The Fiction of Solidarity: Transfronterista Feminisms and Anti-Imperialist Struggles in Central America Transnational Narratives." *Feminist Studies* 34, no. 1/2, The Chicana Studies Issue (Spring-Summer 2008): 199–226.

Sandoval-Sanchez, Alberto and Nancy Sternback. *Stages of Life. Transcultural Performance and Identity in the U.S. Latina Theater*. Arizona: U of Arizona P, 2001.

Smith, Sidonie and Julia Watson. *Reading Autobiography: A Guide for Interpreting Life Narratives*, second edition. Minnesota: U of Minnesota P, 2010.

Strehle, Susan. *Transnational Women's Fiction. Unsettling Home and Homeland*. New York: Palgrave Macmillan, 2008.

Suárez, Lucía M. *The Tears of Hispaniola: Haitian and Dominican Diaspora Memory*. Florida: U P of Florida, 2006.

Wallas, Guillermina. *Entre dos Américas: narrativas de Latinas en los '90s*. Lanham: U of America P, 2000.

Waldinger, Roger and David Fitzgerald. "Transnationalism in Question. *American Journal of Sociology* 109, no. 5 (March 2004): 1177–95.

Wucker, Michelle. "Edwidge Danticat: A Voice for the Voiceless." *America Magazine* 52, no. 3 (May/June 2000): 40–46.

Part II

TV AND FILM

Chapter 4

"Postfeminist Supergirl" Turned Superspy

Crossing Borders and New Identities in El tiempo entre costuras

Barbara Minter

Recently, the small screen has become one of the most popular and widely used media. However, with the inclusion of streaming, the definition of what constitutes television has evolved over the years. In a world that is becoming increasingly globalized, the term transnationalism seems to have become more of a buzzword that lacks consensus, thus leaving itself open to criticism. It is a concept that can be used both figuratively and literally. Though we can certainly consider how the globalization of our world allows for more easily crossed borders and less of a focus on nation-states, given the interconnectivity that exists in society, it is important to also understand what it means to *"think transnationally*, to think in a way which crosses borders in a way that does not simply 'add in' countries previously 'overlooked' by Western/ Northern scholarship, but to address the transnational as a field structured by power relations."[1] Walter Mignolo defines border thinking as *"thinking from dichotomous concepts rather than ordering the world in dichotomies."*[2] In considering this definition, it is important to pay attention to the transnational effect that the television industry has on the world, rather than just the Western hemisphere. Thanks to streaming, TV is no longer limited to the country in which it is produced. In fact, many television programs are produced across borders, adding to the transnational effect of this medium. That said, even though a transnational trend in the production of televised content is important in our globalized world, the way in which television is distributed is impactful because it opens television programs to being interpreted beyond their original cultural context, linking together viewers from all over the world to the same program.

Borders have become less defined as well. Although migration is no new concept, there is still much research to be done on how border-crossing and hybridization are linked to transnationalism. T. S. Eliot explains that "the migrations of modern times [which] have transplanted themselves according to some social, religious, economic or political determination, or some peculiar mixture of these." According to Eliot, this results in "the people [taking] with them only a part of the total culture . . . The culture which develops on the new soil must therefore be bafflingly alike and different."[3] These hybrid identities can be observed in many forms—cultural, national, and even through gender roles. In some areas of the world, people are creating more culturally diverse societies, and it is becoming increasingly difficult to pinpoint where each culture begins and ends. Not only are we witnessing a change in regard to a more globalized society, but because these changes also manifest in different ways (i.e., cultural, national, and even gender roles), the rules for these different categories are evolving, forcing industries, such as the television industry, to adjust with them.

National identities—be they more monolithic or hybrid in nature—are a historically recent concept. Even more recently, scholars of the humanities have not only had to take a look at the effects of globalization and migration, but to revisit migratory patterns from the past as well and see how they may have affected previous generations. In popular culture, there has been a trend toward an imaginative re-creation of the past through narratives that populate significant historic moments with the concerns that are much more relevant to today's reality than to anything that happened in the past. It may be for this reason that cultural reproductions of historical accounts are increasing in popularity, thus allowing us to link the past to our present. How is this being translated into popular culture and what can be learned from these cultural productions? Beginning in 2013, one of Spain's most successful private channels, Antena 3, aired its televisual adaptation of María Dueñas's best-selling first novel, *El tiempo entre costuras*. The final episode of the miniseries came out in 2014 and attracted around four million spectators. However, there is very little written on the series, and there is even less about how postfeminism and transnationalism are being utilized in *El tiempo* to question the patriarchal order of societies past and present. I argue that Stéphanie Genz's concept of the "postfeminist supergirl," a female figure that challenges patriarchal gender norms, can be used to demonstrate how Sira Quiroga, the protagonist of the series, utilizes fashion to subvert the patriarchal order of the society in which she lives and continually crosses borders as she changes her identity.

Postfeminism is quite a contradictory term. Given its prefix, this comes as no surprise. Scholars such as Susan Faludi have argued that this version of feminism is detrimental to previous feminist movements, given that for some the concept indicates "not that women have arrived at equal justice, but simply that they themselves are beyond even pretending to care."[4] However, other critics such as Stéphanie Genz offer a contrasting opinion on the matter. In the introduction to their text, *Postfeminism: Cultural Text and Theories*, Stéphanie Genz and Benjamin A. Brabon propose that "the cultural presence, resonance and longevity of postfeminism have become hard to ignore, specifically as it continues to evolve with changes in the political, cultural, and economic environment."[5] Genz and Brabon explain that "rather than implementing a simple frame of definition, [they] discuss diverse manifestations of postfeminism in order to highlight the term's multiplicity and draw connections between these postfeminist expressions."[6] Considering both critics' interpretation of postfeminism, for the purposes of this study, it is important to remember that postfeminism does not have to be seen as a "post" movement at all, like Faludi suggests, but rather as a combination of ideologies. It is precisely because of its complexity that the term "postfeminism" allows for so many different analyses in different contexts. In their book, Genz and Brabon elaborate on a variety of postfeminist identities. However, Genz's single-author book *Postfemininities in Popular Culture*, although published in 2009, may still be even more useful, as it goes into great detail on how these postfeminist identities are incorporated into different popular cultural productions, which continues to be crucial to our very technological society today.

Genz's study goes into great detail about the makeup of these different postfeminist identities, as well as the way in which it is exemplified in a variety of anglophone audiovisual productions. In this chapter, I apply Genz's conclusions to a popular TV series from Spain. One of Spain's recently successful series is the televisual production of *El tiempo entre costuras*, or *The Time In Between*, as it is translated into English on the US Netflix platform. This program inserts the fictional life of Sira Quiroga, a humble seamstress from Madrid, into the very real history of Spain's not-so-distant Civil War. Though in many ways this novel, and thus the series, can be perceived as another piece of historical fiction, a closer and more critical look allows the reader and spectator to see a connection between the past and the present and concentrate more closely on the feminine identity that takes the center stage in both cultural productions. Sira's character portrays an identity that bridges the gap between both the woman she plays from the past and the one today who is viewing her on television.

According to Stéphanie Genz, postfeminism "is indicative of the diversity of contemporary feminisms and the changes in feminist thinking, activism and politics."[7] Genz's interpretation allows us to embrace this diversity, while not forgetting the work that has been done by any feminists in our past and present, which consequently can be associated with the idea of transnationalism. For Genz, postfeminism should not be defined by its prefix "post," but rather by the fact that it incorporates the many schools of thought that have aligned themselves with the various forms of feminism. One of the identities on which Genz expounds in her book *Postfemininities in Popular Culture* is that of the "postfeminist supergirl," which she proposes as contradictory to the "normal" female figure we perceive in popular culture. She is neither "too feminine" nor "too masculine," and she does not take the backseat in her own story. As is demonstrated in Genz's text, this identity can be viewed in various forms.

Though my study focuses on Spain, the nature of the television industry forces us to think about how spectators across borders are affected by this sort of cultural production. Does anyone believe we are living in a "post" society or does Genz's concept of the "postfeminist supergirl" prove that we are truly able to blur the barriers and lines between feminisms as we do with borders through the use of transnational thinking? I echo Genz's argument that the "post" does not necessarily indicate a "post" society. Walter Mignolo's theory on "border thinking" helps us understand how the postfeminist standpoint does not necessarily indicate a "post" society. Because Mignolo's concept requires thinking from more than one side, this mindset allows us to be open to more than one definition. The limits that define each gender's role in a patriarchal society *can* be crossed and challenged. Therefore, the "postfeminist supergirl" is an identity that challenges those very borders, thus bringing together transnational thought and postfeminism, both of which link the past and the present.

The idea of crossing boundaries has always been central to feminist thought. As Liz Bondi demonstrates in her discussion of the intersections between gender and geography, feminist thinkers have produced a significant amount of research that

> points to the way patriarchal gender relations generate gender-specific experiences of space and time, and demonstrates how women in particular negotiate all manner of boundaries, for example between home and work, between private space and public space, between nation-states, between cultures and classes. It also demonstrates how this crossing of boundaries is central to the operation of dominant economic, political and social systems.[8]

The TV series *El tiempo entre costuras* pays particular attention to these intersections. Its protagonist Sira Quiroga exemplifies the identity of a "postfeminist supergirl" who crosses different kinds of borders and invites the viewers to join her on this journey. This kind of imaginative exercise can have great value as a catalyst that can awaken feminist sensibilities. As Bondi argues, "at this point, real and imaginative geographies intersect, in that feminist work concerned with the former has the potential to redefine our theories about, and therefore our imaginative geographies of, the world."[9]

Sira's character also challenges the idea of a class society. Ulrich Beck argues that, in the risk society of the early twenty-first century, the concept of class mobility has lost its meaning:

> First, processes of individualization deprive class distinctions of their social identity. Social groups lose their distinctive traits, both in terms of their self understanding and in relation to other groups . . . As a result of this development, the idea of social mobility (in the sense of individual movement between actual status classes), which until very late in this century constituted a social and political theme of considerable importance for social identity formation, pales into insignificance.[10]

In the series, we observe Sira cross class boundaries with relative ease. After abandoning Madrid shortly before the Spanish Civil War and suffering hardships that led her to take some of the first steps to becoming a "postfeminist supergirl," Sira is quickly able to jump across class divides. By endowing this character with the mentality of a "postfeminist supergirl," the creators of the series invite the viewers to experience class mobility by identifying with her, an exercise which this postfeminist identity facilitates.

Sira Quiroga grows up with a single mother who is a seamstress and learns the same trade, utilizing this seemingly feminine profession in her adult life as a way to challenge the patriarchal model of gender relations. After a long trajectory of rewarding and difficult experiences during and following the Spanish Civil War, Sira returns to Madrid as a new and reinvented woman. It is at this point that the audience is presented with Arish Agoriuq, a Moroccan spy doubling as a high fashion foreign designer working for Nazi sympathizers. The program begins with a flash-forward that sets the narrative in Tétouan in 1936 in the first few minutes of the first episode. Afterward, the camera cuts quickly to a flashback of Sira learning to thread a needle as a young girl with her mother. The series does not focus on historical events, however. Instead, it centers on the protagonist's endeavors set against a very real historical background. The plotline focuses on how Sira moves through each phase of her life, or, in other words, how she crosses frontiers, the most prominent being the shift that occurs during her move from Tétouan to Madrid as an extravagant Moroccan designer. This is the point at which she begins her career not only as a designer, putting into practice all that she had learned as a young girl, but as an international spy, something she never expected to become. It is this position as a spy that allows Sira to transform into the person that she becomes in the second half of the series and that can best be viewed through the lens of Genz's "postfeminist supergirl."

According to Genz, this concept can be defined as an identity that allows a female character to be seen as a "modern-day action heroine [who] does not adhere to the stereotypical 'men act and women appear' polarization but . . . problematizes the critical framework that constructs the notions of passive femininity and active masculinity in terms of diametrical opposition and mutual exclusivity."[11] Among all of the different interpretations of postfeminist individualities, this is an important distinction to make because it allows us to understand this televisual genre. Though many feminists suggest that this brand of postfeminism is detrimental to feminism as a whole, I argue that Genz's concept simply offers another type of strong female personality.[12] For her, these women display an "inherent contradiction" on screen where "the postfeminist Supergirl reshapes and transforms the distinctions between masculinity and femininity, individualism and collectivity, conformity and resistance. The Supergirl displays a feminine body along with a feminist consciousness and a masculine assertiveness and power."[13] The moment in which Sira transforms into Arish and sets foot onto Spanish soil as a Moroccan citizen is truly the point at which the audience is able to see how this humble seamstress begins to embody the "postfeminist supergirl." As Genz argues, all too frequently, female action heroines are portrayed as either too masculine—those women that are able to "get the job done"—or too feminine. Genz's "postfeminist supergirl" subverts this norm and presents an identity that celebrates her femininity and "does not assume a masculine identity in her active/heroic role but she remains garbed in the signifiers of stereotypical feminine attractiveness."[14] Sira/Arish not only demonstrates these qualities but embodies them to the fullest by utilizing a traditionally feminine occupation to carry out her tasks as a superspy. With this she "refuses to be contained within these simplistic and totalizing classifications as she sabotages and collapses the barrier between them, moving *across* binaries in order to establish and impure an ambiguous 'in-betweenness'."[15] This notion is particularly interesting because Sira demonstrates that she not only lives in a state of "in-between" gender roles, but she also does so culturally, as she is able to travel across borders and morph into the different identities that correspond to each location.

When the audience meets Sira for the first time, her work as a seamstress seems to reinforce the patriarchal vision of a woman's role in the art of dressmaking and clothes design. As Cheryl Buckley points out in her analysis of the gendered nature of design, "dressmaking . . . has been seen as a 'natural' area for women to work in. It is viewed as an obvious vehicle for their femininity, their desire to decorate, and their obsession with appearances."[16] Unlike Dueñas's bestseller, the miniseries begins with a flash-forward that tells the spectator that though at first Sira may seem to be nothing more than another submissive Spanish woman living in the first half of the twentieth

century, the many obstacles that await her throughout the trajectory that will
be displayed to the audience on-screen will subvert that traditional image.
The opening scene of this first episode is a flash-forward of Sira getting ready
to make an illegal transaction in Tétouan. The series begins with the following monologue:

> My name is Sira Quiroga, and I am a seamstress. I never imaged that my destiny
> would be to put my life in jeopardy, crossing a city in a foreign country covered
> with guns strapped to my body. But now, I know that destiny is the sum of all
> of the decisions we make in life. Even the ones that seem insignificant in the
> moment. In my case, though it may seem far away, it all started with something
> as small as learning how to thread a needle.[17]

Though the series does not expose this detail right away, the money both
women make in this transaction will later be used to help Sira establish her
business as a designer in Tétouan. This first step that she makes into adult-
hood on her own (with the help of Candelaria) will later lead her to her career
in haute couture design in Madrid, doubling as a superspy. Buckley points
out that dressmaking is presented within the patriarchy as a female trade,
whereas "fashion design . . . has been appropriated by male designers who
have assumed the persona of genius—Christian Dior, Yves Saint Laurent,
and, more recently, Karl Lagerfield."[18] Thus, the illicit action of selling illegal
arms brings Sira greater freedom than she could have imagined.

This moment is incredibly important in the protagonist's life because it is
the first decision she makes as an independent woman and she does not base
her decision on a man or her romantic feelings. Though inevitably the series
does play on the audience's emotions and includes several love stories, the
relationship in which Sira engages after this point is of her own volition. It
is the kind of love story that the contemporary female viewer can connect
with, thus tying together the past and the present through this representation
of the "postfeminist supergirl." Different as these characters might seem, Sira
shares quite a few characteristics with Buffy the Vampire Slayer, a character
Genz uses as a basis for her concept. In order to better understand how Sira/
Arish's character embodies the "postfeminist supergirl," I would like to mention briefly the example she cites in her text. Genz explains in her chapter
"Fighting It: The Supergirl" that "in her slaying function, Buffy is supervised
by the Watchers' Council, a hierarchical and patriarchal command structure
that regards the Slayer as 'the instrument by which we fight'."[19] She further
elucidates that, instead of conforming to the patriarchal rules enforced by the
Watchers' Council for what seems like centuries, "she [Buffy] refuses to be
molded into the Council's image of the perfect Slayer as a regimental soldier
and she decides to disregard their orders and 'do things my way'."[20]

In the concluding episode of *El tiempo entre costuras*, a similar narrative arc is explored. Sira confronts her supervisor, the British agent, Alan Hillgarth. Early in Sira's career as a designer/superspy, Hillgarth gives her explicit rules to follow, which prohibit her from maintaining contact with her best friend, Rosalinda Fox, her lover, Marcus Logan, and her father, all of whom are British sympathizers. Though she does her best to abide by these rules, knowing that they are likely in place to keep her and the rest of the British Intelligence safe, in the final episode, Sira brings the men in her life—her father, Marcus, and Hillgarth—together. During this confrontation, Sira demonstrates that she can assert her will. This conversation is a crucial component in the comparison of Sira to the "postfeminist supergirl" because this is the confrontation that truly transforms her into such a character. She gives her word as a seamstress before that of a spy, placing a greater importance on her female characteristics over the more traditionally "male" characteristics that she embodies as well.

Laura Lee Kemp elaborates on the use of this very traditionally feminine career and identity as a subversive feminist role that fights against patriarchal structures. Kemp views Sira's role as a seamstress as a masquerade, citing a very important moment in the series in which she seemingly admits having been performing all along. Sira explains to the assistants in her sewing workshop that "'in this life it doesn't matter who one is, but rather who they seem to be.'"[21] Sira's admittance of this demonstrates her active role in creating a space for herself in the patriarchal society that surrounds her. She knows that it is unrealistic to try and create a new identity and society other than the one in which she lives, but that does not stop her from utilizing the resources she does have to subvert the norms that have been laid out for her.[22] Though Walter Mignolo's theory on "border thinking" relates more to global dichotomies, such as Western versus non-Western, Genz's theory of the "postfeminist supergirl" allows us to think dichotomously in regards to gender. The identity Genz proposes is female; however, in accordance to patriarchal order, her actions do not align with either gender, but rather oscillate between both societal roles. That said, in order to understand her, we must use "border thinking," we must think transnationally, and we must look through a postfeminist lens.

Another example where the audience can perceive Sira's transformation into the "postfeminist supergirl" turned superspy is the period of time in which she is starting her business in Tétouan. Though at first, she struggles to feel authoritative in this role, this formative moment in her life is where the audience can perceive her growth as a woman. This transitional instant exemplifies that she "seeks to come to negotiate with her inherent paradoxes" and thus "she seeks to come to terms with her own heterogeneity."[23] Moreover, it is through her female friendships with other characters such as

Candelaria and Rosalinda, the real-life British mistress of the also real Juan Luis Beigbeder, that she gains the confidence needed to begin breaking the rules in order to serve the greater good. These examples of female solidarity further exemplify her worthiness as a "postfeminist supergirl" because she does not feel the need to be alone in the world and overcompensate for her womanliness. In fact, she embraces it through these friendships which demonstrate that even though hegemonic discourse argues that women are more powerful and worth more when they attach themselves to a man, female friendships can and should effect social transformations.[24]

These friendships, particularly the one that develops between Rosalinda and Sira, are what gives the protagonist the courage to be more than the simple seamstress she grew up thinking she would always be. This friendship does not only exist as a support system, but it also serves as a connection through which both women will be able to negotiate in their own ways. Sira supports her friend's relationship and even helps her when her abusive husband returns threatening to take her and their son away from all that she loves in Morocco, including her lover Beigbeder. Through Rosalinda's treatment by her husband, the miniseries exemplifies the way in which many women during the first half of the twentieth century were to be seen and not heard. Mary Nash affirms that "the basis of the gender system is substantiated by the polarization of the differences between women and men, and the projection of men as the norm and women as subordinates."[25] *El tiempo* is a Spanish series yet the cast of characters it features is decidedly multinational. Rosalinda is British, yet at the time of her husband's brief return to her and her son's lives, she is living in Morocco and maintaining an amorous relationship with a Spanish diplomat.

This multicultural cast and plotline can be viewed through Homi Bhabha's notion of "in-between." Bhabha explains that "in the midst of the multicultural wars we are surprisingly closer to an insight from T.S. Eliot's *Notes Towards the Definitions of Culture*, where Eliot demonstrates a certain incommensurability, a necessary impossibility, in *thinking* culture."[26] Though he focuses more on cultural hybridity, Bhabha's notion of the "in-between" is an important concept when considering Genz's postfeminist identities, given that they are, as she claims, "inherently contradictory." It is this contradictory nature that allows them to function as feminist identities, given that they do not conform to any sort of norm. In a society that tends to categorize whenever possible, Bhabha's concept of the in-between allows these characters to be analyzed differently, as something more than just another "girlie" televisual figure.

As Genz argues, popular culture leans away from action heroine identities that allow for more indistinct interpretation of what it means to be a woman. The postfeminist supergirl has infiltrated Spanish television and even gone back in time. In *El tiempo entre costuras*, Sira utilizes her femininity in order to carry out her role as a spy, which was considered a traditionally masculine role during the years presented in the series. As a 'postfeminist supergirl' she exhibits both masculine and feminine characteristics; however, throughout the series her feminine qualities take center stage and her femininity is simultaneously glorified.

Thinking transnationally implies thinking beyond borders. This perspective forces a different perception for concepts such as feminism, bringing into the picture Genz's idea of the "postfeminist supergirl." In *El tiempo entre costuras*, Sira's character demonstrates that this type of identity fits perfectly into the contemporary globalized society due to its hybrid nature. Because of how well she embodies this identity, Sira is more capable of moving across borders, both nationally, culturally, and in-between those that define both masculine and feminine genders. Some would say that she defies the odds even more so by having defeated the patriarchy in her own way while being viewed as a Moroccan woman who is perceived as inferior. As I have demonstrated, this oscillation between all of her different worlds exemplifies Bhabha's concept of the "in-between" and proves that such identities are not at a disadvantage but rather an enormous advantage, given the fluidity of their nature. This sort of representation is inspiring to the spectator because of the possibilities that Sira's identity provides. However, in reality as opposed to the screen, one must possess enormous privilege to be able to practice this kind of fluidity. The action heroine that we see in the *El tiempo entre costuras* does, in fact, take from all of her different "homes" to create a new identity, which makes her stronger. Rather than being viewed as a disadvantage, her overtly feminine qualities in *El tiempo entre costuras* allow Sira Quiroga/Arish Agoriuq to triumph. Furthermore, she proves that a woman can save the day with a nontraditional set of weapons, which in her case consists of a sewing machine, beautiful fabrics, sewing scissors, threads, pins, and needles. After all, as Sira Quiroga states in the opening monologue to the series, it all began for her with what seemed to be a simple lesson on how to thread a needle but actually ended up transforming into a journey crossing borders and challenging identities.

NOTES

1. Christina Scharff and Rosalind Gill, *New Femininities: Postfeminism, Neoliberalism, and Subjectivity* (New York: Palgrave Macmillan, 2011), 9. Note that the author used italics in their original text as a means of emphasis.

2. Walter Mignolo, *Local Histories/Global Designs: Coloniality, Subaltern Knowledges, and Border Thinking* (Princeton: Princeton UP, 2000), 85. Note that the author used italics in their original text as a means of emphasis.

3. T. S. Eliot, *Notes Towards the Definition of Culture* (New York: Harcourt, Brace & Co, 1943), 64.

4. Susan Faludi, *Backlash, The Undeclared War Against American Women* (New York: Three Rivers P, 1991), 86.

5. Benjamin A. Brabon and Stéphanie Genz, *Postfeminism: Cultural Texts and Theories* (Edinburgh: Edinburgh UP, 2018), 24.

6. Brabon and Genz, *Postfeminism: Cultural Texts and Theories*, 24.

7. Stéphanie Genz, *Postfemininities in Popular Culture* (New York: Palgrave Macmillan, 2009), 32.

8. Liz Bondi, "Gender and Geography: Crossing Boundaries," *Progress in Human Geography* 17, no. 2 (1993): 241.

9. Bondi, "Gender and Geography," 241.

10. Ulrich Beck, *Risk Society: Towards a New Modernity* (London: SAGE, 1991), 100.

11. Genz, *Postfemininities in Popular Culture*, 152.

12. Genz cites several examples in her text regarding the fact that postfeminism has received a substantial amount of backlash. Tania Modleski in particular writes about "texts that, in proclaiming or assuming the advent of postfeminism, are actually engaged in negating the critiques and undermining the goals of feminism" (3).

13. Genz, *Postfemininities in Popular Culture*, 155.

14. Genz, *Postfemininities in Popular Culture*, 158.

15. Genz, *Postfemininities in Popular Culture*, 155.

16. Cheryl Buckley, "Made in Patriarchy: Toward a Feminist Analysis of Women and Design," *Design Issues* 3, no. 2 (1986): 5.

17. Note that this Spanish to English translation is my own. Here is the original quote in Spanish: "Me llamo Sira Quiroga, y soy costurera. Nunca imaginé que mi destino sería jugarme la vida cruzando una cuidad de un país extranjero con un traje de pistolas sobre mi piel. Pero ahora sé que el destino es suma de todas las decisiones que tomamos en nuestra vida. Incluso las que en su momento parecen insignificantes. En mi caso, por lejano que me parezca ahora, todo empezó con algo tan pequeño como aprender a enhebrar una aguja."

18. Buckley, "Made in Patriarchy," 5.

19. Genz, *Postfemininities in Popular Culture*, 161.

20. Genz, *Postfemininities in Popular Culture*, 161.

21. Note that this Spanish to English translation is my own.

22. In this context, I would like to mention Josefina Ludmer's article "Tretas del débil." The article elaborates on Sor Juana Inés de la Cruz's use of her feminine qualities as tools with which she was able to subvert the rules that bound her as a woman and a nun and ultimately achieve her goal of being able to write. I find this study fascinating because it serves as a real-life model of how, for centuries, women have been able to find a way to subvert patriarchal order by utilizing the parameters laid out for them. Ludmer's article is inspiring and demonstrates that such notions have existed and will continue to exist in our world and that we must continue to study them.

23. Genz, *Postfemininities in Popular Culture*, 159.

24. bell hooks, "Sisterhood: Political Solidarity between Women," *Feminist Review* 23 (1986): 127.

25. Mary Nash, "Experiencia y aprendizaje: la formación histórica de los feminismos en España," *Historia social* 20 (1994): 152. Note that this Spanish to English translation is my own. Here is the original quote in Spanish: "La base del sistema de género se fundamenta en la polarización de las diferencias entre mujeres y hombres, y la proyección del hombre como norma y de las mujeres como subordinadas."

26. Homi K. Bhabha, "Culture's In-Between," in *Questions of Cultural Identity*, ed. Stuart Hall and Paul du Gay (London: SAGE, 2011), 53.

BIBLIOGRAPHY

Anderson, Benedict. *Imagined Communities: Reflections on the Origin and Spread of Nationalism.* New York: Verso Books, 2006.

Beck, Ulrich. *Risk Society: Towards a New Modernity.* London. SAGE, 1991.

Bhabha, Homi K. "Culture's In-Between." In Questions of Cultural Identity, edited by Stuart Hall and Paul du Gay, 53–60. London: SAGE, 2011. doi: 10.4135/9781446221907.n4.

Bondi, Liz. "Gender and Geography: Crossing Boundaries." *Progress in Human Geography* 17, no. 2 (1993): 241–46.

Buckley, Cheryl. "Made in Patriarchy: Toward a Feminist Analysis of Women and Design." *Design Issues* 3, no. 2 (1986): 3–14.

Dueñas, María. *El tiempo entre costuras.* Madrid: Planeta, 2009.

El tiempo entre costuras. "Amor y otras verdades." 1.01. Directed by Iñaki Mercero. Written by María Dueñas (novel) and Susana López Rubio (screenplay). Antena 3, October 21, 2013.

El tiempo entre costuras. "Episode #1.17." 1.17. Directed by Norberto López Amado and Iñaki Mercero. Written by Susana López Rubio (screenplay), Alberto Grondona (screenplay) and María Dueñas (novel). Antena 3, March 4, 2014.

Eliot, T. S. *Notes Towards the Definition of Culture.* New York: Harcourt, Brace & Co, 1943.

Faludi, Susan. *Backlash, The Undeclared War Against American Women.* New York: Three Rivers P, 1991.

Genz, Stéphanie, and Benjamin A. Brabon. *Postfeminism: Cultural texts and theories.* Edinburgh: Edinburgh UP, 2018.

Genz, Stéphanie. *Postfemininities in Popular Culture.* New York: Palgrave Macmillan, 2009.

Gill, Rosalind, and Christina Scharff. *New Femininities: Postfeminism, Neoliberalism, and Subjectivity.* New York: Palgrave Macmillan, 2011.

hooks, bell. "Sisterhood: Political Solidarity between Women." *Feminist Review* 23 (1986): 125–38.

Kemp, Laura Lee. "The Re-construal of 'La Costurera': A Feminist Re-interpretation of the Role of the Seamstress in *El tiempo entre costuras / The Time Between the Seams* (2013)." *Studies in Spanish & Latin American Cinemas* 13, no. 2 (2016): 159–75.

Ludmer, Josefina. "Las tretas del débil." *Representaciones, emergencias y resistencias de la crítica cultural: Mujeres intelectuales en América Latina y el Caribe,* edited by Nelly Prigorian and Carmen Díaz Orozco, 245–51. Buenos Aires: CLACSO, 2017.

Mignolo, Walter. *Local Histories/Global Designs: Coloniality, Subaltern Knowledges, and Border Thinking*. Princeton: Princeton UP, 2000.

Nash, Mary. "Experiencia y aprendizaje: la formación histórica de los feminismos en España." *Historia social* 20 (1994): 151–72.

Chapter 5

Lucrecia Martel's Salta Trilogy

A (Trans)National Bildungsroman of Female Sexuality

Java Singh

Lucrecia Martel is part of the *Nuevo Cine Argentino*[1] (*NCA*) that includes filmmakers like Anahí Berneri, Pablo Trapero, and Lisandro Alonso. As with any grouping that brings together diverse poetics and rhetoric, the practitioners of *NCA* offer "heterogenous cinematic designs," sharing "a distancing from the established aesthetics of the films of renowned Argentine cineastes of the previous decade and also with [. . .] more commercial cinema."[2] Three key elements contribute to the 'newness' of the *NCA*. First, its filmmakers adopt a novel perspective in their criticism of the violence perpetrated by the state during the military dictatorship's "Dirty War" in Argentina (1976–1983). They tend "to avoid the allegorical narratives, political posturing, and denouncement of injustice that had marked the films of their predecessors" and equally refuse "to buy into the 'feel good'[3] memory politics of Kirchnerism."[4] Secondly, as Geoffrey Kantaris has pointed out, *NCA* is "a cultural reaction to the widespread imposition of neoliberal 'structural adjustment' policies with their attendant immiseration—a kind of *de facto* financial dictatorship."[5] Whereas the first two distinguishing aspects of *NCA* represent its ideological stance against authoritarian government and neoliberalism, the third is a rhetorical shift. The politics of *NCA* is articulated mainly through a grammar of staccato spatial contrapositions and nonverbal soundscapes, while conventional strategies involving character, plot, and dialogue are deprioritized.

This chapter examines how Lucrecia Martel's Salta trilogy, an epitome of *NCA*, succeeds in establishing accessible referential frameworks for transnational comprehension despite being anchored in recent Argentinian history and politics. The three films show stylistic and generic consistency

137

when visualized as parts of an anthology. The films' naturalist inflection and the collective female bildungsroman that Martel builds through them are vital to generating a transnationally accessible referential framework. Stylistically, the director links the women's confinement to their transnationally recognizable microenvironments: disconnected rural areas and inward-looking provincial towns that have been left to decay because they do not fit into the narrative of a dynamic globalization.[6] These zones project plurivocal images that criticize Argentina's authoritarian structures and its bourgeois neoliberalism while presenting the region of Salta as a microcosm of any unequal society. Martel's transnational reach is enabled by the innovative use of the generic elements of the bildungsroman. During the formative transition from girl to woman, varying modes and degrees of sexual expressions are portrayed that suggests a strong correlation between self-fulfillment and self-expression. Moreover, the indigenous working woman is counterposed to the bourgeois white woman to bring out the intersectionality of race, class, and feminism. This creates a recognizable transnational referentiality on two parameters: first, an intragender division of labor based on race, caste, provincial, or immigrant status is at the foundation of many hierarchized societies; secondly, the change in the degrees of freedom that a woman claims as she matures is also a common feature of any social structure wherein patriarchal attitudes are dominant. Thus, the chapter addresses an epistemological concern: whether cultural representations of globally relevant issues can be approached through techniques and tactics that do not obliterate the local, do not seek recourse to universalizing tropes, and do not homogenize regional specificities into the global monolith.

The Salta trilogy draws out the global and the national from the local. Like other *NCA* films, Martel's cinema recalls the national trauma caused by the years of oppression during the "Dirty War," but her cultural imaginary is not fueled by a condemnation of the military, paramilitary forces, and extrajudicial militia. She brings into focus the role of the bystanders who did not participate in the violence but, in a way, allowed its propagation by their silence or betrayals. The bystanders' (di)stance ensured not only their own survival but also that of the oppressive regime. Martel emphasizes their complicity by foregrounding symbols of silent acceptance of injustices such as the complaisant homemaker Tali in *La ciénaga* (*LC*) and of betrayal for survival, as is the case with the young Josefina. The latter incriminates her best friend in *La niña santa* (*NS*). In an interview, Martel said that she is more shocked at the negation of recent history by those who were 'not' involved in the repressive apparatus than at the ruthlessness of the dictatorship during that time.[7] In her opinion, the motivations of a military junta that inflicted "cruelty, death and violence" are less inexplicable than the attitudes of those who did not perpetrate or witness the abuses, but willingly embrace the collective and selective social amnesia about the dictatorship years.[8]

A powerful scene from *La mujer sin cabeza* (*MSC*) showcases Martel's methods of recalling the human rights abuses of the "Dirty War." In the film, set in contemporary Argentina, some twenty-five years after the end of the military dictatorship, "a clinical dissection of the mechanisms through which the operations of 'disappearance' were conducted, (is) refracted through the events following a hit-and-run accident."[9] The accident happens when Vero, a sophisticated, 'upper-class' white woman, hits something on the road. She is not sure whether it is a boy or a dog. Without any firm evidence, she convinces herself that she has not killed a boy, and only hit a dog. A few days later, when she hears reports that a boy's dead body was recovered from the location of the accident, she dismisses it as mere coincidence. Nobody knows the facts of the boy's death, and nobody wants to find out because he came from a poor indigenous family. The boy is a hybridized symbol of the immiserated sections of Argentinian society—the marginalized indigenous population and the 'disappeared' persons during the military dictatorship. Martel uses subtle clues to show the perdurance of "the terrible national id that [underlay] the repressive national superego" in the 1970s military rule and the present-day neoliberal regime in Argentina.[10] The song "Soleil, Soleil" plays in the background on Vero's car stereo just before the accident happens. The song used to be popular among "people who were not participating politically—who ignored the dictatorship."[11]

Like the disappearances during the dictatorship, the boy's 'disappearance' does not cause any inconvenience to the bourgeois section of society. A few phone calls from Vero's family to the police and the hospital staff are all that is needed to destroy any records that might suggest her involvement in the incident. Vero is linked inconclusively to the death of the boy, and none of the other family members is guilty of any violence. Their distance from the actual crime, their race, and their social class create a contrapuntal symbolism to the dead boy. Vero and her family represent the bystanders who believed themselves to be extraneous to the violence of dictatorship, as well as the white bourgeois class who are indifferent to the visible impoverishment and precarity of people in their close proximity. Martel explains in an interview that "what was important or relevant wasn't finding out whether she actually killed somebody but her reaction to what happened."[12] By leaving the details of the boy's death vague, Martel shows the perdurance of a collective unwillingness to acknowledge the fact of visible violence—political, social, and economic, in the society.

Apart from providing an oblique musical reference to the dictatorship, the materiality of the collision metonymizes economic disparity: a car runs over the poor, indigenous boy who comes in the way on a road between a city and a shantytown. The road that is meant to connect the two locations, in fact, separates them, and the subaltern on the road is invisible to the class that has access to mobility. Through the song and the imagery, Martel establishes an enduring nonverbal, acoustic, and spatial continuity between the bystanders to the violence of the military dictatorship in the past and the economic dictatorship in the present day. As Rok Spruk points out, "Argentina has never finished the transition to open democracy under the rule of law. Even though Argentina formally transitioned to democracy in 1983, institutional breakdowns [. . .] remain deeply embedded in the political culture."[13] The privileged economic status of the traditional elite classes continued undisturbed across the regime change.

Martel's decentered spatial strategy brings attention to the plight of the people who inhabit the margins of her country. Martel chooses 'other spaces,' far from the metropolitan center, as settings for her films. Her films are counted among those, "which have utilized the rural landscape to mark questions of social marginality."[14] Martel self-identifies as a regionalist. She was surprised when a director from "a very different culture" wrote her to convey his admiration for *MSC*, which the director declares as her "most Argentinian" film:

> I think that it is my most Argentinian film, and I would even say the most *salt-eña*, or in any event, Northern. I think that it is amazing that there are foreign critics who find a lot of value in it. There was even a director from a very different culture from ours who, moved by the film, wrote to me after Cannes; [. . .] I am surprised [by this] because I believe that one cannot understand it without certain codes.[15]

In Martel's opinion, certain regional codes are necessary to understand the film. She explains that for the audience in northern Argentina, the film has several pertinent local references, such as the mention of Monsignor Pérez—a bishop from Salta who had served during the military dictatorship—that would be lost on viewers elsewhere. While her hesitation about whether the film can have its full impact without a grasp of the local references is a relevant concern, the political-as-personal undertone of her films ensures cross-cultural and transnational validity.

Elizabeth Ezra and Terry Rowden identify three prerequisites for the emergence of transnational cinema. The first is the prevalence of a cinematic literacy that goes beyond the appreciative consumption of national or regional narratives that audiences can identify as their own; the second, an accessibility to referential frameworks devoid of national and cultural peculiarities, and third, an enhanced permeability of national borders aided by technology.[16] When one seeks to examine the Salta trilogy against the second prerequisite of the absence of national and cultural peculiarities, the portrayal of race relations comes to the forefront. The racial imbalance undergirds all three films in the trilogy. Indigenous children are shown ambling aimlessly near a dangerous swamp and working odd jobs in exchange for food and clothes. Indigenous women are servants in the bourgeois households, and they are either berated constantly and accepted grudgingly, or completely ignored. In Argentina, the racial discrimination carries the centuries-old weight of colonial exploitation. However, in the films, the regional specificity of race-based class formations does not turn into a "cultural peculiarity," it can be recognized as a feature of other cultures as well. For example, in India, though racial discrimination is not a vestige of its colonial history, it is relatable through caste-based discriminations.[17]

A solipsistic global middle class[18] that is "deeply integrated into global capitalism," that plays a "key role in the new liberalized economies and benefit(s) from the neoliberal transitions of the economies," is a concomitant of globalization.[19] Though the characters in the Salta trilogy are drawn from provincial middle classes, they are nevertheless secondary beneficiaries of neoliberal economics. They are socially privileged by being white in a formerly colonized society and financially privileged due to their links, though tenuous, to the neoliberal economy through specialized large-scale agricultural production in *LC* and well-paid urban professions in *NS* and *MSC*. On account of its severe art movie aesthetics, the usage of the Gothic as a transnational story space, and the ability to make transnational connections through local imagery and the referential frameworks highlighted in this chapter, Martel's cinema transgresses national frontiers.[20] The regionally coded referential frameworks of race-based class formations and privileged middle classes allow for a coherent transnational crossover.

The referential framework within which this chapter builds its argument is the containment of female sexuality in a heteronormative familial context. This line of analysis, while highlighting the transnational reach of the gender framework, does not aim to convey "that the national simply becomes displaced or negated [. . .] in fact the national continues to exert the force of its presence even within transnational film-making practices."[21] Martel's decidedly local flavor is not packaged as commodified merchandise that seeks to "administer comfort and illusion."[22] Merchandised cinema does not necessarily rely on a glittery star cast or on overstated theatrics to commodify the ideas it seeks to convey. Cineastes can also commodify those ideas by their reification in easily relatable tropes such as selfless motherhood and innocent childhood. Merchandise strives for aesthetic perfection at the cost of complexity, and its facile imagery aligns itself with the "homogenizing imaginaries of transnational capital."[23] Cinema as merchandise cannot free itself from endorsing established conventions such as designating the home as a place of domestication and motherhood as a self-subsuming identity.[24] Martel subverts the conventional notions of both home and motherhood. In *LC* and *NS*, the home is also place of business. Helena runs the hotel where she also lives, and Mecha manages the pepper production on the ranch that is also her home. In *MSC*, the home is a site of madness for both Vero and the senile Tía Lala. Vero's concussion from the accident causes unexpected emotional outbursts, and her bedridden aunt muddles the past and the present.

Moreover, Martel's films do not present a universalizing idea of motherhood. The mothers in the trilogy are differentiated combinations of the three archetypes identified by Gloria Anzaldúa: "Guadalupe, the virgin mother who has not abandoned us, la Chingada (Malinché), the raped mother whom we have abandoned, and la Llorona, the mother who seeks her lost children and is the combination of the other two."[25] Helena, Vero, and Mecha, as overtly sexual women, may be seen as abandoned mothers—the *chingadas* whose husbands and grown-up sons and daughters are distant from them. They are also the *lloronas* because they seek emotional connections with children. Helena is shown sharing an ice cream with a young child in the hotel kitchen, Vero volunteers at a dental camp in a school, and Mecha is troubled by the delay in her youngest child's surgery. Mirta, the only indigenous mother in the trilogy, is a dry, caustic martinet who is openly hostile to her daughter. The daughter Miriam responds to her mother's harsh criticism by threatening to poison Mirta. There is nothing of the *llorona* in Mirta; she is entirely the abandoned *chingada*. Tali represents the conventionally lauded motherhood of Guadalupe. Her pure and chaste motherhood may be equated with the nineteenth-century, Sarmientian *civilización*, and in contrast, the sexualized mother with the antipodal *barbarie*. The *chingada* is barbaric because she destroys the settled idea of a 'civilized,' unselfish, and asexual motherhood. Martel's films bring the *chingada-madre* antinomy to the twenty-first century to dismantle it entirely. In the process, she ruptures the "domestication of perception." Commenting on her aim to "distort" perception, Martel says that,

> the domestication of perception is the path to political conservatism. On the other hand, any distortion of perception–this is my feeble hope–is what generates a disruption in the setting, and this perhaps enables, though I am not saying always, another way of conceiving reality.[26]

Conflating the civilized-mother with the barbaric-*chingada* is as necessary for dislodging a settled position for the woman in society as for interrogating conservative political attitudes. Martel's mothers are far removed from the majoritarian notions of motherhood as a selfless vocation that leads to salvation. As portrayed in the trilogy, motherhood, in fact, lessens the self.

The rejection of majoritarian constructs is a key element of the trilogy's transnationality. When a narrative operates with a majoritarian script, the local is merely a synecdoche for the global. In it, selfless love for the child would define and save the mother from loneliness, depression, and their own sexuality. In contrast, the local in transnational cinema is not a synecdoche for the global, and it has to be read allegorically. For example, a mother engulfed in her child's existence could be a representation of exclusion, isolation, self-deception, and even decadence. Martel enunciates a clearly minoritarian stance on motherhood in *NS*. In the film, a group of girls deliberate upon the topic of the divine calling. Some of the questions they raise are: How will they recognize their role in God's plan? How will they know what their vocation is? Whether the divine plan is a plan for their salvation? In this context, one of the girls suggests that a mother who saves her child by sacrificing her own life is responding to her vocation. The youngest girl in the group contradicts her—the least tutored in gender roles—who declares, "Pero madre no es una vocación." Martel, by exploring as many as seven maternal relationships in the trilogy, makes it clear that motherhood is not a divine vocation, it is a stage in life that women should be free to outgrow mentally just as they do biologically with the onset of menopause.

Martel's depiction of family relationships, especially of the woman as mother, has a naturalist register—it is imposed upon her as a biological imperative, often obliterating all aspects of her individuality. Martel portrays the mothers' sexual frustrations as channeled into troubled relationships with their daughters on the one hand, and an incestuous desire for their son, brother, cousin, or father, on the other. The evocation of the women's shrunken ambits through a realist, microscopic examination of their microenvironment suggests a naturalist register that is antithetically coded in both regional specificity and transnational expansiveness. Locating the films in the "long tail" of nineteenth-century naturalism, wherein they "re-semanticize"[27] it for the twenty-first century, Spicer-Escalante argues that the "transnationality of Hispanic naturalism" is indisputable.[28] The Salta trilogy meets the naturalist requirement of high fidelity to reality by visualizing its settings microscopically. The camera moves slowly, often coming to rest in close-ups of showers and sinks in bathrooms, a noisy table fan failing to dispel the sultry February heat. It pauses upon dimly lit bedroom corners that forebode illicit sexuality, tin-roofed shanty dwellings that emblematize state negligence, and on crowded streets that offer impunity to sexual aggressors. Though these scenes are distinctly representative of a provincial Salta, contrasting it with the fast-paced metropolis of Buenos Aires, their imagery could well belong to provincial areas in distant countries. The link between an environment market by hopelessness, declining economic prospects, inability to participate in the hypermobility of globalized commerce and an inward, incestual withdrawal is discernible transnationally.

Martel's documental approach heightens the naturalist tone and allows an almost unmediated interaction between the viewer and the film. Even a viewer who is distant from the film's setting is intimately drawn into the reality portrayed on the screen. The absence of conspicuous costumes, quirky characters, and fortuitous coincidences bridges the distance between the screen-text and the viewer. Martel complies with the obligation of authenticity in a documentary by depriviliging the use of artifice. She deliberately avoids symmetrically composed frames, and there is an untidiness in her camerawork that suits the depiction of everyday clutter in her characters' lives. The inclusion of unusual elements in *LC* like naming the ranch *La Mandragora* after the mandrake root, a plant with hallucinogenic and aphrodisiac properties, and the theremin in *NS*, a musical instrument that is played without touching does not dilute documental verisimilitude because the dramatic defamiliarization is consistent with the film's particular inflexion: the aphrodisiac plant echoes Mecha's unsatiated desire, and the played-but-not-touched theremin reflects Amelia's ambiguity about her first sexual experience. Martel's sporadic insertion of curiosities uses the "reality of drama" to invoke "the drama of reality."[29] True to naturalist conventions, the characters in Martel's trilogy are examples of the "*homo lubricus* confined in a community subdued by mistaken norms, by a sexual and social morality disavowed by naturalists."[30] However, trapped in a community subjugated to moral imperatives, the women in the trilogy do not resign themselves to their condition. They constantly chafe at the leash that ties them to conformity.

As if trying to address not only the misrepresentation of women in cinema but also their underrepresentation, Martel offers an extensive array of female characters. Across the entire trilogy, seventeen characters merit comment in a discussion of the portrayal of female sexuality. The women in the trilogy can be subdivided into six groups based on the acknowledgment, expression, and performance of their sexuality. The groups trace the advancement of female sexuality as the woman progresses from early puberty to maturity. Due to the chronological parity within the groups, they are termed 'ages.'

The age of decadence is represented by the three mature women and the potential for it by three young ones. The aging beauties—Mecha, Vero, and Helena—are portrayed by actresses who are considered visibly attractive. The legendary Graciela Borges plays Mecha. A glamorous Mercedes Morán portrays Helena. Morán's transformation from the perennially stressed, self-effacing housewife, Tali, in *LC* to the languid seductress in *NS* is uncanny, to say the least—it is also a signal that to this filmmaker, sexuality is crucial to vitality. Maria Onetto plays Vero. Though a highly respected theatre actress, Onetto was not well known in the cinema world when Martel decided to cast her as the lead in the film. Martel chose her because the character's heightened visibility as a tall blonde woman in Salta makes Vero's project of staying hidden abortive from the very outset. Explaining her choice, Martel says:

> María has [. . .] an obvious body, which was very necessary for the film. A tall, white, obvious body of a woman in a place where she is trying to remove her trace in the perpetration of something [criminal]. I liked the idea that the person who is trying to find the perfect cover is someone who cannot be hidden, because, in Salta, such a tall blonde is not at all common.[31]

Martel "de-hierarchizes the senses, privileging the non-visual over the ocular-centric regimes in which Helena (Mercedes Morán)—a kind of parody of the femme fatale, of feminine to-be-looked-at-ness—is enmeshed."[32] Not only Helena but Mecha and Vero also parodize the femme fatale—their visible bodies are ideal tools for seduction. Yet, their seductive allure remains invisible to their husbands; it evokes reciprocity only in incestuous relationships. Relying on Judith Bulter's construct, Deborah Martin affirms that these parodic performances cover a "range of disobedience" that the interpellating law produces.[33] The interpellating law that these women disobey is that they must wear the veil of invisibility as wives and mothers. Instead of complying with the expectation, the femme fatales stay within family structures in, "a parodic inhabiting of conformity" that produces a "slippage between the discursive command and the effects."[34]

If incestual attraction may be considered a measure of decadence, then there is an incremental enhancement of decadence as the narrative of the anthology moves from the country estate in *LC* to a small-town hotel in *NS* and then, to the city in *MSC*. In the country estate, Mecha's grown-up son curls up intimately with her like an infant, in the home-hotel, Helena sleeps in the same bed as her brother. In the city, Vero, protected by urban anonymity, acts upon her incestuous attraction by conducting an affair with her brother-in-law. The femme fatales expose their decadent environment by choosing incest over complete desexualization. The level of dissimulation increases as the narratives move from *barbarie* of the countryside to the *civilización* of the city, and so does the potency of decadence. Explaining why she sees a positive valence in decadence, Martel says that,

> it's hard to think of characters being propelled by action or having a direction. What we are speaking of is decadence, in the Argentine sense of it. I think of decadence as a positive value, especially if one thinks of the previous order as confining and exclusionary. The sooner the demise of the values that organize the world, the better. That's what we're living through in Argentina. It's like the triumph of decadence and therefore, an interesting period.[35]

The decadent relationships constitute strategies of rebellion. Martel meant for these women to feel alive through their sexuality: "La película tiene una carga sexual, una sensualidad un poco desbordada, hasta incestuosa en algunos casos, que le da el único aspecto feliz que siento que tiene la película, porque veo que hay algo vivo."[36] Whereas in nineteenth-century Latin American *naturalismo* lovers were torn apart to avoid the consummation of the incestuous relationship, in the trilogy, incest makes for a happy togetherness in the age of decadence.

On the other hand, Inés, the young Josefina, and the young Vero are likely to slip into an 'unhappy' decadence because they refuse to recognize the lack in their lives. Inés is the voice coach in *NS*. She recasts the voice modulation class as a religious group where the girls sing hymns, discuss the path to salvation, and learn how to look out for 'the sign' from God. Inés's quest for refuge in Scripture is hypocritical because she is using the garb of religiosity to hide her sexual adventures. The young Josefina abets the pretense of her own sham celibate purity. When Josefina's mother walks in on Josefina and her boyfriend while they are having sex, she distracts her mother with salacious gossip about her friend to avoid being censured for promiscuity. In the face of her insincere behavior, her subsequent promise to Amalia that she will always take care of her seems duplicitous. The third girl trapped in 'unhappy' decadence is the young Vero in *LC*. She is consumed by jealousy for José's partner Mercedes. In her incestuous attraction for her brother, Vero seems to be subconsciously imitating her mother. Her story of "La Rata Africana," the fictitious animal that eats up all the cats in a bloody feast, clearly points to José, who is the object of the sexual desires of three women. Given her mother's hysteria, she must sense that incestual attraction is self-destructive, yet she sustains it. Hypocrisy, deceit, and jealousy are the dominant emotions in the age of bitterness.

The next group, comprised of ostensibly stable-settled women, represents the age of stagnation. Tali from *LC* is the busy caregiver. She is seen cooking for her children, cheering up her ill friend, and trying to restore the balance with her calmness when mother and daughter get into an ugly fight. On repeated occasions, Tali is shown making plans for a journey to Bolivia to buy cheap school supplies for her children, but she does not end up traveling because her husband thwarts her plans. His insidious foiling of her travel plans is a clear indication of his desire to control her. He does not allow her to step out of the domestic space, even temporarily. This incident represents the end of Tali's diligently mounted domestic equilibrium. In its aftermath, she smokes in front of her young children, even though young Luci hates the smell and holds his breath to avoid it. Soon after, Luci will fall to his death from a ladder that his mother had put against the patio wall. Her son's death represents the final blow to Tali's stability.

The stable woman in *NS* is the unnamed frumpy, gullible mother who appears to be so excited by the molestation of Amalia, her daughter's best friend, that she does not notice that her own school-age daughter was having sex just before giving her news of the scandal. She turns her back to her daughter's boyfriend as he gets dressed hurriedly. Her gesture is symbolic of her unwillingness to face the truth. It is easier for her to focus on Amalia's molestation because it reaffirms her decision to keep her daughter safe from harm within the confines of her home. In her estimation, her domestic confinement saves her from predators like Dr. Jano. Josefina's mother is blind to the fact her daughter is sexually active and, therefore, by the mother's standards, unsafe, even inside her home. The mother has a perpetual need to seek justification for her 'domesticated perception.' In a conversation with her family, she talks about the "los hermanos Correa" as examples of the worst that can befall a person:

Mother: And I hope that you don't have to go through what happened to the Correa brothers, who kept at it until they destroyed their mother. And look where they are!
Boy: Where are they?
Mother (baffled by the question, after a pause): One is divorced.
Boy (sarcastically): And the other lives in Spain; he has a two-year scholarship.
Mother: There you have it! The other one, out of the country.[37]

In Josefina's mother's estimation, divorce and living abroad destroy the family unity that is the glue of middle-class respectability. Her despair at the Correa brothers' circumstances expresses her discomfort with transnational displacement. Her self-image as a sex-less, selfless, and undesiring woman proves to be false when a naked man falls into her balcony. Josefina's mother cannot stop staring at him in fascination. She has been sublimating her sexual deprivation into religious obsession and constant carping about her maid. She uses the racist term *china* to refer to her maid. Even though she finds the maid so dirty that she does not allow her to use a bathroom in the house, she cannot dismiss her. Like the maid, physical longing is dirty but indispensable. The stable mother in *NS* can sustain her stability only by obfuscating reality.

The older Josefina, the stable-stagnant woman in *MSC*, is the polar opposite of Tali. She is also a homemaker, but she is completely self-absorbed: she is unruffled by her daughter's chronic jaundice or her old aunt's madness. The cocoon-like safety of her bourgeois life gives her unshakeable certainties. Even though Candita, her daughter, frequently shuts herself in her room with Cuca, her biker friend, the mother refuses to accept her daughter's homosexuality. She disguises her objections to her daughter's gay friends as disapproval for their 'mannish' behavior: "machoneando con la moto." She expresses sympathy for a friend because he has a 'mannish' daughter she calls "machona de la hija." Candita's jaundiced frailty, delicate body structure, and soft-spoken demeanor make her definitively 'feminine' and, therefore, in her mother's opinion, immune to homosexuality. Josefina's claim to stability is built on a false premise. If she is forced to accept Candita's lesbianism, her state of equilibrium will be shaken.

Isabel, the indigenous maid in *LC*; Miriam, the indigenous cook who wants to be a masseuse, in *NS*; and Cuca, the lesbian biker from a poor barrio in *MSC* represent subaltern border enclaves in the hegemonic bourgeois territory. As young, confident, and purposeful women, they constitute the age of liberation. They live on their own terms, their lack of privileges does not make them bitter, and they hold on to their dignity. Isabel leaves her job at La Mandrágora when it gets too unpleasant; Miriam openly defies her mother's authority when she declares that her ambitions are different from the mother's expectations; Cuca does not bother to be polite to her girlfriend's mother. When these subalterns talk to authority, they are not deferential. The women in the age of freedom express their sexuality confidently. Isabel rejects the advances of her employers' son and fights him off when he tries to force himself on her during the village dance. Miriam's ambition to become a masseuse shows that she is comfortable touching naked bodies, and Cuca is not discouraged by her lover's family's cold attitude toward her.

The group of the three youngest girls represents the age of vitality. The adulatory Momi, the jaundiced Candita, and the neurotic Amalia are alive with the spirit of exploration. These young girls recognize their sexuality and pursue their desires. The age of agency is embodied in the two mature women, Mercedes and Mirta. Mercedes runs a successful trading business and lives with the man to whom she is attracted, even though he is the son of her former lover. Mirta runs the hotel and knows that she is invaluable to the establishment. Unlike the decadent women, Mercedes and Mirta break free from social entrapment. They generate affinities with the world at large. They do not deplete their self-worth by constantly appraising their sexual appeal.

The seventeen characters discussed above represent six stages in the formation of female sexuality. The 'formation' starts in the age of vitality, where, as a girl-child, the woman explores, expresses, and pursues her desire. The exploratory stage may meet with a quick end by deteriorating into the age of bitterness where she lies, deceives, and gives in to jealousy, or it may progress to an age of liberation where the woman accepts her sexuality and develops reciprocal love relationships. In the age of stagnation, the woman sustains her domestic idyll by constant self-deception. In the age of agency, the woman's sexual satisfaction or the absence of it does not weigh in disproportionately on her self-perception; in contrast, in the age of decadence, the woman rebels against being controlled by indulging in incestuous relationships. The films trace two divergent trajectories in the ages of woman: a positive progression constituted by vitality-liberation-agency and destructive negativity of bitterness-stagnation-decadence.

Through the trajectory of female sexuality, Martel deftly traces the historical arc of her country over the last two centuries. The age of vitality parallels the idealist romantic conception of the nation shortly after the onset of independence in the nineteenth century. In the next century, the age of liberation resonates with the socialist promise of the early Peronist years, the age of stagnation with the subsequent disillusionment with the Peronistas, and the military dictatorship years are marked by lies and deception like the age of bitterness. The twentieth-century fin de siècle neoliberal program held the promise of an age of agency wherein the country would benefit from stronger linkages with the global financial and product markets. However, by the start of the twenty-first century, the national scenario had quickly deteriorated to an age of decadence marked by corruption and disregard for the plight of marginal classes. Martel's primary tool for evoking the link between female sexuality and the nation is her spatial strategy. Therefore, it is worthwhile to take a close look at one specific instrument in her spatial tool kit: the swimming pool.

Instead of treating the formation of sexuality linearly, Martel presents it in simultaneity. Her technique for coeval representations of the diverse ages of woman can be illustrated through her use of the spatial tool of *la pileta*, the swimming pool. Commenting on the use of water as a cinematic technique, Deleuze observes that, "water is the most perfect environment in which movement can be extracted from the thing moved or mobility from movement itself."[38] Martel upends the mobility of water by pouring it into a concrete tank. Her "liquid perception" is muddied with dregs of rot, creating a "perception-image" suspended in colloidal murkiness.[39] The spatial imagery of the swimming pool inhabits critical moments in each film in the Salta trilogy in distinct ways.

In *LC*, in general, the "treatment of space privileges stagnation and stasis over movement or transition," but it is the pool specifically that is a participatory witness to the family's inexorable decay.[40] "The swimming pool in *LC* takes part in social categorization and class division," and the water also acts as the medium for a dialogue with the self.[41] The closely placed shots of a swamp where a cow is sinking to her death and a dirty pool where Mecha sits drunk, barely able to hold her head upright, highlight the congruence between the swamp and the pool and between Mecha's body language and the cow's helpless submission to the suction of the bog. The water body remains a "symbol of stagnation" despite the mutation of a slushy marsh in the 'barbaric' woods into a swimming pool in the 'civilized' ranch.[42] However, the stagnation does not present an insurmountable obstacle for everyone. In the second pool scene, Momi, the younger daughter, dives into the pool. Momi's submergence under the turbid pool waters covered by rotting leaves signifies her knowledge of "dirty realities ignored by others."[43] The vital girl-woman is the only one who is shown diving into the pool. The decayed woman, Mecha, and the bitter girl-woman, Vero, sit on its edge but never step in. The stable woman, Tali, goes near the pool only to get her children out of it. Thus, the greater the distance of the woman from the pool, the greater is her alienation from her sexuality.

In *NS*, the first framing of the pool is almost monochromatically blue— Helena's swimsuit, cap and robe, the waterproof cushions on the deck chairs, swimming trunks of the men, and of course the water are all blue. The blue is contrasted with the white walls and floors of the pool area. The setting strongly evokes the blue and white colors of the Argentinian flag. The absence of any other color turns the frame into a static photograph from the past that will not admit any variability in its composition. The resort is the nation. It is trying to survive in a changing economic scenario. The doctors who have come to attend the conference at the hotel represent the speculative investors who tried to profit from their country's economic crisis. The doctors start their day with drinks by the pool. They seem more intent on the pursuit of pleasure than knowledge. The rapacious intent of the profiteers is embodied in Dr. Vesalio, who molests a fellow woman attendee. All the people present in the hotel during the conference belong to the same province. The doctors are from nearby areas in Salta. Dr. Jano even attended the same school as Helena and her brother. Despite their regional ties, they are deprived of a sense of community. Under the force of liquid modernity, brought on by neoliberal globalization, the community links are like "zipped harnesses . . . and their selling point is the facility with which they can be put on in the morning and taken off in the evening."[44] The pool is a witness that the community in *NS* marked by betrayal, lasciviousness, and insincerity. Even after breaking Amalia's confidence, Josefina swims with her. The doctors leer at Helena while she does her daily laps in the pool. Dr. Jano plays at being the loyal husband and concerned father as he dries his son's hair and chats with his wife and daughter at the poolside. The pool represents the fluidity that dissolves traditional community and family ties.

In *MSC*, the pool scene contrasts the self-positioning of Vero and her sister Josefina. Josefina stands in the water with her shoulders and head above it because she does not want to get wet. Josefina feels she can control the events around her, whereas Vero, because of the lasting shock of the recent accident, knows that the unexpected will disorder her arranged life. Unlike her stable sister who gets into the pool/marriage but does not get wet/satisfied, the decadent Vero seems transformed after noticing the beautiful wetness of the pool/nation from the outside. She drives out to the unfamiliar, poor barrio on the outskirts to give Cuca a lift, and she invites the boy who washes her car to have a snack and gives him used clothes. Vero's engagement with the marginalized classes whom she did not notice before suggests a hope for a way out of decadence for the nation.

Martel's emphatic and novel use of liquid perception emphasizes the impact of liquid modernity on social structures. According to Zygmunt Bauman, modernity has been a project of liquefication from the start. To begin with, it 'melted' solids like "traditional loyalties, customary rights, and obligations," and eventually, "left the whole complex network of social relations unstuck."[45] The Salta trilogy examines the changes in a woman's social positionality under modernity's liquefying forces. Modernity has freed the woman from the obligation to be the fragile virgin when she is young and to be the iron anchor of the family when she is mature. However, this freedom is not synonymous with emancipation in the films. Modernity creates the desirable impact of emancipation for the younger woman in the age of vitality, and the older woman in the age of agency. In contrast, the younger women in the age of bitterness and the older woman in the age of decadence turn into liquified anchors and become indistinguishable from the flotsam and jetsam cast aside on the liquid surface. They have the agential freedom, but not the capabilities to free themselves from incestual bonds. The decadent, bitter women mirror not only Martel's contemporary Argentina but any country that, in the grip of neoliberal economic fervor, has witnessed "the renunciation, phasing out or selling off by the state of all the major appurtenances of its role as the principal . . . purveyor of certainty and security."[46]

When the Salta trilogy is seen as part of a whole anthology, it becomes a bildungsroman of female sexuality and the nation. In order to justify this generic categorization, two aspects merit explanation. First, sexual maturation is not shown through the events in the life of a single character. Instead, it is presented as a progression in a collectivity. Though the traditional understanding of the genre demanded a focus on individual growth, there is no longer a consensus on that aspect: "Some critics emphasize individuality and individual change of the self in the process of formation, whereas others look more at milieu, regarding the condition of the protagonist actively involved in the social world as essential."[47] Olga Bezhanova has also questioned the centrality of individuality in a bildungsroman by articulating a subgenre of the collective bildungsroman that experiments with multiple narrative voices.[48] Secondly, the bildungsroman normally follows a diachronic narrative style that demonstrates a sequence of changes in the life of the protagonist. Martel's synchronic depiction of the various ages of woman should be seen as an innovation in, rather than a break from, the stylistic conventions of the bildungsroman. The issue of the inappropriate latter half of the portmanteau—'roman'—also needs to be addressed. The trilogy is not a novel but, given that film criticism borrows heavily from literary criticism, this may be considered one more entry in the extensive terminology that the two fields share in common.

The transnational accessibility of the Salta trilogy derives from three key elements. Its structure as a collective bildungsroman that associates the sexual formation of the woman with her emancipation makes it relatable to any society where patriarchy continues to limit the woman's capability for agential action. The naturalist inflection in the narrative, manifested through the close camerawork, foregrounds transnationally recognizable microspaces. Finally, its coding of Argentina's historical journey through the stages of romantic idealism, spurious populism, military rule, and economic immiseration in the grammar of female sexuality speaks to marginalized populations everywhere who are excluded from the rhetoric of neoliberal prosperity. The reason cited by Bong Joon-ho for the transnational relevance of his film *Parasite*, despite its distinctive "Koreanness," is also true of the Salta trilogy. The films evoke an emotional connect regardless of their regional specificities because "we all live in the same country called capitalism" and because the most influential province in that country is called patriarchy.[49]

NOTES

1. The term *NCA* gained currency in the 1990s with the release of *Historias Breves* (1995), *Rapado* (1996), and *Mundo Grúa* (1999). The change in the country's cinematic trend received international attention in 2001 when Argentine filmmakers marked their presence at Cannes after a thirteen-year hiatus. The festival included films by Lisandro Alonso and Lucrecia Martel. Before 2001, the last Argentinian film that was screened at Cannes had won the best director award for Fernando Solanas in 1988. His film *Sur* was set against the backdrop of the Falklands War that had been instigated by the military dictatorship in 1982.

2. Wolfgang Bongers, *Interferencias del archivo: Cortes estéticos y políticos en cine y literatura* (Frankfurt: Peter Lang, 2016), 139.

3. In his inaugural address on the occasion of his election as president of Argentina in 2003, Néstor Kirchner pressed the need for staying focused on the future without going into the details of past governmental failures: "No es necesario hacer un detallado repaso de nuestros males" (Kirchner 2003). Under the Kirchner administration, the criminals of the "Dirty War" were brought to justice, and the government adopted a decidedly socialist outlook in its policy framework. However, for the *NCA* filmmakers, the improvements on the legislative, judicial, and economic fronts under Kirchernism did not make for an easy closure on the past. They did not subscribe to the idea of a monolithic feel-good narrative, instead they continued the exploration of the national trauma.

4. María M. Delgado and Cecilia Sosa, "Politics, Memory and Fiction(s) in Contemporary Argentine Cinema: The Kirchnerist Years," in *A Companion to Latin American Cinema*, eds. Maria M. Delgado, Stephen M. Hart, and Randal Johnson (Chichester: Wiley Blackwell, 2017), 242.

5. Geoffrey Kantaris, "From Postmodernity to Post-Identity Latin American Film after the Great Divide," in *A Companion to Latin American Cinema*, eds. Maria M. Delgado, Stephen M. Hart, and Randal Johnson (Chichester: Wiley Blackwell, 2017), 152.

6. The widespread, violent protests against the government's economic policies in Argentina in 2001 and more recently in Chile in 2019 show neoliberal frameworks stretch the veneer of prosperity of a few over the misery of many. Though these demonstrations broke out in the national capitals, they speak to the precarity at large of marginal groups in the provinces and rural areas as well. See *Clarín* and *La Nación* for reportage on the protests.

7. Lucrecia Martel, "La mala memoria," interview with Mariana Enríquez. August 17, 2008. https://www.pagina12.com.ar/diario/suplementos/radar/9-4766-20 08-08-17.html; accessed February 12, 2018.

8. Ibid.

9. Delgado and Sosa, "Politics, Memory and Fiction(s)," 243.

10. Donald Shaw, *The Post-Boom in Spanish American Fiction* (New York: SUNY Press, 1998), 10.

11. Lucrecia Martel, "Shadow of a Doubt," interview with Amy Taubin. *Filmcomment*, July-August 2009, https://www.filmcomment.com/article/shadow-of -a-doubt-lucrecia-martel-interviewed/; accessed January 28, 2018.

12. Ibid.

13. Rok Spruk, 2019. "The Rise and Fall of Argentina." *Latin American Economic Review* 28, 16 (2019): n.p. https://doi.org/10.1186/s40503-019-0076-2.

14. Claudia Sandberg, "Maximiliano Schonfeld's Films of the Volga Germans in Entre Ríos: About the Neoliberal Devil in Argentine Cinema," in *Contemporary Latin American Cinema: Resisting Neoliberalism?* eds. Claudia Sandberg and Carolina Rocha (New York: Palgrave Macmillan, 2018), 244.

15. Lucrecia Martel, "La mala," translation mine.

16. Elizabeth Ezra and Terry Rowden, *Transnational Cinema: The Film Reader* (Abingdon: Taylor and Francis, 2006), 3–5.

17. Rina Chandran, "India's Low-caste Dalits Rally to Demand End to 'Unclean' Jobs," *Reuters*, August 1, 2016, n.p. https://www.reuters.com/article/us-india-prot ests-caste-idUSKCN10C2RB; accessed February 4, 2020.

The traditional Indian social structure was comprised of a hierarchical arrangement of four castes wherein the lowest was assigned tasks that were deemed 'unclean,' such as cleaning sewers and disposal of dead animals. Even in contemporary India, Dalits remain at the bottom of India's social hierarchy and their struggle for integration into the narrative of development is politically charged.

18. For more perspectives on the differences between the traditional middle class and the new middle class, see *The Global Middle Classes* (2012) by R. Heiman et al.

19. Hagen Koo, "The Global Middle Class: How Is It Made, What Does It Represent?" *Globalizations*, 13:4 (2016): 443, doi: 10.1080/14747731.2016.1143617.

20. Paul Julian Smith, "Transnational Co-productions and Female Filmmakers: The Cases of Lucrecia Martel and Isabel Coixet," in *Hispanic and Lusophone Women Filmmakers: Theory, Practice and Difference,* eds. Parvati Nair, Julián Daniel Gutiérrez-Albilla (Manchester: Manchester UP, 2013), 13.

Margaret McVeigh, "Different but the Same: Landscape and the Gothic as Transnational Story Space in Jane Campion's *Sweetie* (1989) and Lucrecia Martel's *La Ciénaga* (2001)," *Critical Arts*, 31:5 (2017): 144.

21. Will Higbee and Song Hwee Lim, "Concepts of Transnational Cinema: Towards a Critical Transnationalism in Film Studies," *Transnational Cinemas* 1:1 (2010): 10.

22. Theodor W. Adorno, *The Culture Industry: Selected Essays on Mass Culture* (London and New York: Routledge, 1991), 24.

23. Kantaris, "From Postmodernity," 151.

24. This perfect merchandize might look like Alfonso Cuarón's *Roma* that reifies the idea of nostalgic belonging in the trope of selfless motherhood. *Roma*, as a meticulously aesthetic representation of the male gaze, offers a stimulating counterpoint to Martel's trilogy. Both *Roma* and the trilogy focalize the racial difference of the female experience, but Martel's films do not permit an "easy cross-cultural crossover of her explorations of class, race, history," and gender (White 2015, 187). Cuarón chooses the *chingada-madre* as a viable binary, and even in the twenty-first century offers motherhood as the ultimate refuge from being the *chingada*. In *Roma*, the child protagonist's Hispanic mother and the indigenous maid seek refuge in motherhood. Rejected by the husband and lover, the women turn into asexual devoted mothers.

25. Gloria Anzaldúa, *Borderlands/La Frontera: The New Mestiza* (San Francisco: Aunt Lute, 2007), 52.

26. Lucrecia Martel, "La mala," translation mine.

27. Whereas the novels of nineteenth-century fin de siècle writers attest their understanding of "determinism, heredity and instinct in society, elements that conspired against the idealized nature of the world that the romantic generation had espoused" (Spicer-Escalante 18), the films of twentieth-century fin de siècle *NCA* cineastes use the same elements to manifest the falsity of neoliberal claims of widespread betterment.

28. Juan Pablo Spicer-Escalante, "The 'Long Tail' Hypothesis: The Diachronic Counter-Metanarrative of Hispanic Naturalism," in *Au Naturel:(Re)Reading Hispanic Naturalism*, eds. J. P. Spicer-Escalante and Lara Anderson (Newcastle upon Tyne: Cambridge Scholars Publishing, 2010), 18.

29. Ana del Sarto. "Cinema Novo and New/Third Cinema Revisited: Aesthetics, Culture and Politics," *Chasqui. Special Issue on Brazilian and Spanish American Literary and Cultural Encounters*, 34:1 (2005): 85.

30. Pura Fernández. *Eduardo López Bago y el naturalismo radical: La novela y el mercado literario en el siglo XIX* (Amsterdam: Rodopi, 1995), 230, translation mine.

31. Lucrecia Martel, "La mala," translation mine.

32. Deborah Martin, *The Cinema of Lucrecia Martel* (Manchester: Manchester UP, 2016) 56.

33. Ibid., 64.

34. Ibid., 64.

35. Lucrecia Martil, "Mí Límite límite es el pudor, no lo que va a pensar el público," interview with Ernesto Babino. September 17, 2005, accessed February 9, 2018, http://ernestobabino.blogspot.com/2005/09/ entrevista-lucrecia-martel-director a.html.

36. Ibid.

37. *La Niña Santa*, directed by Lucrecia Martel (Argentina: Lita Stantic Producciones, 2004), DVD.

38. Gilles Deleuze, *Cinema 1: The Movement Image*, trans. Hugh Tomlinson and Barbara Habberjam (Minneapolis: U of Minnesota P, 1986), 77.

39. Ibid.

40. Martin, *The Cinema*, 34.

41. María Mercédez Vázquez Vázquez, "New Geographies of Class in Mexican and Brazilian Cinemas: *Post Tenebras Lux* and *Que horas ela volta?*" in *Contemporary Latin American Cinema: Resisting Neoliberalism?* eds. Claudia Sandberg and Carolina Rocha (New York: Palgrave Macmillan, 2018), 73.

42. Pedro Lange-Churión, "The Salta Trilogy: The Civilised Barbarism in Lucrecia Martel's Films." *Contemporary Theatre Review*, 22:4 (2012): 472.

43. Laura Podalsky, "Out of Depth: The Politics of Disaffected Youth and Contemporary Latin American Cinema," in *Youth Culture in Global Cinema*, ed. Timothy Shary and Alexandra Seibel (Austin: University of Texas P, 2011), 109.

44. Zygmunt Bauman, *Liquid Modernity* (Cambridge: Polity, 2006), 169.

45. Ibid., 3–4.

46. Ibid., 184.

47. Petru Golban, *A History of the Bildungsroman* (Newcastle upon Tyne: Cambridge Scholars Publishing, 2018), 10.

48. Olga Bezhanova, *Growing Up in an Inhospitable World: Female Bildungsroman in Spain* (Tempe: AILCFH, 2014), 11.

49. Bong Joon-ho, "The Master Speaks," interview by Stephen Hathoff, *Birth. Movies.Death*, October 16, 2019, accessed February 8, 2020, https://birthmoviesd eath.com/2019/10/16/bong-joon-ho-discusses-parasite-genre-filmmaking-and-the -greatness-of-zodia.

BIBLIOGRAPHY

Adorno, Theodor W. *The Culture Industry: Selected Essays on Mass Culture*. London and New York: Routledge, 1991.

Anzaldúa, Gloria. *Borderlands/La Frontera: The New Mestiza*. San Francisco: Aunt Lute, 2007.

Bauman, Zygmunt. *Liquid Modernity*. Cambridge: Polity, 2000.

Bezhanova, Olga. *Growing Up in an Inhospitable World: Female Bildungsroman in Spain*. Tempe: AILCFH, 2014.

Bongers, Wolfgang. *Interferencias del archivo: Cortes estéticos y políticos en cine y literatura*. Frankfurt: Peter Lang, 2016.

Chandran, Rina. "India's Low-caste Dalits Rally to Demand End to 'Unclean' Jobs." *Reuters*, August 1, 2016. https://www.reuters.com/article/us-india-protests-caste-id USKCN10C2RB. Accessed February 4, 2020.

Clarin. "El Estallido Social." December 20, 2001. https://www.clarin.com/politica /capital-fuerte-cacerolazo-nocturno-masiva-marcha-plaza-mayo_0_ByIxGrLeCtl .html. Accessed February 2, 2020.

del Sarto, Ana. "Cinema Novo and New/Third Cinema Revisited: Aesthetics, Culture, and Politics." *Chasqui. Special Issue on Brazilian and Spanish American Literary and Cultural Encounters*, 34:1 (2005): 78–89.

Deleuze, Gilles. *Cinema 1: The Movement Image*. Trans. Hugh Tomlinson and Barbara Habberjam. Minneapolis: U of Minnesota P, 1986.

Delgado, Maria M. and Cecilia Sosa. "Politics, Memory and Fiction(s) in Contemporary Argentine Cinema: The Kirchnerist Years." In *A Companion to Latin American Cinema*, edited by Maria M. Delgado, Stephen M. Hart, and Randal Johnson, 238–268. Chichester: Wiley Blackwell, 2017.

Ezra, Elizabeth and Terry Rowden. *Transnational Cinema: The Film Reader*. Abingdon: Taylor and Francis, 2006.

Fernández, Pura. *Eduardo López Bago y el naturalismo radical: La novela y el mercado literario en el siglo XIX*. Amsterdam: Rodopi, 1995.

Golban, Petru. *A History of the Bildungsroman*. Newcastle upon Tyne: Cambridge Scholars Publishing, 2018.

Heiman, Rachel, Carla Freeman and Mark Liechty, eds. *The Global Middle Classes: Theorizing through Ethnography*. Santa Fe: School for Advanced Research, 2012.

Higbee, Will and Song Hwee Lim. "Concepts of Transnational Cinema: Towards a Critical Transnationalism in Film Studies." *Transnational Cinemas* 1:1 (2010): 7–21.

Joon-ho, Bong. "The Master Speaks." Interview by Stephen Hathoff. *Birth.Movies. Death*. October 16, 2019. Accessed https://birthmoviesdeath.com/2019/10/16/ bong-joon-ho-discusses-parasite-genre-filmmaking-and-the-greatness-of-zodia. Accessed February 8, 2020.

Kantaris, Geoffrey. "From Postmodernity to Post-Identity Latin American Film after the Great Divide." In *A Companion to Latin American Cinema*, edited by Maria M. Delgado, Stephen M. Hart, and Randal Johnson, 150–66. Chichester: Wiley Blackwell, 2017.

Koo, Hagen. "The Global Middle Class: How Is It Made, What Does It Represent?" *Globalizations*, 13:4 (2016): 440–53. doi: 10.1080/14747731.2016.1143617.

La ciénaga. Directed by Lucrecia Martel. 2001; Argentina: Lita Stantic Producciones, 2001. Prime Video.

La mujer sin cabeza. Directed by Lucrecia Martel. 2008; Argentina: El Deseo, 2008. Prime Video.

La nación. "Caos en Chile." October 20, 2019. https://www.lanacion.com.ar/el-mund o/caos-chile-manifestantes-incendiaron-edificio-del-diario-nid2298820. Accessed February 2, 2020.

La niña santa. Directed by Lucrecia Martel. 2004. Argentina: Lita Stantic Producciones, 2004. DVD.

Lange-Churión, Pedro. "The Salta Trilogy: The Civilised Barbarism in Lucrecia Martel's Films." *Contemporary Theatre Review*, 22:4 (2012): 467–84.

Martel, Lucrecia. "La mala memoria," interview with Mariana Enriquez. August 17, 2008. https://www.pagina12.com.ar/diario/suplementos/radar/9-4766-2008-08-17 .html. Accessed February 12, 2018.

———. "Mi límite es el pudor, no lo que va a pensar el público," interview with Ernesto Babino. Septrember 17, 2005. http://ernestobabino.blogspot.com/2005/09/ entrevista-lucrecia-martel-directora.html. Accessed February 9, 2018.

———. "Shadow of a Doubt," interview with Amy Taubin. *Filmcomment*, July-August 2009. https://www.filmcomment.com/article/shadow-of-a-doubt-lucrecia -martel-interviewed/. Accessed January 28, 2018.

Martin, Deborah. *The Cinema of Lucrecia Martel.* Manchester: Manchester UP, 2016.

McVeigh, Margaret. "Different but the Same: Landscape and the Gothic as Transnational Story Space in Jane Campion's *Sweetie* (1989) and Lucrecia Martel's *La Ciénaga* (2001)." *Critical Arts*, 31:5 (2017): 142–55.

Podalsky, Laura. "Out of Depth: The Politics of Disaffected Youth and Contemporary Latin American Cinema." In *Youth Culture in Global Cinema*, edited by Timothy Shary and Alexandra Seibel, 109–30. Austin: University of Texas P, 2011.

Roma. Directed by Alfonso Cuarón. 2018; n.p.: Espectáculos Fílmicos, 2018. Netflix.

Sandberg, Claudia. "Maximiliano Schonfeld's Films of the Volga Germans in Entre Ríos: About the Neoliberal Devil in Argentine Cinema." In *Contemporary Latin American Cinema: Resisting Neoliberalism?* edited by Claudia Sandberg and Carolina Rocha, 231–248. New York: Palgrave Macmillan, 2018.

Shaw, Donald. *The Post-boom in Spanish American Fiction.* New York: SUNY Press, 1998.

Smith, Paul Julian. "Transnational Co-productions and Female Filmmakers: The Cases of Lucrecia Martel and Isabel Coixet." In *Hispanic and Lusophone Women Filmmakers: Theory, Practice and Difference*, edited by Parvati Nair, Julián Daniel Gutiérrez-Albilla, 12–24. Manchester: Manchester UP, 2013.

Spicer-Escalante, Juan Pablo. "The 'Long Tail' Hypothesis: The Diachronic Counter-Metanarrative of Hispanic Naturalism," In *Au Naturel:(Re)Reading Hispanic Naturalism*, edited by J. P. Spicer-Escalante and Lara Anderson, 11–37. Newcastle upon Tyne: Cambridge Scholars Publishing, 2010.

Spruk, R. "The Rise and Fall of Argentina." *Latin American Economic Review* 28:16 (2019): n.p. https://doi.org/10.1186/s40503-019-0076-2.

Vásquez Vásquez, María Mercédez. "New Geographies of Class in Mexican and Brazilian Cinemas: *Post Tenebras Lux* and *Que horas ela volta?*" In *Contemporary Latin American Cinema: Resisting Neoliberalism?* edited by Claudia Sandberg and Carolina Rocha, 65-82. New York: Palgrave Macmillan, 2018.

White, Patricia. *Women's Cinema, World Cinema.* Duke UP, 2015.

Part III

VISUAL AND PERFORMING ARTS

Chapter 6

Reimagining the *Borderlands*

Intersectionality and Transnational Queering of Laura Aguilar's Self-Portrait Three Eagles Flying

Rosita Scerbo

Laura Aguilar, daughter of a first-generation Mexican American man and a mixed-race mother, was an acclaimed Californian photographer who worked mainly in the genre of portraiture and self-portraiture. Her lesbian identification has traces of both male and female identities and her culture is a mixture of many different races and cultures. By transcending beyond the limits of US and Mexican cultures, Aguilar's art expression gives voice to the people of the Borderlands. This essay looks at one of Laura Aguilar's most appreciated works in the context of Chicano feminist studies, *Three Eagles Flying* (1990). This self-portrait explores the construction of her multiple identities. The visual artist's inner struggles were related not only to her sexuality but also to her cultural and ethnic heritage (Leimer 30–31). In a single image, Aguilar manages to critically embrace and include all the power relations inherent to intersectional perspectives: race, gender, sexuality, class, and ability. *Three Eagles Flying* externalizes the author's inner struggles that were related not only to her sexual ideology but also to her cultural and ethnic heritage and to the mental and physical disorders that characterized her existence. The symbolic elements in *Three Eagles Flying* constitute an interplay with the meaning of the artist's last name, since *águila* means "eagle" in English. Aguilar never felt supported by her family as a person and as an artist. Depression was a faithful companion of her life, and the photographer had to find a way to escape from this reality and turn her suffering into a work of art that allowed her to communicate and make herself visible.

In this context, intersectionality serves as a helpful analytical lens[1] to investigate how multiple inequalities may be portrayed to represent the "complex ontology" of characters.[2] Laura Aguilar's visual art deploys multiple, complex, and simultaneous identities, displaying the experience of marginalized subjects who live in what feminist theorist Anzaldúa defines as *Borderlands*. Intersectionality has become the expression used to designate the theoretical and methodological perspective that seeks to account for the cross- or overlapping perception of power relations. This approach allows us to investigate the intersections between race and gender, and class and gender. Moreover, this perspective explores the consequences of the relationships among the social groups involved. This concept gives voice to the political contributions of black and brown feminism as methods of decolonizing epistemic approaches. In US academic contexts, intersectionality seems to have become the most widespread feminist approach[3] that allows female social activists to talk about either multiple or interdependent identities or inequalities.[4] On the other hand, in the field of structuralist feminism, Patricia Hill Collins[5] was the first to speak of intersectionality as a paradigm, while it was Ange-Marie Hancock[6] who proposed a formalization of this paradigm, understood as a set that encompasses both normative theory and empirical research.

This double genealogical affiliation historically imputed to intersectionality is configured differently according to national contexts. Scholars from different countries look at intersectionality in a different way based on their personal and historical experience. For example, while in the United States most of the academic studies that apply intersectionality theories are strongly influenced by black feminism, in Europe intersectionality is rather linked to postmodern thinking.[7] For female activists and artists like Laura Aguilar, the question of race is central, as well as the struggle that the black and brown body experiences in the United States and Mexico. Therefore, Aguilar uses her art to express these concerns.

Laura Aguilar was able to explore the real and symbolic disputes within the different identities that characterized her as an individual and as an emblem of modern feminism.[8] She was able to do so through her revolutionary photographic work. In *Tree Eagles Flying*, we can observe her partially nude body wrapped in the American flag and tied with ropes, while the flags of the United States and Mexico hang, respectively, on her left and right side. The Mexican flag hides her head. The central image of the flag, which is the Mexican eagle, covers her face. The eagle represents, using Barthes's terms, 'the studium' of Aguilar's photo, an element that indicates historical, social, or cultural meanings extracted through the semiotic analysis of the illustration.[9] In this case the eagle can be read as a unifying component, which brings together the two identities of the photographer, the American and the Mexican, both linked to this emblematic image. This powerful image lends itself to an intersectional study, a look that puts the focus on the power relations produced at the crossroads of inequalities[10] such as class, gender, or race, among others[11] and that allows us to examine the categories and their relationships in order to know how privileges and oppressions, agency and empowerment are configured from a situated perspective[12] very individual's life is built on the basis of social and structural organizers that hierarchize our experiences.[13] In the case of Laura Aguilar, the self-portrait *Tree Eagles Flying* makes the spectator reflect about the connection between "here" and "there," which characterizes the transnational experiences of migrants.[14]

In the image, Aguilar's body is tied with heavy cords representing the lack of freedom suffered by her community of Mexican American migrants that after crossing the border of their home country find hostility in new, unfriendly territories. Waldinger and Fitzgerald argue that these "communities conform to the root meaning of transnational—extending beyond loyalties that connect to any specific place of origin or ethnic or national group."[15] Migrants living in-between states, such as the case of people leaving in the border between Mexico and the United States are often wrongly suspected of dual loyalty.[16] Their migratory identity raises questions regarding the allegiance and political bona fides of these persons whose social identities are largely framed by their connections to two states.

The terms of national belonging are almost always the subject of conflict; variations in political culture ensure that they also differ from one nation-state to the other.[17] My reading of *Tree Eagles Flying* is that this is the reason why Aguilar is blindfolded and almost her entire face hidden. She lost her identity and her visibility as a human being because of the migratory nature of her personal experience. Her self-portrait resembles the collective condition in which millions of Mexican Americans live today. The anthropologists Glick-Schiller, Basch, and Szanton-Blanc defined this situation as 'immigrant transnationalism.' The notion of transnationalism was also identified as the social connections existing between receiving (United States) and sending country (Mexico); and 'transmigrants' is the denomination assigned to the migrants who have links to both countries.[18] In 1987, Douglas Massey et al. published the book *Return to Aztlan* that became the point of reference in the scholarship of migration and transnationalism, establishing the dynamic nature of migration and migrants that are considered members of "binational communities."[19]

Aguilar's self-portrait represents perfectly this extraneous condition. The spectator observes a naked female body, tied and wrapped in the flags of Mexico and the United States. The Chicana artist is challenging the belief system that "expects immigrants to have a single identity, national allegiance, and representation in one national polity."[20] According to my reading, Aguilar, in the process of making both flags part of her body, contradicts this approach. To the contrary, her worldview seems to be more in line with the position described by Glick-Schiller and Fouron and that identifies international migrants as "transnational, as persons with two homelands."[21]

The Borderlands between Mexico and the United States is an open wound that stands to define hegemonic spaces and establish a third border dimension. When Gloria Anzaldúa uses the term Borderlands with a capital B, she relies on a concept that goes beyond the Texas/Mexico border. Anzaldúa uses the idea of a bridge as something that at the same time can separate individuals with hybrid identities and connect them to each other as well. The 'bridge' is seen by many Mexican American scholars and artists as an opening to a space both uncomfortable and alien to them. All Anzaldúa narratives are based on multiple experiences to create a collective story that transcends the social barriers among different groups of people. While identity politics relies on specific categories of identity, spiritual activism requires that we free ourselves from all these barriers.

Like Anzaldúa, many other Chicana authors and artists create prose, poems, and works of art that detail the invisible frontiers that exist between Latinos and non-Latinos, men and women, heterosexuals and homosexuals, and other groups. In *Three Eagles Flying*, the Borderlands between Mexico and the United States is the pressing topic that Aguilar aims to investigate. In this piece, Laura Aguilar's body is wrapped in the American and the Mexican flag. The self-portrait alludes to the ways in which transnational migration can have a particularly punishing effect on Hispanic women who suffer some of its worst consequences. In this context, María José Magliano dedicates a lot of attention to the relation between intersectionality, transnationalism, and migration. The author points out that discussions about intersectionality have become central to theoretical elaborations on gender and migration. Therefore, she analyzed the potential of the theory of intersectionality to advance our thinking about social processes and experiences, specifically international migration and the experiences of female migrants of color.[22]

According to Floya Anthias, intersectionality in relation to migration processes has been formed by various axes of inequalities. One of the most significant points she highlights is that in international migrations, gender, class, national origin, race, ethnicity, age, immigration status, and religion can influence the daily lives of women and men and have a decisive impact on their access to rights and opportunities, as well as on the situations of privilege or exclusion that derive from these circumstances. Anthias states that women suffer multiple discriminations inside the migration processes and confirms the complexity and diversity of realities of migrants, especially underlying the different experience between male and female expatriates or asylum seekers. She points out the centrality of emphasizing the gender dimension and taking into account the ethnized and racialized character of emigrants, while stressing that it is not possible to understand the categories of ethnicity and migration without considering the gender and class of migrants.[23] Therefore, what Laura Aguilar with her revolutionary work attempts to transmit is that we cannot isolate gender issues without considering in the same debate other identity categories, such as race, sexuality, ethnicity, and class. In the words of Pierrette Hondagneu-Sotelo, "gender does not exist in isolation but is always part of a scheme in which race, nationality, occupational integration and socioeconomic class positions are related in a particular way, and the analysis of all this reflects the nuances of this intersectionality."[24] This approach helps us appreciate that we cannot analyze migratory experiences if we do not take into consideration the gender of the migrants. Through her self-portrait, Aguilar emphasizes, in particular, the position of Hispanic women crossing the border between Mexico and the United States.

The different dimensions of *Three Eagles Flying* show us that gender, as confirmed by Hondagneu-Soleto, is not an isolated reality, but works in intersection with social class, ethnicity, nationality, and other categories that encourage different forms of discrimination. These images challenge normative conceptions about the invisible large, brown, immigrant, female body. In the figure 6.1 below, the artist's nude body becomes an emblem of rebellion against the colonization of Latinas' corporality. This artistic piece has, at the same time, a deep personal and national meaning, in which Aguilar's experience turns into a sort of collective autobiography. The photographs themselves draw upon numerous intersectional conflicts, alluding to her skin color, her limited language abilities as a child who was incapable to negotiate between English and Spanish, her body weight, and her challenges as a binational lesbian who navigates between two cultural and racial identities.

The past two decades have witnessed the emergence of literary and artistic contributions by Latina lesbians in the cultural scene of the United States. Laura Aguilar is well known for her portraits, mostly focused on people from

Figure 6.1   Laura Aguilar, "Three Eagles Flying" (1990), Three gelatin silver prints, 24 × 20 inches each. *Source*: © Laura Aguilar Trust of 2016.

marginalized communities, including LGBT people, Latinas, and obese individuals. Her work focuses on the human form and challenges contemporary social constructs of beauty. Aguilar worked actively as a photographer from the 1980s onward. She often used the self-portrait to accept her own body by challenging the social norms of sexuality, class, gender, and race. This is the reason why one of the most outstanding features of her work is the genre of the self-portrait. As Amelia Jones explains, "the self-portrait photograph performs a kind of visual autobiography, promising to deliver a particular 'subject' (in this case the author her-or himself) to the viewer through a visual 'text' narrated in the first person."[25] Self-portraiture in photography becomes fundamental for women artists, who struggle to articulate themselves as authors rather than as objects of male artistic creation. Historically, women's bodies are subordinated to a gaze by male subjects that renders them submissive.[26] Aguilar can challenge this situation photographically, creating her own visual and autobiographical narrative. She thus becomes a subject instead of maintaining her situation as a feminine 'object' that is speechless and dominated by the patriarchal imaginary.

During the decades of the 1970s and 1980s, the masculine gaze was studied by many theorists who agreed to define it as aggressive and penetrating. For example, we can refer to Laura Mulvey's essay dedicated to the formative theorization of the male gaze, in which the author clarifies that "woman stands in patriarchal culture as a signifier for the male other, bound by a symbolic order in which man can live out his fantasies and obsessions . . . by imposing them on the silent image of woman still tied to her place as bearer, not maker, of meaning."[27] Through a visual representation of Chicano feminist aesthetics, Aguilar dismantles and rebuilds the female body, claims an independent space that had never been conquered, and offers new interpretations and revealing perspectives of Chicano identity that have to do with an unconventional body size and a homosexual identification. Aguilar poses an artistic disturbance of the patriarchal hegemonic discourse, which contributes to the fact that Chicana artists and writers remain invisible or marginal if compared to male colleagues.[28] The photographer proposes, in this way, a new model of femininity that exceeds the limits imposed by the male gender: "Men act, and women appear. Men look at women and women watch themselves being looked at."[29]

When it comes to focusing on Aguilar's subversive work, it is essential to mention her prestigious exhibition "Show and Tell" which is the only individual representation of a Chicana artist on the Pacific coast. The pieces included in this exhibition document how her visual language was built throughout her career. Her work contributes to Chicana artistic and cultural production while at the same time explores new themes within feminist criticism and the typical interests of border theories. One of these new themes explored by Aguilar is related to the struggles that brown women experience based on their geographic location, among other factors. In this context, spirituality is the powerful weapon these female activists use to overcome their situation of poverty in rural areas. Agricultural work is a traditional aspect of migrants' lives together with other underpaid jobs that normally nationals don't do. Both Aguilar's parents come from humble origins. Aguilar's experience in the United States started as daughter of Paul Aguilar, a welder by trade, and Juanita Grisham that was a housekeeper, both of Mexican descent. The majority of low-income immigrant families saw their hands tied to the crop, during the rise of the United Farm Workers Union. Aguilar's photographic work was always connected with the land, with nature as a nurturer, and it always focused on her family history. With respect to the relevance of spirituality in the Mexican and Chicana identity, Ruth Trinidad Galván in "Campesina Epistemologies and Pedagogies of the Spirit: Examining Women's *Sobrevivencia*" shows that women farmers suffer discrimination based on their geographical, class, and ethnic status, and their only option is to rely on their own resources to survive. Farmer life is a reality that many first and second generations of Mexican Americans are familiar with, as many Chicana writers and artists come from low-income families and suffered severe economic struggles growing up. Trinidad Galván analyzes specific peculiarities of these women, such as intuition, which is made up of personal experiences as well as beliefs, traditions, and ancestral sources of the community, including dreams, and signs of nature such as moon phases.[30] Many Chicana authors and artists see in all aspects of Chicano and Mexican spirituality a source of these women's strength. Trinidad Galván, like Aguilar, Anzaldúa, and other queer Chicana feminist scholars, such as Rosaura Sánchez and Emma Pérez, among others, believe in the possibility of effecting social change through struggle. Women through their powerful artistic creations have shown that change can be possible and that they can challenge traditional societal structures.

One way of challenging hegemonic social systems is to demonstrate how the image of the obese body, as portrayed in Aguilar's autobiographical visual narrative, can be considered queer. Bodily shape, after all, often stands as yet another source of inequality. The genesis of obesity studies as an academic field began with the liberation movement that emerged in the United States at the end of the 1960s. This current arose from civil rights and, especially, from women's liberation movements. The first activists within this trend were groups of women aware of the problem of obesity who were seeking solutions that would address the specific needs and problems faced by fat women, whom dominant strains of feminism often ignored. Within my queer reading of her work, it is important to point out that Aguilar in only one image was able to embrace and include all the power relations inherent to intersectional perspectives.

According to LeBesco, a series of similarities/parallels can be established in the medical, psychological, social, and representation treatments of 'fatness' and 'queerness.' LeBesco argues that both fatness and queer identity have been medicalized, pathologized, and stigmatized.[31] Fatness and queerness have been targeted by public health campaigns and other interventions that seek to administer, cure, and attempt to eliminate them. These discourses produce fat and queer bodies (and queer fat bodies, as in the case of Aguilar) as unacceptable both physically and morally. To explain the reasons that inspire and support the comparison between these two concepts, it is important to note, however, that with the term 'queer' one does not simply want to describe the desire a person feels toward an individual of the same sex. On the contrary, the term 'queer' can be a description or refer to an action; an orientation and a practice; a mode of political and critical research that seeks to expose assumptions that are taken for granted, declassify clear categories, and undo the supposedly fixed definition of bodies, gender, desire, and identities. As Eve Kosofky Sedgwick argues, 'queer' can refer to: the open mesh of possibilities, gaps, overlaps, dissonances and resonances, lapses and excesses of meaning when the constituent elements of anyone's gender, of anyone's sexuality aren't made (or can't be made) to signify monolithically.[32] Aguilar's photography can be defined as queer based on many considerations. As Grosz states, "any account of embodiment is also always an account of sexuality."[33]

The self-portrait analyzed here is an example of the many uses of the symbolic image of a bird that is often present in Aguilar's visual art. The birds in some of her photographs are immortalized sitting on a series of cactus alluding to the Mexican identity. The eagle in particular appears on the coat of arms of Mexico, as are the links of that bird with the oral history of the Aztecs: an eagle sitting on a cactus and eating a snake. According to Manuel Gonzales's perspective, the symbolization around the bird's image can be read as an emblem of the identity of Mexicans related to the migratory aspect that characterizes the life experience of many of these individuals.[34] On the other hand, Claude Lévi-Strauss, in *The Savage Mind*, also seeks an explanation of this symbol, this time using the feeling of interdependence that unites many species of birds that can somehow resemble the system that governs the communities of human beings. The author explains that birds are historically given human Christian names because they can be permitted to resemble men in many ways:

They are feathered, winged, oviparous, and they are also physically separated from human society by the element in which it is their privilege to move. As a result, they form a community which is independent of our own but, precisely because of this independence, appears to us like another society, homologous to that in which they live a family life and nurture their young; they often engage in social relations with other members of their species; and they communicate with them by acoustic means recalling articulated language.[35]

Aguilar seems to be putting into practice the principles theorized by Lévi-Strauss in the process of highlighting the relation between birds and human beings. Through these symbolic elements, Aguilar is trying to create connections and alliances among opposing minority groups, while at the same time she is making visible different level of oppressions. After all, intersectionality is part of a postmodern project that conceptualizes identities as multiple and fluid and meets the Foucault's perspective of power to the extent that both put the emphasis on dynamic processes and deconstruction of standardizing and homogenizing categories. In terms of historical trajectory, Laura Aguilar's visual work seems to support and promote many of the perspectives related to intersectional studies. The origin of the term intersectionality lies in the theories articulated more than two centuries ago by thinkers such as Olympia de Gouges, in France. In *The Declaration of Women's Rights*, the author compared colonial domination with patriarchal domination and established analogies between women and slaves (De Gouges n. pag.). The same happened in many Latin American countries, where intersectionality became a way to read the reality of the social and sexual oppression that women were suffering. Some Latin American writers and artists used intersectionality theory from an early date. In Peruvian literature, the most significant contribution was made in 1899 by Clorinda Matto de Turner, thanks to her book titled *Aves sin nido (Birds Without a Nest)*. This text revealed the sexual abuses perpetrated by local governors and priests against indigenous women, pointing out the vulnerability generated by their ethnic/racial and gender status in this context. In Brazil, some artistic works started the conversation about intersectionality in women-related issues. One important example is the cubist painting *A Negra* (1923) by Tarsila do Amaral, which represents a naked black woman with hypertrophied lips and breasts and has been interpreted as an allegory of the situation of black nurses in Brazilian society.[36] It can be beneficial to point out that both examples reveal the views that some white women who belong to Latin American elites have about oppressions related to race, gender, and class issues experienced by indigenous and black women.

Laura Aguilar's body in *Three Eagles Flying* represents these multiple oppressions. As a lesbian, obese woman, coming from a low-income family and suffering from different level of discriminations, she became the voice and face of intersectional feminism. Bare-breasted and bound by heavy rope, she wants to transmit her struggle—the same struggle that ethnic women are experiencing between the American and the Mexican lands. To try to understand the identity that Aguilar is trying to portray, we could turn our attention to the origin of Foucault's theories about poststructuralism, which leads us to look at the concept of identity not only as a space in which the individual is subjective and interact with the outside world but also as a political notion that is fundamental for those strategies of power through which human beings are made subjects. From the reading of Foucault, the identity is unveiling as a device of domestication.[37] The nation-state, which is a form of governmentality that was theorized in the eighteenth century and exported from Western Europe to all regions of the world throughout the nineteenth and twentieth centuries, arose in order to accommodate industrial capitalism. It encouraged a massive migration from the countryside to the city, a strengthening of the bourgeoisie along with the decline of the old nobility, and a development of a positivist mentality. This new form of governmentality created a multitude of biopolitical ways of exercising control.

Newer theory on transnationalism dialogues with concepts such as state sovereignty and territoriality through the proclamation of a borderless world and an "end of geography" and separations. Wendy Brown's *Walled States, Waning Sovereignty* discuss these contradictory bordering practices, focusing on the recent spate of construction of new walls, fences, and other barriers. The book resonates with the themes explored in Aguilar's photography emphasizing mainly the issues surrounding the US-Mexican and Israeli-Palestinian borders. Brown points out that this trend of wall building can be found around the world in almost every political context and strongly criticizes these practices: "It is the weakening of state sovereignty, and more precisely, the detachment of sovereignty from the nation-state, that is generating much of the frenzy of nation-state wall building today. Rather than resurgent expressions of nation-state sovereignty, the new walls are icons of its erosion."[38] Nations and states generally justify the construction of these barriers as a response/protection against some sort of nonstate threat, such as smuggling, illegal migration, terrorism, and drugs trafficking, all issues that help to legitimize the fear of the foreign "other." As Brown confirms, these new walls commonly exhibit differential rigidity based on ethnicity, religion, wealth, citizenship, and education, increasing the physical and spiritual separations that already exists among different populations. In this context, Aguilar represents metaphorically the control that the nation-state has over an individual. She does so through the image of her hands and body trapped and immobilized with heavy ropes. In *Tree Eagles Flying*, we are not able to see her face; the national flag covers any recognizable features of her physiognomy. She has lost her identity in the middle of the fight between the different levels of inequalities she is representing. She is invisible, as a woman and as a citizen of a nation.

Aguilar's work contributes to a political debate that resonates with the similar discussions that exist in different Latin American countries. One prominent case is the one of Brazil initiated in the 1960s. Many of public discussions in this period focused on the problems black women were facing as topics of political debate within the Brazilian Communist Party.[39] Various activists and intellectuals, like Maria Beatriz do Nascimento, Luiza Bairros, Jurema Werneck, Thereza Santos, Lelia González, and Sueli Carneiro, among others, promoted the theory of the triad of oppression, that is to say "race-class-gender" to articulate the differences between Brazilian women that the dominant feminist discourses had been ignoring. Similarly, Aguilar promotes visibility and recognition for the brown indigenous women that live in the *Borderlands* between the American and the Mexican territory. In this context, it is essential to emphasize that intersectionality-based approaches reveal two issues: first, the multiplicity of experiences of sexism lived by different women, and second, the existence of social positions that do not suffer from marginalization or discrimination because they embody the norm itself, such as patriarchal masculinity, supremacist whiteness, or heteronormativity. For this reason, the very concept of intersectionality was coined in 1989 by the African American lawyer Kimberlé Crenshaw in the context of the discussion of a specific legal case, with the aim of making clear the legal invisibility of the multiple dimensions of oppression experienced by the black workers of an American company called General Motors. When Crenshaw first used this term, her objective was to highlight the fact that in the United States black women were exposed to violence and discrimination on grounds related to both race and gender. However, above all, she aimed to create specific legal categories to help face women discrimination in multiple and varied levels.

The Argentine philosopher María Lugones introduces the concept of intersection relationship[40] that can be useful to interpret Laura Aguilar's *Three Eagles Flying*. The notion of the intersection of oppressions theorized by Lugones has been widely disseminated academically because of her reading of intersectionality as a mechanism of control, immobilization, and disconnection. For Lugones, this concept stabilizes social relations and fragments them into homogeneous categories. Moreover, it creates fixed positions and divides social movements, instead of fostering coalitions between them. Based on this interpretation, the immobilized and restricted body of Aguilar in *Three Eagles Flying* represents exactly this metaphoric position. Lugones's approach (2005) explains that the intersection of inequalities shows us an emptiness, an absence, where the black (or in the case of Aguilar, the brown) woman should be, because clearly neither the traditional heterosexual "woman" category nor the "black" category include her. The most valuable contribution given by Lugones has to do with the moment in which this vacuum has been identified. For the author, once this happened, that is to say, once this emptiness has been identified, it must act politically. In this regard, Lugones proposes the logic of fusion as a lived possibility of resisting multiple oppressions by creating circles resistant to power from within, at all levels of oppression, and coalition of identities through complex dialogues from the interdependence of nondominant differences.[41]

This coalition of identities can be observed in Laura Aguilar's photographic work that creates dialogue and conversation, merging the US and the Mexican national identity's experience. In conclusion, it is essential to direct attention to the enormous contribution that the field of intersectionality studies is providing to feminist research and scholarship. Women authors and artists, like the Mexican American photographer Laura Aguilar, identified the importance of integrating intersectionality into the development of feminist and activist work. She demonstrated how it is not enough to create a dialogue with categories of domination according to gender dimensions. We cannot forget that the powerful Western patriarchal system is, indeed, articulated and constructed around other classifications, from social classes, racial and ethnic groups, to sexual identities and nationalities.

NOTES

1. Nash, Jennifer. "Re-thinking Intersectionality," in *Feminist Review* 89, no. 1 (2008): 12–13.

2. Phoenix, Ann, and Pamela Pattynama. "Intersectionality," *European Journal of Women's Studies* 13, no. 3 (2006): 187.

3. Brah, Avtar, and Ann Phoenix. "Ain't I a Woman? Revisiting Intersectionality," in *Journal of International Women's Studies* 5, no. 3 (2004): 75.

4. Bilge, Sirma. De l'analogie à l'articulation: théoriser la différentiation sociale et l'inégalité complexe," *L'homme et la société* 2–3, no. 1 (2010): 44.

5. Collins, Patricia H. "Social Inequality, Power, and Politics: Intersectionality and American Pragmatism in Dialogue," *The Journal of Speculative Philosophy*, 26, no. 2, (2012): 444.

6. Hancock, Ange-Marie. "Intersectionality as a Normative and Empirical Paradigm," *Politics and Gender* 3, no. 2 (2007): 248.

7. Bilge, Sirma. "Théorisations féministes de l'intersectionnalité," *Diogèn* 225, no. 1 (2009): 74–75.

8. Perez, Daniel. "Chicana Aesthetics: A View of Unconcealed Alterities and Affirmations of Chicana Identity through Laura Aguilar's Photographic Images," *LUX* 2, no. 1 (2013): 1.

9. Perez, "Chicana Aesthetics," 22.

10. Crenshaw, Kimberlé. "Demarginalizing the Intersection of Race and Sex: A Black Feminist Critique of Antidiscrimination Doctrine, Feminist Theory, and Antiracist Politics," in *Feminist Legal Theory: Readings in Law and Gender edited by Barlett, Katharine T. et al.* (New York: Routledge, 2018), 58.

11. Collins, "Social Inequality," 242–43.

12. Platero, Rachel Lucas. "¿Es el análisis interseccional una metodología feminista y queer?," in *Otras formas de (re)conocer. Reflexiones, herramientas y aplicaciones desde la investigación feminista* (Bilbao: Instituto Hegoa, 2014), 82.

13. Platero, Rachel Lucas. *Intersecciones: cuerpos y sexualidades en la encrucijada.* (Barcelona: Bellaterra, 2012), 22.

14. Waldinger, Roger, and David Fitzgerald. "Transnationalism in Question," *American Journal of Sociology* 109, no. 5 (2004): 1177–78.

15. Waldinger and Fitzgerald, "Transnationalism in Question," 1178.

16. Waldinger and Fitzgerald, "Transnationalism in Question," 1185.

17. Waldinger and Fitzgerald, "Transnationalism in Question," 1178.

18. Glick-Schiller, Nina, Linda Basch, and Cristina Szanton-Blanc. *Towards a Transnational Perspective on Migration: Race, Class, Ethnicity, and Nationalism Reconsidered* (New York: New York Academy of Sciences, 1992), 25–52.

19. Dinerman, Ina R. *Migrants and Stay-at-Homes: A Comparative Study of Rural Migration from Michoacan, Mexico* (La Jolla: Center for US-Mexican Studies, U of California, 1982), 78.

20. Guarnizo, Luis, Alejandro Portes, and William J. Haller. "Assimilation and Transnationalism: Determinants of Transnational Political Action among Contemporary Migrants," *American Journal of Sociology* 108, no. 1 (2003): 1211.

21. Glick-Schiller, Nina, and Georges Fouron. "Everywhere We Go, We Are in Danger: Ti Manno and the Emergence of a Haitian Transnational Identity," *American Ethnologist* 17, no. 2 (1990): 341.

22. Magliano, María José. "Interseccionalidad y migraciones: potencialidades y desafíos." *Estudios Feministas* 23, no. 3 (2015): 693.

23. Anthias, Floya. "Género, etnicidad, clase y migración: interseccionalidad y pertenencia translocalizacional," in In *Feminismos periféricos* (Granada: Alhulia, 2006), 66.

24. Anthias, Floya. "Género, etnicidad, clase y migración: interseccionalidad y pertenencia translocalizacional:, in *Feminisismo periféricos* edited by Rocío Medina Martín (Granada Alhulia, 2006), 66.

25. Hondagneu-Sotello, Pirrette. "La incorporación del género a la migración: 'no solo para feministas ni solo para las familias," in *El país transnacional: migración mexicana y cambio social a través de la frontera* (Mexico: UNAM, 2007), 426.

26. Jones, Amelia. "Performing the Other as Self: Cindy Sherman and Laura Aguilar Pose the Subject," in *Interfaces: women, autobiography, image, performance* (Arbor: U of Michigan P, 2005), 69.

27. Jones, "Performing the Other as Self," in *Interfaces: women, authobiography, image, performance* edited by Ellen G. Friedman (Arbor: U of Michigan P, 2005), 69.

28. Mulvey, Laura. *Visual and Other Pleasures* (Houndmills, Basingstoke; New York: Palgrave Macmillan, 2009), 15.

29. Kafka, Phillipa. *(Out)Classed Women: Contemporary Chicana Writers on Inequitable Gendered Power Relations* (Westport: Greenwood Press, 2000), 12.

30. Berger, John. *Ways of Seeing* (London & New York: BBC / Penguin Books, 1972), 47.

31. Trinidad Galván, Ruth. "Campesina Epistemologies and Pedagogies of the Spirit: Examining Women's Sobrevivencia," in *Chicana/Latina Education in Everyday Life: Feminista Perspectives on Pedagogy and Epistemology* (New York: State U of New York P, 2006), 169.

32. LeBesco, Kathleen. *Revolting Bodies? The Struggle to Redefine Fat Identity* (Amherst: U of Massachusetts P, 2004), 7–8.

33. Sedgwick Kosofky, Eve. *Tendencies* (Durham: Duke UP, 1993), 8.

34. Grosz, Elizabeth. *Volatile Bodies: Toward a Corporeal Feminism. Theories of Representation and Difference* (Bloomington: Indiana UP, 1994), viii.

35. Gonzales, Manuel G. *Mexicanos: A History of Mexicans in the United States* (Bloomington: Indiana UP, 2009), 266.

36. Lévi-Strauss, Claude. *The Savage Mind (La Pensée Sauvage)* (London: Weidenfeld & Nicolson, 1966), 204.

37. Vidal, Edgard. "Trayectoria de una obra: 'A Negra' (1923) de Tarsila Do Amaral. Una revolución icónica" *Artelogie* 1, no. 1 (2011): 1.

38. Allen, Ansgar, and Roy Goddard. "The Domestication of Foucault: Government, Critique, War," *History of the Human Sciences* 27, no. 5 (2014): 28.

39. Brown, Wendy. *Walled States, Waning Sovereignty* (New York: Zone Books, 2010), 28.

40. Barroso, Costa, Barroso, Carmen, and Costa, Albertina De Oliveira. *Mulher, Mulheres* (São Paulo: Cortez Editora: Fundação Carlos Chagas, 1983), 73–88.

41. Lugones, María. "Multiculturalismo radical y feminismos de mujeres de color," in *Revista Internacional de Filosofía Política* 25 (2005): 61.

BIBLIOGRAPHY

Allen, Ansgar, and Roy Goddard. "The Domestication of Foucault: Government, Critique, War." *History of the Human Sciences* 27, no. 5 (2014): 26–53.

Anthias, Floya. "Género, etnicidad, clase y migración: interseccionalidad y pertenencia translocalizacional." In *Feminismos periféricos*, edited by Pilar Rodríguez, 49–68. Granada: Alhulia, 2006.

Anzaldúa, Gloria. *Borderlands = La Frontera*. 2nd ed. San Francisco: Aunt Lute Books, 1999.

Barroso, Costa, Barroso, Carmen, and Costa, Albertina De Oliveira. *Mulher, Mulheres*. São Paulo: Cortez Editora: Fundação Carlos Chagas, 1983.

Barthes, Roland. *Camera Lucida: Reflections on Photography*. New York: Hill and Wang, 1981.

Berger, John. *Ways of Seeing*. London & New York: BBC / Penguin Books, 1972.

Bilge, Sirma. "Théorisations féministes de l'intersectionnalité." *Diogèn* 225, no. 1 (2009): 70–88.

———. "De l'analogie à l'articulation: théoriser la différentiation sociale et l'inégalité complexe." *L'homme et la société* 2–3, no. 1 (2010): 43–65.

Brah, Avtar, and Ann Phoenix. "Ain't I a Woman? Revisiting Intersectionality." *Journal of International Women's Studies* 5, no. 3 (2004): 75–86.

Brown, Wendy. *Walled States, Waning Sovereignty*. New York: Zone Books, 2010.

Crenshaw, Kimberle. "Demarginalizing the Intersection of Race and Sex: A Black Feminist Critique of Antidiscrimination Doctrine, Feminist Theory, and Antiracist Politics." In *Feminist Legal Theory: Readings in Law and Gender*, edited by Katharine T. Bartlett and Rosanne Kennedy, 57–80. New York: Routledge, 2018.

Collins, Patricia H. "Social Inequality, Power, and Politics: Intersectionality and American Pragmatism in Dialogue." *The Journal of Speculative Philosophy*, 26, no. 2 (2012): 442–57.

Collins, Patricia H. *Black Feminist Thought: Knowledge, Consciousness, and the Politics of Empowerment.* 2nd ed. New York; London: Routledge, 2000.

Dinerman, Ina R. *Migrants and Stay-at-Homes: A Comparative Study of Rural Migration from Michoacan, Mexico.* La Jolla: Center for US-Mexican Studies, U of California, 1982.

Foucault, Michel, Michel. *The Birth of Biopolitics Lectures at the Collège de France, 1978–79,* edited by M. Senellart et al. Basingstoke / New York: Palgrave Macmillan, 2008.

Glick-Schiller, Nina, Linda Basch, and Cristina Szanton-Blanc. *Towards a Transnational Perspective on Migration: Race, Class, Ethnicity, and Nationalism Reconsidered.* New York: New York Academy of Sciences, 1992.

Glick-Schiller, Nina, and Georges Fouron. "Everywhere We Go, We Are in Danger: Ti Manno and the Emergence of a Haitian Transnational Identity." *American Ethnologist* 17, no. 2 (1990): 329–47.

Gonzales, Manuel G. *Mexicanos: A History of Mexicans in the United States.* Bloomington: Indiana UP, 2009.

Gouges, Olympe de. "Declaración de los derechos de la mujer y de la ciudadana." *Culturamas: La Revista de Información Cultural en Internet* September 7, 2012. Accessed November 26, 2019. http://www.culturamas.es/blog/2012/09/07/decl aracion-de-los-derechos-de-la-mujer-y-de-la-ciudadana-1791-por-olympe-de-go uges/

Grosz, Elizabeth. *Volatile Bodies: Toward a Corporeal Feminism. Theories of Representation and Difference.* Bloomington: Indiana UP, 1994.

Guarnizo, Luis, Alejandro Portes, and William J. Haller. "Assimilation and Transnationalism: Determinants of Transnational Political Action among Contemporary Migrants." *American Journal of Sociology* 108, no. 1 (2003): 1211–48.

Hancock, Ange-Marie. "Intersectionality as a Normative and Empirical Paradigm." *Politics and Gender* 3, no. 2 (2007): 248–54.

Hondagneu-Sotelo, Pirrette. "La incorporación del género a la migración: 'no solo para feministas ni solo para las familias.'" In *El país transnacional: migración mexicana y cambio social a través de la frontera,* edited by Marina Ariza y Alejandro Portes, 423–51. Mexico: UNAM, 2007.

Jones, Amelia. "Performing the Other as Self: Cindy Sherman and Laura Aguilar Pose the Subject." In *Interfaces: women, autobiography, image, performance,* edited by Sidonie Smith, 79–82. Ann Arbor: U of Michigan P, 2005.

Kafka, Phillipa. *(Out)Classed Women: Contemporary Chicana Writers on Inequitable Gendered Power Relations.* Westport: Greenwood Press, 2000.

Keating, AnaLouise. *EntreMundos/AmongWorlds: New Perspectives on Gloria Anzaldua.* New York: Palgrave Macmillan, 2005.

LeBesco, Kathleen. *Revolting Bodies? The Struggle to Redefine Fat Identity.* Amherst: U of Massachusetts P, 2004.

Lévi-Strauss, Claude. *The Savage Mind (La Pensée Sauvage).* London: Weidenfeld & Nicolson, 1966.

Lugones, María. "Multiculturalismo radical y feminismos de mujeres de color." *Revista Internacional de Filosofía Política* 25 (2005): 61–76.

Magliano, María José. "Interseccionalidad y migraciones: potencialidades y desafíos." *Estudios Feministas* 23, no. 3 (2015): 691–712.

Matto De Turner, Clorinda. *Aves sin nido.* Barcelona: Linkgua, 2013.

Massey, Douglas S., Rafael Alarcón, Jorge Durand, and Humberto González. *Return to Aztlan: The social process of international migration from Western Mexico.* Berkeley: U of California P, 1987.

Mulvey, Laura. *Visual and Other Pleasures.* 2nd ed. Houndmills, Basingstoke; New York: Palgrave Macmillan, 2009.

Nash, Jennifer. "Re-thinking Intersectionality." *Feminist Review* 89, no. 1 (2008): 1–15.

Perez, Daniel. "Chicana Aesthetics: A View of Unconcealed Alterities and Affirmations of Chicana Identity through Laura Aguilar's Photographic Images." *LUX* 2, no. 1 (2013): 1–8.

Phoenix, Ann, and Pamela Pattynama. "Intersectionality." *European Journal of Women's Studies* 13, no. 3 (2006): 187–92.

Platero, Rachel Lucas. *Intersecciones: cuerpos y sexualidades en la encrucijada.* Barcelona: Bellaterra, 2012.

———. "¿Es el análisis interseccional una metodología feminista y queer?" In *Otras formas de (re)conocer. Reflexiones, herramientas y aplicaciones desde la investigación feminista*, edited by I. MendiaAzkue et al., 9–98. Bilbao: Instituto Hegoa, 2014.

Sedgwick Kosofky, Eve. *Tendencies.* Durham: Duke UP, 1993.

Trinidad Galván, Ruth. "Campesina Epistemologies and Pedagogies of the Spirit: Examining Women's Sobrevivencia." In *Chicana/Latina Education in Everyday Life: Feminista Perspectives on Pedagogy and Epistemology*, edited by Dolores Delgado Bernal, C. Alejandra Elenes, Francisca E. Godinez, and Sofia Villenas, 131–48. New York: State U of New York P, 2006.

Waldinger, Roger, and David Fitzgerald. "Transnationalism in Question." *American Journal of Sociology* 109, no. 5 (2004): 1177–95.

Vidal, Edgard. "Trayectoria de una obra: 'A Negra' (1923) de Tarsila Do Amaral. Una revolución icónica." *Artelogie* 1, no. 1 (2011): 1–19.

Chapter 7

The Transformative Experience of the New Continent in Maruja Mallo's Art

María Alejandra Zanetta

Maruja Mallo (Vivero, Lugo, 1902—Madrid, 1995) is one of the most interesting artists of the Spanish avant-garde. At the age of twenty, she moved to Madrid to study painting at the San Fernando Academy of the Arts. While attending the academy, she befriended many artists, thinkers, writers, and poets connected to the famous *Residencia de Estudiantes*, such as the surrealist painter Salvador Dalí, the poet Federico García Lorca, and the filmmaker Luis Buñuel. La *Residencia de Estudiantes* in Madrid offered one of the most vivid and prolific experiences of scientific and artistic creation and exchange in interwar Europe. From its beginnings, it was conceived as a house open to creation, thought, and interdisciplinary dialogue very similar to the model of English colleges. The model of teaching in the Residence was based on direct contact between teachers and students, collective effort, and personal responsibility.[1] Mallo thrived in the liberal-minded, collaborative, and experimental environment of the Residence. From the beginning of her career Mallo questioned and rejected the masculine construction of "the feminine" and challenged the restrictive social norms that were intended to keep women out of the political, intellectual, and artistic activity of the time. Politically, Mallo opposed the conservative classes and the church who supported the reactionary monarchy of Alfonso XIII (1886–1931) and the dictatorial government of General Miguel Primo de Rivera (1923–1930).[2] In relation to Mallo's political thinking, Shirley Mangini explains that Mallo vehemently rejected the lack of humanity exhibited by the aristocracy and the conservative class who ignored the hardships of the lower classes and did nothing to improve the living conditions of the neediest people.[3]

On April 14, 1931, the Spanish Second Republic was proclaimed after the deposition of King Alfonso XIII. Mallo supported the newly democratically elected government and enthusiastically embraced its ideals of social justice

177

and its progressive agenda. Mallo wholeheartedly believed that the social reforms enacted by the Spanish Republic would enable the formation of a new egalitarian and inclusive social system for Spain. Unfortunately, these social reforms were met with dread by the same reactionary and conservative forces that had backed the monarchy of the deposed king and the dictatorship of General Miguel Primo de Rivera. In 1936, a military coup supported by the conservative establishment, the army, and the church, and led by General Francisco Franco started the Spanish Civil War. The bloody confrontation, which lasted until 1939, culminated with the defeat of the democratically elected Republican government and the establishment of a brutal fascist dictatorship under General Francisco Franco.

Due to her vocal support of the Spanish Republic, and aware of the serious threat that she would face if she were to stay in Spain, Mallo managed to flee the country in 1937. When Mallo arrived in Buenos Aires in 1937, she was leaving behind the horrors of the Spanish Civil War. Mallo was deeply affected by the traumatic moments she had experienced during the last months she had spent in Galicia, hidden from the nationalist forces of the Franco regime who were executing and incarcerating her comrades and loved ones.[4] The egalitarian social order that the Spanish Republic had tried to establish, one in which Mallo deeply believed, crumbled in front of her eyes. The American continent, with its diverse races, religions, and geographies presented itself as a beginning full of promise, the possibility of a new life. Mallo was deeply moved by the exuberance of America's nature, especially the magnificent shells she collected with the poet Pablo Neruda[5] while exploring with him the Chilean beaches of the Pacific.[6]

During her long exile in South America, which lasted until 1964, Mallo frequently visited Uruguay and Brazil. During those trips, she became very interested in the syncretism of Afro-Uruguayan and Afro-Brazilian religions and in the powerful and visually striking rituals of Candomblé, a religion found primarily in Brazil and in Uruguay with elements derived from African cultures.[7] Mallo had always been interested in spiritual and philosophical traditions as an alternative to the Judeo-Christian tradition, and therefore, the animism of Candomblé exerted a powerful attraction over her. Mallo was a fierce opponent of the Catholic Church, both as a political institution and as a belief system. The artist believed that the church as a political institution that supported the fascist regime of Franco and of the Nationalist party had a nefarious influence in Spain and was complicit in maintaining an unjust social order that only benefited a few while oppressing the majority. Mallo also considered that the church's belief system reinforced and propagated oppressive gender norms that segregated women and kept them chained to their so-called biological destiny.

From the very beginning of her artistic career, Mallo employed her art both to condemn the patriarchal and conservative social order that excluded women and the working classes, and to propose new systems of beliefs that would enable the emergence of a truly democratic world. The series of paintings under the titles *Naturalezas Vivas*, *Retratos Bidimensionales*, and *Máscaras*, which were created during her American exile, are both a result of her transnational experience and a continuation of Mallo's long-standing search for a truly republican order. A few months before the outbreak of the civil war, Mallo began to paint the series *La religión del trabajo*, which she later continued in exile. These paintings visually articulate Mallo's unwavering faith in the eventual victory of the democratic values that were under attack by the repressive forces that toppled the Republican government. In *La religión del trabajo*, Mallo visually communicates the spiritual values of the new social order. In one of her lectures titled "Proceso histórico de la forma en las artes plásticas," Mallo describes the purpose of artistic creation. For her, art provides the iconography that expresses a new spiritual and social order:

> The new civilization, in bringing with it a new humanity bearing a new mythology, a new social and material structure, had to provide a new plastic order, new forms of expression . . . Nature, history and art are eternally linked together. Consciously or unconsciously, art is a form of propaganda. Revolutionary art is a weapon used by society in full possession of its faculties against one that is disintegrating. The new art is not a weapon but a result; it is the incarnation, the symbol, of a new society.[8]

Therefore, the paintings in this series embodied the principles she considered essential to overcome, once for all, inequality, exclusion, and oppression in all its forms.

The first group of paintings of *La Religión del trabajo* were directly inspired by the Workers' March that took place in Madrid on May 1, 1936, only two months before the outbreak of the Spanish Civil War. During that event, Mallo was captivated by the sight of a worker marching and holding a loaf of bread in her hand. Mallo explained the significance of this event in 1977 in an interview with Juan Manuel Bonet:

> On May 1st, 1936 we watched from Columbus square the popular worker's march. Watching a procession of notables pass by, I realized that if the Republic depended on these men, however honest as they were, it was doomed. In contrast, the proletarian groups marched with impressive decision. Suddenly an arm appeared, holding, as in Eucharistic consecration, a huge loaf of bread. That's where the picture comes from . . . that Castilla la nueva, so different from the sinister Castilla la vieja, is what inspired *El canto de las espigas*, which I painted in Buenos Aires.[9]

For Mallo, the image of the worker holding the loaf of bread symbolized the emergence of a proletarian order that would carry out the revolutionary project that Mallo dreamed for Spain. The painting *El canto de las espigas*,[10] as Mallo states, was directly inspired by this vision. In this painting, Mallo represents the Greek goddess Demeter, at the time of her transformation into wheat. Demeter was the goddess of the harvest and of fertility, and presided over the cycle of life and death associated with the natural order. Wheat, for Mallo, was the symbol of a humanistic and egalitarian order. In relation to the meaning of wheat in this painting, Mallo explains that wheat is "the universal vegetable, symbol of social struggle, terrestrial myth. It is the physical manifestation of a belief that arises from the severity and grace of the two Castillas, from my materialistic faith in the triumph of the fish, in the rule of the wheat spike."[11] The materialistic faith Mallo refers to is her unwavering belief in the republican project. Mallo dedicated this series to the fishermen and peasants of her beloved country, who, for her, embodied the democratic ideal of the Spanish Second Republic. Moreover, the wheat spikes motif was one of the most widespread symbols of the Spanish Republic.[12] Therefore, the archetype of the telluric mother symbolizes the rise of a new social arrangement alternative to the patriarchal society that had failed to establish a democratic system. In order to achieve social justice and to eliminate oppression, humankind needed to find a new way of moving forward, leaving behind the exploitation of people and nature.[13] The telluric and permeable trinity represented in this painting, with her body completely open to nature, personifies the natural network that connects all species, as expressed by the artist through the network of spikes that envelops the deity.

La religión del trabajo reflects Mallo's profound admiration for the natural order. As she expressed many times, she wanted to emulate nature, to paint like nature.[14] Nature, for Mallo, personified a supreme intelligence that rationally maintained the universal balance on the concepts of complementariness and connectivity. This balance is based on what is known as the Golden ratio or Divine proportion, a mathematical formula that is found throughout the universe; from the spiral of a Nautilus seashell to the helixes of galaxies. In the paintings of *La religión del trabajo*, these ideas are visually articulated through the way in which Mallo geometrically arranges the compositional space, the symbols she employs, and the characterization of the divinities that populate these canvasses. The female protagonists, who exhibit somewhat androgynous features, look like ancestral goddesses of matriarchal religions closely connected with the natural order. Mallo seems to propose a new materialistic principle that is defined as contrary to the patriarchal religion of European Christian culture. Unlike the Catholic imagery where the role of women is reduced to that of mother and wife, in Mallo's new mythology we find ourselves in front of a universe of ambiguous beings with the potentialities of both genders in themselves. The androgyny of these figures relates to the symbolism of the hermaphrodite, a being that incorporates within itself the possibilities of both genders. The hermaphrodite is the result of the application of the symbolism of the number two to the human being, thus creating a fully integrated personality despite its duality.[15] This harmonious integration sharply contrasts with the emphasis that the patriarchal order places on difference and exclusion through the categorization of the feminine as a different and inferior "Other."[16] Mallo's new religion proposes a new world in which opposition, exclusion, and imbalance are replaced by complementariness, inclusion, and harmony.

In time, and due to the impact of the new natural American surroundings, Mallo substituted the androgynous characters of the *Religión del trabajo* with natural elements alluding to the same principle of the union of opposites. The paintings of this new America-inspired series, entitled *Naturalezas Vivas*, further develop the idea of a harmonious new order inextricably united with the natural world previously expressed in *La Religión del trabajo*. In these paintings, we can clearly see the deep impression that the exuberance of the beaches of the Atlantic and Pacific oceans, their vegetation, and their seashells made on Mallo. In *Naturalezas Vivas*,[17] Mallo once again found hope in the natural order, the only alternative to the destructive irrationality of the androcentric and anthropocentric value system. Mallo was very influenced by the Pythagorean school of thought as well as by the ideas of the Uruguayan painter and theorist Torres García, whom she met in 1933. In his writings, Torres García advised "to keep the measure and affirm that essential faith, as the Pythagorean wanted, in universal harmony, since our improvement can only be obtained by the acquiescence to the intelligence and the soul of the harmonious laws that govern the universe."[18] The vertical arrangement of the elements in these paintings reminds us of tribal totems. The totem represents a mystical bond within a group. In prehistoric societies, totems were crucial religious symbols built to maintain social cohesion and to transmit the cultural values of the community. Mallo's totems convey a new concept of humanity which does not conceive itself as the center of the universe but as a part of the cosmic order. In this way, when representing plants, seashells, and marine animals in a relationship of interdependence, the artist reminds us of the importance of a model of coexistence based on respect, collaboration, and equality. The concept of cosmic balance is represented once more with the union of masculine and feminine elements. The masculine polarity is denoted by conches or algae that end in tips or elongated shapes of clear phallic connotations. These invariably connect vertically with feminine elements, symbolized by seashells, marine stars, eggs with permeable centers that closely resemble the female genitalia.

Mallo reminds us of the need to adopt a concept of nonhierarchical identity based on heterogeneity and inclusion. Inher art, Mallo expresses many
of the ideas that would be later articulated by ecological feminist, therefore
anticipating one of the main principles of ecofeminist thought which states
that, it is precisely the hierarchical and individualistic conception typical
of the androcentric mind, that justifies the exclusion and abuse of all those
considered inferior, starting with the natural world. The message of these
paintings is very similar to that of deep ecologists for whom humanity's failure to identify with the rest of nature is the result of a masculine viewpoint
from which the world is perceived and organized. This branch of ecological
feminism believes that anthropocentrism is the cause that has led humanity
to its separation from nonhuman nature and to the environmental crisis that
threatens the survival of the planet.[19] As an alternative, they propose a process
of personal transformation based on the cultivation of a "biocentric" perspective which expands the identification of oneself with the entire natural world.
It is evident that Mallo decided to adopt a similar biocentric perspective when
she created the *Naturalezas Vivas* series in order to articulate most clearly her
condemnation of the patriarchal order and of what the Australian philosopher
Val Plumwood would decades later define as its logic of domination.[20]

At the same time as *Naturalezas Vivas*, Mallo created a series of paintings of female heads, representative of different racial types, which she titled
Retratos bidimensionales.[21] These monumental feminine heads, geometrically
constructed, and representing different races, become cosmic symbols of a new
inclusive egalitarian order inspired by the natural and racial diversity she found
in the American continent. Regarding the egalitarian dream that Mallo expresses
in these paintings, art historian Estrella De Diego raises the possibility that
Mallo's interest in the concept of race could have been partly inspired by Ruth
Benedict and her book entitled *Raza*, which was published in Spanish in Mexico
in 1941. Benedict, an American anthropologist, was, according to De Diego,
"very influenced by her passionate egalitarianism among human races."[22] As
Carlos L. Bernárdez points out, these paintings of female heads express "a dream
of a superior humanity, synthesis of all races, the opposite of any racism."[23]

At the same time Mallo painted *Retratos bidimensionales*, she created
the series titled *Máscaras*. This fourth series, which was deeply influenced
by the magical rituals of Candomblé, continues to express the same idea of
an egalitarian social order inextricably bound to nature. As José Luis Ferris
explains, Mallo was very attracted to the religions of the indigenous peoples
of the Americas and spent short periods in indigenous villages to learn their
ways of life and their religions: "From Brazil to Peru, there was magic and
esoteric arts, the delicious crossbreeding of America and Africa, the ethnicities at a pure crossroads, La Macumba, Vodú and Candomblé, the African
rites resounding in the New Continent to enrich the inexhaustible imagery of

Maruja Mallo."[24] The *Máscaras* paintings emerge, therefore, from Mallo's personal contact with the religious ceremonies of Vudú, Candomblé, and Macumba.

The Afro-Brazilian religion of Candomblé reflects Brazil's cross-national mestizo identity and symbolizes the aspirations of Brazil to become a fully racially integrated nation. The concept of Brazilian identity has been reformulated in large part by the efforts of Brazilian Regionalism, which, since 1930, has proposed an image of Brazil as a country proud of its mulatto or mestizo identity.[25] From 1930, as J. Lorand Matory explains, Candomblé became the ideal to aspire to as a nation. By the 1980s, Candomblé became the emblem "of the regions' status as an exemplar and bastion against alienation and marginalization of people of numerous regions, races, classes, and genders in Brazil."[26]

The social aspect of Candomblé must have resonated strongly with Mallo and her lifelong search for a true egalitarian order. In addition to its democratic nature, Candomblé is a religion that empowers its followers to find happiness and balance in the here and now and not in the afterlife. Like many other belief systems alternative to the Judeo-Christian tradition, Candomblé is a practical, here-and-now belief system that does not separate the spiritual and material aspects of human beings.[27] Mallo, like her friend, the philosopher María Zambrano, rejected the imbalance and alienation caused by the exclusionary value system of the rationalist patriarchal mind. Far from rejecting the materiality of life as inferior to the realm of thought and spirit, and realizing that human existence is a situated one, Mallo and Zambrano strongly believed that any living organism could not aspire to find harmony and happiness in a realm separated from the physical world. The "poetic reason" ("razón poética") postulated by Zambrano as an alternative to the prevailing rationalism of her time was a new methodology suitable for the elaboration of a humanistic anthropological philosophy committed to understanding life and helping humans find the truth in the here and now. Zambrano's philosophy proposed overcoming the dualisms of Cartesian rationalism. These dualisms, based on oppositional hierarchies, privileged the aspects related to reason—associated with masculine attributes—and discredited nonrational forms of knowledge considered "feminine." Mallo and Zambrano believed that this androcentric premise, built upon an interpretation of human nature that assumed the universality of a masculine model of humanity, produced a selfish vision of humankind that promoted individual fulfillment at the expense of nature or any other living organism considered inferior.[28] Therefore, the concept of an afterlife in a detached spiritual world was very problematic for Mallo because it devalued the natural world and appeased the masses with the promise of a paradise to be achieved through sacrifice, resignation, and acceptance of a profoundly unjust social order.[29]

As a religion for the living, as opposed to a religion of salvation directed toward the hereafter, Candomblé "resonates with the power to improve the lives of people during their brief passage through *aiè* (the world of mortals). Dedicated to the liberation of mortals during this and not the next life, Candomblé has a powerful appeal for the descendants of Africans as well as for an increasing number of Brazilians of European ancestry."[30] Mãe Val, the spiritual leader of the *Terreiro de Cobre*, one of the places of worship in Salvador Bahia, sees Candomblé as resistance to all forms of oppression. When the followers gather in the terreiro to worship with her, they do so to bring spiritual strength to their lives, to gather spiritual energy, and to help them in their social struggle. It is in the sacred space of the *terreiro* that Candomblé practitioners collect their energies and empower themselves to face their individual and collective problems.[31] Consequently, when Mallo came in contact with Candomblé, she was immediately fascinated by the intertwining of material and spiritual transcendence. For her, Candomblé came to embody the new egalitarian and democratic order she dreamed of for Spain, and a symbol of the ability of all men and women to overcome their obstacles and to transcend their limitations in the here and now.[32]

Another aspect of Candomblé that mirrored Mallo's thinking relates to its nonanthropocentric and nonandrocentric nature. One of Candomblé's most important principles is the belief that every living organism has to live in harmony with its surroundings, feeding and benefiting from the universal energy that connects them all in a harmonious whole. In many ways, Candomblé has many points of connection with Torres García's Universal Constructivism and with theosophy. For Torres García, the Universal man is "a synthesis of the highest human aspiration . . . The Universal Man occupies the greater side of the Golden Rule. The Universal Man is a trinity: it is the universal reason: it is the universal moral spirit of nature; and it is the universal physical life, forming those three things a unit: the cosmos. Universus: an indivisible whole."[33] In Torres García's constructive universalism, as in theosophy, another important source of inspiration for Mallo, the most crucial principles are based on the equality of all, regardless of differences of gender, race, or religion and on the respect for all living forms. Nature is central to these systems of thought, and universal harmony depends on the harmonious coexistence of all beings. In Candomblé's cosmology, *axé* is the vital force of existence: "As the life-giving nutrient of the material and spiritual realms, *axé* represents power, energy, and strength. Without it, existence would be paralyzed, deprived of possibility and action. All that is material and spiritual—divinities, humans, plants, animals, or rocks—is endowed with its own innate level and quality of *axé*."[34] Happiness and harmony can only be achieved when our energy connects with the existential energy of the cosmos and of all living things. As J. Lorand Matory explains, for many Brazilians,

Candomblé, as a religion of nature, embodied the opposite of all the bad of the constituted social order and civilization:

> Environmentalism is only the latest transnational movement with which Candomblé, has entered into dialogue . . . There have been several references in the Candomblé, to the veneration of "nature" (to nature), both as a term for one's personal "nature" and as a construction of nonhuman flora, fauna, and minerals. These days, Mãe Aninha, the founder of the African purist Opô Afonjá temple, is regularly quoted as saying something like, "Don't even pluck a single leaf or snap the smallest branch from a tree, for it is like breaking an arm. A tree is like a person, and must be respected as such."[35]

It is interesting to note that the same concept of interconnectivity among species is essential in theosophy and occultism and it is expressed very similarly by H. P. Blavatsky, the cofounder of the Theosophical Society in 1875.[36] As Helen V. Zahara explains in relation to the thought of the Russian occultist, in the mundane existence of every day "all men are truly brothers" and "to injure another is to injure oneself, and that our responsibility towards life in all its forms, in all kingdoms of nature, is much greater than we may have realized."[37] These two main characteristics of Candomblé echoed Mallo's vision of a nonandrocentric and anthropocentric social order based on inclusiveness, social justice, and respect. America, for Mallo, equated to a new beginning in a new continent far from the old and crumbling European social order. Therefore, Candomblé was perceived by her as the religion of this new world, the possibility of transformation and rebirth both in a literal and symbolic way.

If we observe the paintings of this period, we notice that they represent religious rituals which take place by the sea (figure 1). One of the most important deities or *orixás*, in Candomblé, is the Goddess Yemanjá, who originally comes from the ancient Yoruba mythology as the goddess of the ocean. According to the spiritual concepts of Candomblé, Yemanjá represents

Figure 7.1   Maruja Mallo, "Cuatro máscaras" (c. 1948). *Source*: © 2019 Artists Rights Society (ARS), New York/VEGAP, Madrid.

the essence of motherhood. Every year in February, thousands of Yemanjá devotees participate in a colorful celebration in her honor. Dressed in the traditional white garb, Yemanjá's followers gather on the beaches or on the river banks to leave her offerings. Dancing in a circle, singing ancestral Yoruba chants, and praying, her devotees sometimes enter into a trance and become possessed by the spirit of the goddess.[38] As O'Connell and Airey explain, the art of African, American, and Oceanian indigenous cultures evolved in intimate association with religion and magic. Tribal art, rarely of a decorative nature, expresses the common desire of humanity to live in harmony with the natural and supernatural forces to which they are exposed and on which they depend for their survival. The masks are often linked to shamanistic ritual practices and are designed to transform the wearer and connect it with the magical powers of the spiritual world.[39] When we observe Mallo's *Máscaras* paintings, we see that she places the masks either in the middle of the water (figures 2, 3, and 4) or in a liminal space between the sea and the beach (figure 1). The sea, for Mallo, connotes the idea of returning to the origin and, like in Candomblé, is associated with the maternal womb, with the primordial waters, with the origin of life, and with the evolution of the species. If we consider the importance of the mask as a ritual object destined to connect the human being with superior spirits, and the symbolism of the sea as the origin of life and the evolution of the species, Mallo seems to be emphasizing the changing character of the individual, from which humanity evolves

Figure 7.2   Maruja Mallo, "Máscaras" (s/f). *Source*: © 2019 Artists Rights Society (ARS), New York/VEGAP, Madrid.

to its highest evolutionary stage. The concept of the sea as the primordial water from which a new superior humanity emerges is also articulated in the murals Mallo painted for the movie theater Los Ángeles in Buenos Aires around the same time she painted the *Máscaras* series. In these murals, the five races are the result of the highest evolutionary stage in which humanity finally has learned to coexist harmoniously with each other and with all living organisms. Mallo depicts these five races dancing in a circular motion which is aligned with the cosmic movement of rotation.[40] Therefore, the highest evolutionary stage for Mallo would be one that is free at last from restrictive categorizations and exclusions.

It is interesting to note that in the Yoruba diaspora, and especially in Bahia, Yemanjá is "polythetic, that is, she is named and defined through a combination of features and meanings rather than through one monotypic attribute."[41] Moreover, the liminal quality of these ritualistic spaces also emphasizes fluidity and openness over clear demarcations and separating borders. The symbolic nature of liminality is, according to Arnold Van Gennep, closely connected with the rites of passage in which the subject occupies a transitional space.[42] Furthermore, one of the essential characteristics of liminal situations is the tendency to erase social hierarchies and to emphasize nature over culture.[43] As we have previously discussed, the notion of fluidity as a metaphor of a nondualistic, inclusive, and egalitarian order was already employed by Mallo in her painting *Canto de las espigas*, from the series *La Religión del trabajo* and remained a constant in her art until Mallo's death.

Mallo's concept of fluid identity resembles Iris Marion Young's idea of the self as a nonautonomous and permeable entity. In her book *Justice and the Politics of Difference*, Young suggests that "one of the main contributions of poststructuralist philosophy has been to expose as illusory this metaphysic of a unified self-making subjectivity, which posits the subject as an autonomous origin or an underlying substance to which attributes of gender, nationality, family role, intellectual disposition, and so on might attach."[44] Consequently, the choice of a liminal space in which to place both the ritual masks and Yemanjá's devotees represents Mallo's longlife dream of a new democratic order for a new humanity that transcends any sort of demarcations. As Roger Sansi points out, one of the most fundamental characteristics in Candomblé is a concept of self and body that is open and fluid. Fluidity is what allows Candomblé practitioners to heal and transform themselves during the rituals:

> The notion of the body in circulation in this context . . . is not exactly the biomedical body, but the body as a site of encounters of different agencies. To have an open body (*corpo aperto*) means to be open to external influences, at different levels, from illness, to the evil eye (*mal olhado, feitiço*) of other persons, to the influence of a shade or dead person (*encosto*).[45]

In this sense, the embodied experience of spirit possession and transformation essential to Candomblé challenges the concept of identity as a self-contained entity and replaces it with a relational concept of the self deeply connected with, and dependent upon, the energetic fields to which the body is exposed to even before its birth.[46] This model of relational identity resembles, in turn, the primordial union that the child experiences with the mother during the so-called pre-Oedipal stage. During this stage, the child experiences his or her identity as fluid and connected with the one of the mother. As the child grows older, the fluidity and openness characteristic of this stage is replaced by the Oedipal phase of identity formation in which exclusivist and hierarchical demarcations between self and other are taught and reinforced by society.[47] Therefore, the fact that these ceremonies take place by the sea in a sacred liminal space dedicated to the Goddess Yemanjá points to the concept, always present in Mallo's work, of human transcendence directly linked to a new idea of humanity free from the exclusionary model of the androcentric and anthropocentric mind.[48]

If we look again at the *Máscaras* paintings, we notice that Mallo repeatedly paints two masks side by side. Candomblé adherents are connected to two deities representing dichotomous forces. In order to achieve psychological

Figure 7.3   Maruja Mallo, "Máscaras" (1942). *Source*: © 2019 Artists Rights Society (ARS), New York/VEGAP, Madrid.

and spiritual balance, both dualities need to be incorporated within the self. This idea resembles the Chinese concept of the Yin and Yang which describes how opposite or contrary forces are actually complementary, interconnected, and interdependent in the natural world, and how they give rise to each other as they interrelate to one another.[49] Mallo expresses this ideal of complementarity through the facial expressions in the masks (happiness/sadness) and through their contrasting colors (white/black, blue/red). Therefore, Mallo's masks seem to represent the physical provinces of the *orixás* (Candomblé's deities), and their corresponding temperaments, which, as Voeks explains, "are clearly divisible between those that are hot- and those that are cool-tempered. This primary opposition—hot versus cold, fire versus water, masculine versus feminine—is a fundamental feature of the religion of the *orixás*, as it is practiced in Bahia, and of its attendant health and healing functions."[50]

Another motif in Mallo's art that reappears in this series is the symbolism of the numbers three and five. When we observe several of the *Máscaras* paintings, we notice that the triangle, the geometrical representation of the number three, is prominently featured in many of them. The triangle, either formed by the Candomblé practitioners who are dancing (figure 3), or by the shells positioned on top of the masks (figure 2), geometrically organizes the composition. The Pythagorean triangle symbolizes the wisdom associated with man's unity. For the Pythagoreans, the number three contains in itself the beginning, the middle, and the end. Likewise, the three was, for Pythagoras, the number of the construction of the universe. The three, in Hinduism, is represented spiritually with the third eye or Dangma, which indicates the purified soul, one that has reached the highest degree of purification.[51] As mentioned before, Mallo, from a very young age, had been interested in systems of thought and religions alternative to the Judeo-Christian tradition, such as Buddhism, Hinduism, occultism, constructive universalism, and phytagorism, and she freely combined symbols taken from all these traditions in order to express her own personal vision. Therefore, the symbolism of the two masks in conjunction with the triangular shape alludes to the process of individual transcendence necessary for the individual to become one with the harmonious cosmic order, the all-encompassing and indivisible reality. It is also important to note that the triangle is often represented in connection with shells (figure 2). The shell is a symbol associated with the feminine deity and with fertility, while the spiral in its center symbolizes the cycles of life, growth, death, and resurrection. In Candomblé, "cowry shells" are used by the priestesses during the divinatory ceremony *jogo de búzios* in which the two main deities that are within each human being are identified.[52] Therefore, the shells are very important in the evolutionary process of each individual because, if these deities are not properly identified, the *axé*, or energy that connects the practitioner with his/her divinities and with the

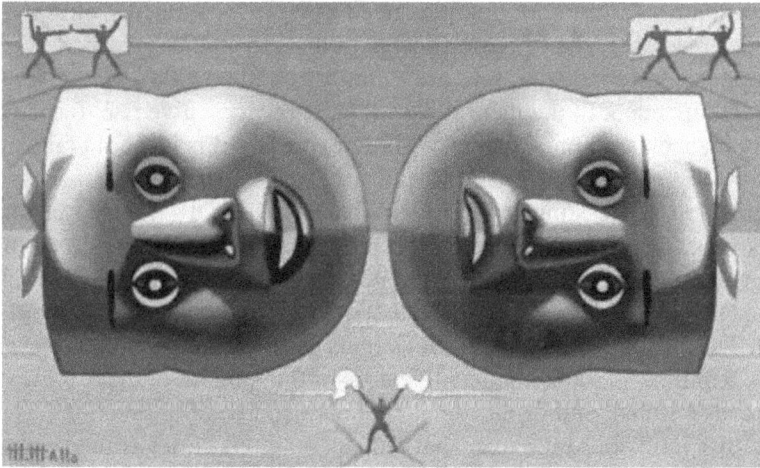

Figure 7.4   Maruja Mallo, "Dos máscaras" (1952). *Source*: © 2019 Artists Rights Society (ARS), New York/VEGAP, Madrid.

cosmos, would not flow properly, and therefore, it will impede the process of transformation and growth. Consequently, if we consider all the symbolism Mallo combines in her paintings, we notice once again that the artist proposes a new social order linked to a matriarchal system based on horizontal, fluid, and nonhierarchical relationships.

If we observe these paintings in more detail, we also notice that the triangle formed by the dancing characters is also connected to the number five since the five dancers are the ones who form the said geometrical form (figures 3 and 4). According to the Pythagoreans, five is the number of the center, of harmony and balance. It was thus the figure of the hierogamias, the marriage of the celestial and masculine principle (symbolized by the number three), and of the ground principle of the feminine mother (symbolized by the number two). It is also the symbol of mankind (with the arms separated, the body seems arranged in five parts in the form of a cross), of the universe (two axes, one vertical and one horizontal passing through the same center), and of order and perfection. Finally, the number five symbolizes the divine will that can only desire order and perfection.[53] Therefore, if we consider the symbolism attached to the number five, it is logical to conclude that the five figures in the painting are engaged in a collective ritual that connects them, and their material world, with the spiritual realm inhabited by the divinities. Attaining harmony and transcendence amounts, for Mallo, to the overcoming of all dualities under the guidance and protection of the maternal principle. It is important to note that these five figures are androgynous. This aspect, in addition to the numerical symbolism and to the location of the ritual in a womb-like space connected with the sea and with Yemanjá, reinforces the message of overcoming androcentric and anthropocentric systems of thought. The only way in which humanity could truly evolve, in Mallo's opinion, would be by embracing a new nonandrocentric order guided by the maternal principle since, as Miriam Johnson has noted, "femininity, in its maternal aspects, encourages the more androgynous principle while a masculine paradigm promotes differentiation and stratification between the sexes."[54]

Another important aspect of Candomblé ritual is the ceremonial dance. The process of overcoming limitations, and of connecting with both the energy of the universe and of the divinities, occurs during the circular dance or *roda*. This essential component of Candomblé ritual is also represented in many of the paintings of this series (figures 1, 3, and 4). Dance, as a symbol of the perfect integration between mankind and the cosmic order, is not only present in the *Máscaras* series, but is also the subject of previous paintings such as the ones with the titles *Bailarines o Bailarinas*.[55] In the *Máscaras* series, the *roda* is the symbolic realization of the continuity of the life cycle and, as the physical manifestation of the Yoruba cosmos, it makes visible the Yoruba concepts of *Orun* (spiritual realm) and *Ayé* (the material world):

> The Yoruba believe that Orun and Ayé exist in symbios is best illustrated by the continuity of the circle, which points of intersections embedded within. Orun is the center for otherworldly forces such as the orisa, and Ayé, the world, is the center for humanity. Priest and priestesses physically inhabit Ayé, but with the knowledge accrued through years of training, they are the conduits that bring Orun into the material plane. In ceremonies, while dancing in the roda, the devotees traverse between Orun and Ayé during possession asking the deities to manifest themselves in this physical plane.[56]

Moreover, the circle, in a universal way, is the symbol of the celestial and expresses the limitless. Connected to the symbology of the circle, we find the idea of perfection, homogeneity, and absence of distinction or division.[57] The circular dance materializes the divinity and makes it tangible to the community and the devotee. Consequently, dance and the circle, in which it happens, represent a space of transcendence and renewal: "The dance form allows the supplicant to touch, talk, and feel the presence of the divine, promoting communal bonding as adherents unite in the knowledge that they share in the protection and receive guidance from forces with transcendental knowledge."[58]

Furthermore, as Daniels explains, the circle is associated with Yemanjá. Therefore, the circle transforms itself into the primordial matrix in which a new humanity and a new social order are gestated. For Daniel, Yemanjá "radiates energy both inward and outward, inward around and among those of her faith and nation, but also outward to the uninitiated members."[59] The experience of communitas felt and shared by her devotees in this symbolic protective womb allows for a sense of empowerment that transcends the ritual space and affects the participants and the community in a very real and material way.[60] The communal experience of interacting with the divinity allows practitioners to free themselves from the norms that regulate the social order and to imagine and negotiate new forms of existence:

> Candomblé initiates work for the community and the society, and the efficacy of this work manifests in the transformative impact beyond the ritual ground. The discourse of power shifts in the Foucauldian order to the multidirectional narrative that the orisas represent. Power thus becomes creative and righteous agency . . . because it is an intangible force that affects all that it encompasses; it is no longer unidimensional, symptomatic of the powerful/powerless dyad, but flowing outward, touching and transforming all who are open to it, just like the axé of the orisas as possession passes from one person to the next. Power, then, it is in the hands of those with transcendental authority, not just those in the political realm.[61]

The *roda* is then the material and symbolic locus from which a new democratic order emanates. This meaning is reinforced by another symbol that frequently appears in the Máscaras paintings: the butterfly.[62] The butterfly is one of nature's perfect examples of transformation and growth. Since ancient times, and in different cultures, it symbolizes change. Its dance reflects the need for movement from where we are to our next phase of being. The chrysalis is the egg that contains the potentiality of being. The butterfly that comes out is a symbol of resurrection.[63] Therefore, the butterfly in association with the mask, and with the guiding and empowering force of the divinity and the community, represents the process of transformation and transcendence that the children of Yemanjá experience during the communal rituals in her honor.

After analyzing all the symbolic elements present in the paintings Mallo created during her exile in Latin America in relation to Mallo's previous series, to the principles of Candomblé religion, and to the deep impact that the new American surroundings had in her, we can conclude that the message that Mallo articulates is one of unwavering hope and faith in humankind. Mallo's lifelong search for social justice and her visceral rejection of any type of oppression transcended national borders and was fueled by what could be described as a feeling of universal solidarity. Her militancy through her art, which she used both to address injustice regardless of where and how it occurred, and to propose new ways to relate to one another, reveals that Mallo's sense of responsibility knew no borders. Maruja Mallo's art is a clear testimony to the continuous search for overcoming our human limitations and for achieving a more balanced and harmonious existence. It is no accident that the artist felt a strong attraction toward the racial diversity of the Americas and toward Candomblé. The biomorphic characters of *Naturalezas Vivas*, the different racial types in her portrait series, and the symbolism of the *Máscaras* paintings, visually capture the idea of the definitive and transcendental connection between humans and the cosmos, an aspiration that drove Mallo's artistic career since its beginning. Mallo's art was always fueled by her hope for the humankind's future and in its ability to transcend its limitations. Her essential optimism is deeply moving and becomes an inexhaustible source of inspiration for all of us who still believe in the transformative capacity of art.

NOTES

1. José Luis Ferris, *Maruja Mallo. La gran transgresora del 27* (Madrid: Ediciones Temas de Hoy, 2004), 58–60.

2. Miguel Primo de Rivera y Orbaneja (Jerez de la Frontera, Cádiz, 1870–Paris, 1930) was a Spanish military man and a dictator. In the 1920s, he was appointed captain general of Valencia, Madrid, and Barcelona. As captain general of Barcelona, Primo de Rivera had to confront several serious problems of public order that plagued the city, such as anarchist terrorism, the boom of Catalanism, and ministerial instability. In reaction to these problems, Primo de Rivera staged a coup in 1923, which put the Constitution on hold, dissolved Parliament, and established a dictatorship (1923–1930). With the complicity of King Alfonso XIII and the approval of a large part of the employers, the clergy, the army, and the conservative forces, Primo de Rivera headed a Military Directory that concentrated in its hands all the powers of the State and excluded professional politicians. His dictatorship came to an end in 1930 when, unauthorized by the military high command and by the king, he was forced to resign. He went into exile in Paris where he remained until his death.

3. Shirley Mangini, *Maruja Mallo*, (Barcelona: CIRCE, 2012), 133.

4. In relation to the trauma associated with the memories of the Civil War, during an interview in 1937, Mallo responded quite aggressively when one reporter asked her if she remembered her childhood: "Doesn't it embarrass you to ask me such stupid questions? Asking me this when I have just escaped from death! Asking me such questions! When my eyes can still see those mutilated children, those murdered men, those women running and crying. I remember nothing, nothing can be remembered . . . except that my country is choking, choking on its own blood" Adriana Piquet, "Maruja Mallo: Drama y verbena." *Atlántida. Ilustración Mensual Argentina* (September 1937): 38.

5. Pablo Neruda (1904–1973) is regarded as one of the greatest poets of Chilean, Latin American, and world literature of the twentieth century. While acting as consul of Chile in Madrid from 1934 to 1936, he frequented the circle of writers and intellectuals of the so-called Generation of 1927, many of whom lived at the *Residencia*

de estudiantes, and became a close friend of the poet Federico García Lorca. In 1971, Neruda was awarded the Nobel Prize for literature.

6. Remembering the profound impact that the American world caused in her art, Mallo wrote: "I feel more complete since I have lived in America . . . In this immense continent that offered me . . . the joy of living in the face of the agony of dying. It was the dawn that revealed new visions, surprises and concepts: the clarification that pushed me like a great waterfall." Juan Pérez de Ayala, "Vida vibrante," in *Maruja Mallo. Naturalezas Vivas. 1941–1944* (Madrid: Galería Guillermo de Osma, 2002), 23.

7. "Brazil witnessed the forced immigration of over four million African souls during its colonial and imperial history, roughly eight fold the number that reached the United States. Uprooted principally from Yoruba-speaking areas of Nigeria and from Angola, they found themselves in a social and physical environment altogether alien. Forced to adapt to the rigors of slave existence and the life ways of an evolving Portuguese civilization, African slaves lost much of what constituted their material culture. They succeeded, however, in introducing significant elements of their religious and ethno medical systems. In the northeastern state of Bahia, Yoruba slaves and freedmen had successfully transplanted the seeds of their belief system by the early nineteenth century. Candomblé, as the religion came to be called, expanded geographically and numerically to the point that today it represents a powerful cultural influence in the region." Robert A. Voeks, "Candomblé Ethnobotany: African Medicinal Plant Classification in Brazil," in *Ethnobotany. A Reader*, ed. Paul E. Minnis (Norman: U. of Oklahoma P, 2000), 148.

8. Maruja Mallo, "Proceso histórico de la forma en las artes plásticas." In *Maruja Mallo, 59 grabados en negro y 9 láminas en color 1928-1942,* estudio preliminar por Ramón Gómez de la Serna (Buenos Aires: Losada, 1942), 38.

9. Juan Manuel Bonet, "La forma expresa el contenido de una época." *El País, Archivo: hemeroteca Digital* (January 30, 1977): n/p. The English translation is mine.

10. To see "Canto de las espigas," please visit the virtual gallery dedicated to Mallo's work at the Museo Nacional Centro de Arte Reina Sofía https://www.museoreinasofia.es/en/collection/artwork/canto-espigas-song-spikes. To see additional paintings of this series, like the one entitled "Figuras" go to https://www.museoreinasofia.es/en/collection/artwork/figuras-figures-1.

11. Wheat is "the universal vegetable, symbol of social struggle, terrestrial myth. It is the physical manifestation of a belief that arises from the severity and grace of the two Castillas, from my materialistic faith in the triumph of the fish, in the rule of the wheat spike." Maruja Mallo, "Lo popular en la plástica española (a través de mi obra) 1928–1936," in *Maruja Mallo, 59 grabados en negro y 9 láminas en color 1928-1942,* estudio preliminar pro Ramón Gómez de la Serna (Buenos Aires: Losada, 1942), 43). The English translation is mine.

12. Arturo del Villar, explains that wealth spikes appeared prominently featured in the most popular representation of the Spanish Second Republic: "A matron dressed in the Greek way, wearing a long white dress, a red cloak on her shoulders and the Phrygian cap on her head, holds the tricolor flag with her left hand, and with her right

a balanced scale. Behind her appears a lion, along with the three republican slogans, and to the right we see included various symbols of human progress and work: an airplane, a merchant ship, a locomotive, an anvil, some books, a painter's palette, and a bundle of ears of wheat with the sickle." Arturo del Villar, *Maruja Mallo, pintora del pueblo, testigo de lo que hicieron en Galicia* (Madrid: Biblioteca de Divulgación Republicana, 2009), 21. The English translation is mine.

13. Mallo had previously expressed her condemnation of the patriarchal order in a series of paintings that preceded *La Religión*. Her condemnation of the patriarchal society and of the conservative social establishment can be clearly seen in the paintings grouped under the titles *Verbenas* and *Cloacas y Campanarios*. To expand of the meaning behind these series, please consult Zanetta's *La subversión enmascarada* (Madrid: Biblioteca Nueva, 2014).

14. In the lecture titled "Lo popular en la plástica española (a través de mi obra) 1928–1936" Mallo describes her desire to emulate in her art the harmonious laws that regulate nature: "It was nature that began to attract me, the desire to find a new order. In order lies the intimate structure of nature and man, the living mathematics of the skeleton. In nature . . . I analyzed the structure of minerals and plants, the variety of transparent and biological forms, synthesized in numerical and geometrical order; in a living an universal order." Maruja Mallo, "Lo popular," 46.

15. Juan Eduardo Cirlot, *Diccionario de símbolos* (Barcelona: Ediciones Siruela, 2004), 80.

16. For an in-depth analysis of Maruja Mallo's art, please consult both Zanetta's *La otra cara de la vanguardia: Estudio comparativo de la obra artística de Maruja Mallo, Ángeles Santos y Remedios Varo* (Lewiston: Edwin Mellen P, 2006) and *La subversión enmascarada.*

17. To view the paintings of this series, please visit the online catalog *Maruja Mallo. Naturalezas Vivas. 1941–1944.* http://www.guillermodeosma.com/images/pdf/MARUJA%20MAYO%20BAJA.pdf. Accessed December 9, 2019. The paintings *Naturaleza viva, Naturaleza viva con estrella de mar,* and *Naturaleza viva. Vida vibrante,* reproduced, respectively, in pages 38, 41, and 45 in this catalog, are one of the most representative of this series.

18. Torres García, Joaquín. *Escritos,* ed. Juan Fló (Montevideo: Arca Editorial, 1974), 30. The English translation is mine.

19. For further reading on this subject, please consult, among others, Frederic L. Bender, *The Culture of Extinction: Toward a Philosophy of Deep Ecology* (Amherst, New York: Humanity Books, 2003); Jim Cheney, "Eco-Feminism and Deep Ecology," *Environmental Ethics* 9, No 2 (Summer 1987): 115–45; William Devall, and George Sessions, *Deep Ecology: Living As if Nature Mattered* (Salt Lake City: Gibbs M. Smith, Inc. 1985).

20. According to the Australian philosopher Val Plumwood (1939–2008) the "logic of domination" develops in four stages. The first is the establishment of dualisms in the Derridian sense of hierarchical opposition between mind and body, reason and nature. Such dualism would be clearly represented in Platonic rationalist philosophy. The second stage corresponds to Descartes's dualism, which strips all mental capacity of nonhumans, and Locke's concept of productive work as the basis

for the legitimate individual appropriation of nature. The third stage is identified as appropriation through systematic instrumentalization. The ego, defined as selfish rationality, seeks the usefulness of Nature. The Other is reduced to merchandise status. Finally, the fourth and final stage, the one we are living, proceeds to devour the Other. In Plumwood's words, "the world is no longer only conceived instrumentally, but completely instrumentalized. The objective is the implementation of the Cartesian dream of total control over the alien and the complete destruction of any resistance that the earth may oppose." Plumwood, *Feminism and the Mastery of Nature* (London an New York: Routledge, 1993), 193.

21. One of the most representative examples of this series is the one entitled "La cierva humana." This painting, part of the permanent collection of the Museo Benito Quinquela Martín in Buenos Aires, has been featured in a recent exhibition organized by this museum and reviewed by the journal *La voz de Galicia*. To see a reproduction of the painting as well as the review, please visit: https://www.lavozdegalicia.es/noticia/cultura/2019/01/07/cierva-humana-maruja-mallo-vuelve-maravillar-buenos-aires/0003154685547549530 8899.htm. Accessed December 9, 2019. To see more examples of the *Retratos bidimensionales* series, visit the online catalog *Maruja Mallo. Orden y Creación*. 14 septiembre–10 noviembre, 2017 (Madrid: Galería Guillermo de Osma, 2017), 30–38. http://www.guillermodeosma.com/pdf/marujamallo.pdf. Accessed December 9, 2019.

22. Estrella De Diego, "Retratos," in *Maruja Mallo, Vigo: Casa de las Artes, septiembre de 2009—enero de 2010; Exposición Madrid, Real Academia de Bellas Artes de San Fernando, 26 de enero—abril de 2010*, ed. Fernando Huici March and Juan Pérez de Ayala (Vigo: Fundación Caixa Galicia, 2010), 83.

23. Carlos Bernárdez, *Maruja Mallo. A pintura da nova muller* (Vigo: Nigratrea, 2010), 76

24. Ferris, *Maruja Mallo*, 282.

25. Lorand Matory, *Black Atlantic Religion. Tradition, Transnationalism, and Matriarchy in the Afro-Brazilian Candomblé*, (Princeton and Oxford: Princeton UP, 2005), 151.

26. Matory, *Black Atlantic Religion*, 168.

27. Robert A. Voeks, *Sacred Leaves of Candomblé. African Magic, Medicine, and Religion in Brazil* (Austin: U of Texas P, 1997), 68.

28. As Janis Birkeland explains, the notion of masculinity that is based on power over others and on its distance from "the feminine" justifies the abuse of power and it fosters "competitive individualism, human chauvinism, instrumentalism, hierarchy, parochialism, and the addiction to power." Janis Birkeland, "Ecofeminism: Linking Theory and Practice," in *Ecofeminism. Women, Animals, Nature*, ed. Greta Gaard (Philadelphia: Temple UP, 1993), 25.

29. Both Mallo and Zambrano believed that the "Sacrificial History" of the old world order would be replaced by a new concept of humanity that resulted from the democratic system that both of them wanted for Spain during the Second Republic. Both painter and philosopher believed that the republican project was the only viable way toward true equality, an equality that did not entail uniformity but the embrace of difference and diversity in all its forms. The key to open the way to a new concept

of human history was to completely eradicate the Sacrificial History that century after century had alienated and abused big segments of the human population and of the natural world. In relation to this Zambrano writes, "It is more obvious than ever that democracy is the only way for the so-called Western culture to continue, and this revelation lays bare, today more than ever, the sacrificial structure of human history. I have gone from the beginning of my life in search of a religion of a non-sacrificial nature. The sacrifice had already been accomplished. Today we see that it has not yielded the fruits of the accomplished sacrifice, but rather we find a chalice that very few are willing to accept." María Zambrano, *Persona y democracia. La historia sacrificial.* (Barcelona: Anthropos, 1988), 7.

30. Voeks, *Sacred Leaves*, 68.

31. Lia Paula Rodrigues, "Space and the Ritualization of Axé in Candomblé," in *Kult 6 – Special Issue Epistemologies of Transformation: The Latin American Decolonial Option and its Ramifications* (Roskilde, Denmark: Department of Culture and Identity. Roskilde University. 2009), 93.

32. Mallo, like Torres García, advocated for a materialistic humanism in which the worker becomes the pillar and center of a new social and religious order. In relation to this, Torres García expressed: "We have proclaimed work as a law of life, and for this we have wanted to give it a religious symbolic meaning . . . The religious sense of work; the transcendence of material living; Well, if I can say that everything is concrete, I also say that everything is spiritual . . . Why the working man, who is aware of his primary role in the world, would want this work to be only a material function, without significance?" Joaquín Torres García, *Estructura* (Montevideo: Biblioteca Alfar, 1935), 126.

33. Torres García, *Escritos*, 29–30.

34. Voeks, *Sacred Leaves* 73.

35. Matory, *Black Atlantic Religion*, 176.

36. It is a well-known fact that Mallo was very influenced by occultism and by many other systems of thought such as Zoroastrianism, Pythagoreanism, and Buddhism, among others.

37. Helen Zahara, "Man-the Miracle of Miracles," in *H. P. Blavatsky and the Secret Doctrine*, ed. Virginia Hanson (Wheaton: The Theosophical Publishing House, 1988), 65.

38. To see a photographic album documenting the ceremonies in honor of Yemanjá in San Salvador de Bahia, Brazil, please visit: Jan Sochor, *Photography Gallery* at https://latin-america.photoshelter.com/search?I_DSC=yemanja&I_COU NTRY_ISO=&I_SORT=RANK&I_DSC_AND=t&V_ID=&G_ID=&C_ID=&_ACT =search. Accessed December 16, 2019.

39. Mark O'Connell and Raje Airey, *Signs and Symbols* (London: Anness Publishing, 2006), 74.

40. With regards to the paintings in this mural Melva Luna writes, "The color expresses, above all, the cosmic vitality, which energizes the races and unifies the peoples . . . The original idea for the formation of the races starts from the oceanic plane; the abyssal depth would become the formidable uterus where the metamorphosis of the jellyfish, star or algae to the mermaid and the angel takes place. The five races are here represented in parallel circular motion with the cosmic rotation. The

ribbons that unite them symbolize the bonds of fraternity for the man of this century."
Melva Luna, "La personalidad pictórica de Maruja Mallo," in *Maruja Mallo,* in *Lyra,*
diciembre de 1945, n/p. Reproduce in *Maruja Mallo,* ed. Juan Pérez de Ayala and
Francisco Rivas (Madrid: Galería Guillermo de Osma, 1992). 88. The original article
was published in *Lycra* magazine with no pagination. It was later reproduced in
Peerez de Ayala y Rivas.

41. Mikelle Smith Omari-Tunkara, *Manipulating the sacred. Yoruba Art, Ritual,
and Resistance in Brazilian Candomblé* (Detroit: Wayne State UP, 2005), 72.

42. Arnold Van Gennep, Arnold. *The Rites of Passage.* Trans. Monika B. Vizedom
and Gabrielle L. Caffee (Chicago: U of Chicago P, 1960), 10.

43. Victor Turner, "Passage, Margins, and Poverty: Religious Symbols of
Communitas," in *Dramas, Fields and Methaphors. Symbolic Action in Human
Society* (Ithaca: Cornell UP, 1974), 253.

44. Iris Marion Young, *Justice and the Politics of Difference* (Princeton: Princeton
UP, 1990), 45.

45. Roger Sansi, "Shires, substances, and miracles in Afro-Brazilian Candomblé,"
Anthropology & Medicine 18, no. 2 (August 2011): 273–74.

46. In relationship to this aspect of Candomblé, Seligman explains:

"The process of self-transformation in Candomblé mediumship is an embodied one. The
transformations that mediums experience is not merely intellectual, but experiential—they
act and feel differently. Second, selfhood is itself fundamentally embodied. Self-transformation is not merely intellectual because self is not just an idea; it is a way of being in the
world that is located at the intersection of mind and body. Third, because self is embodied, transformation of the whole self must involve not only discursive but also embodied
forms of learning. When acquisition of new ideas and beliefs about self is complemented
by forms of training that involve new ways of using and experiencing the body, self-
transformation is particularly profound. Fourth, embodied learning is a biocultural process
and as such involves bodily mechanisms, including psychophysiological ones." Rebecca
Seligman, *Possessing Spirits and Healing Selves. Embodiment and Transformation in an
Afro-Brazilian Religion* (New York: Palgrave Macmillan, 2014), 10.

47. The fluid relationship between the self and the cosmos that characterizes the
concept of selfhood in Candomblé closely resembles the process of gender identity
formation described by Nancy Chodorow. According to Chodorow, the human being
is not born with a perception of gender differences. These emerge throughout the
development of their personality. In contrast to what Freudian theory held, the author
states that the concept of manhood is more conflictive and problematic than originally
believed. Underlying or incorporated into the generic nuclear male identity—what
Chodorow calls "core gender identity"—is an early, nonverbal and primary sense of
undifferentiated union with the mother who continually challenges and undermines
the sense of manhood in the boy. Because of this primary uniqueness and the early
identification of the child with his mother, the generic nuclear identity of the child
and man is perceived as a problem. The child must learn their generic identity as
nonfeminine or nonmother. Subsequently, and due to the primacy of the mother in the
early development of the child, and the absence of available concrete male figures of
the same importance as the mother with whom the child can identify, learning what

it means to be masculine comes to mean learn not to be feminine. Because of these conflicts experienced early in the child's development, having a clear sense of the generic difference, of what is masculine and feminine, and establishing rigid barriers between both categories becomes something of fundamental importance to man in a patriarchal social order. Nancy Chodorow, "Gender, Relation, and Difference in Psychoanalytic Perspective," in *The* Future of Difference, ed. Hester Eisenstein and Alice Jardine (Boston: Barnard College Women's Center, 1980), 13.

48. It is interesting to note that Candomblé is perceived to be a matriarchal religion. Cheryl Sterling states that "the perception of matriarchal dominance in Candomblé prevails and has become a defining characteristic of the practice. Ruth Landes, who, in *The City of Women*, first documents the centrality of female leadership in the ter-reiros, highlights the divergence of such matriarchal power from society at-large." Cheryl Sterling, *African Roots, Brazilian Rites. Cultural and National Identity in Brazil* (New York: Palgrave McMillan, 2012), 28. It is precisely the divergent role of women in the religion that caused, in part, the negative connotations that the white Brazilian elite held toward Candomblé: "The centrality of African women in the religion also added to its pernicious quality. Inverting the social order, the matriarchal emphasis stood in direct opposition to white male patriarchy and the evolving character deemed appropriate for the Brazilian nation." Sterling, *African Roots*, 48.

49. This idea is also found in the foundations of occult thinking, for which the individual, from reincarnation and karma and operating within their own evolutionary field, is responsible for their own evolutionary process. Sri Madhava Ashish writes that "like everything else, the Individual Self must evolve and grow, passing from unrealized potential to a clear focus in the trans individual light." Sri Madhava Ashish, "The Secret Doctrine as a Contribution to World Thought," in *H.P.Blavatsky and the Secret Doctrine*, ed. Virginia Hanson (Wheaton: The Theosophical Publishing House, 1988), 52. The changing and fluid aspect of humanity is what precisely guarantees its evolution and the possibility of achieving maximum transcendence by uniting with the divine.

50. Voeks, *Sacred Leaves*, 56. In relation to the concept of duality in Candomblé's deities, Chery Sterling writes: "The orisas are multivalent entities, and even though each one has a dominant trait, it is quite feasible for that orisa to invoke the opposite of that defining characteristic. Thus, Oshun can be both love and war, as both energies often exist in complementary engagement." Sterling, *African Roots*, 46.

51. Helena P. Blavatsky, *The Secret Doctrine*, ed. Michael Gomes (New York: Penguin, 2009),13.

52. Sterling, *African Roots*, 47.

53. Jean Chevalier and Alain Gheerbrant, *Diccionario de los símbolos* (Barcelona: Herder Editorial, 1986), 291.

54. Miriam Johnson, "Androgyny and the Maternal Principle," *The School Review* 86, no. 1 (1977): 51–52.

55. Fernando Huici March, "Con el cerebro en la mano," in *Maruja Mallo, Vigo, Casa de las Artes, septiembrede 2009—enero de 2010; Madrid, R.A. Bellas Artes de S. Fernando, enero—abril de 2010*, 71–87 (Vigo: Fundación Caixa Galicia, 2010), 87.

56. Sterling, *African Roots*, 58–59.

57. Chevalier, *Diccionario de los símbolos, 301.*

58. Sterling, *African Roots*, 61. It is interesting to note that Benjamín Péret, the influential surrealist poet that was part of Breton's circle, also found Candomblé and Macumba fascinating. During the years Péret spent in Brazil, he participated in several ceremonies and Candomblé rituals and wrote several essays about these experiences. Péret perceived the dances in these ceremonies as a type of movement that was simultaneously religious and erotic: "In the hypnotic or transcendental quality of the dancing, Péret must have seen a unity of mind and body uncommon in Western religions." Elizabeth M. Ginway, "Surrealist Benjamin Peret and Brazilian Modernism," *Hispania* 75 (September 1992): 548.

59. Yvonne Daniel, *Embodied Knowledge in Haitian Vodou, Cuban Yoruba, and Bahian Candomblé,* (Chicago: U of Illinois P, 2005), 268.

60. As Sterling explains, Candomblé celebrations "profoundly affect the disposed individual in offering a glimpse at the future possibilities of society, the longed-for way of life in which one's Africanness/blackness is not subject to and manipulated by external social and political hierarchies. In this politicization of culture, those struggling for equal voice and choice for Afro-Brazilians enter the debate and use agentative focus of such ritual encounters as a source from which to construct a society in which blackness is not only acknowledge on special days." Sterling, *African Roots*, 86.

61. Sterling, *African Roots*, 86.

62. Examples of *Máscara* paintings with butterflies can be found in the online catalog *Maruja Mallo. 1902–1995.* Juan Pérez de Ayala and Francisco Rivas eds., 67–68 (Madrid: Guillermo de Osma gallery, October 21–December 20, 1992). http://www.guillermodeosma.com/images/pdf/PDF%20-%20Maruja%20Mallo(completo)FINAL.pdf. Accessed December 9, 2019.

63. Chevalier, *Diccionario de los símbolos*, 691.

BIBLIOGRAPHY

Ashish, Sri Madhava. "The Secret Doctrine as a Contribution to World Thought." In *H.P.Blavatsky and the Secret Doctrine*, edited by Virginia Hanson, 47–56. Wheaton: The Theosophical Publishing House, 1988.

Bernárdez, Carlos L. *Maruja Mallo. A pintura da nova muller.* Vigo: Nigratrea, 2010.

Birkeland, Janis. "Ecofeminism: Linking Theory and Practice." In *Ecofeminism. Women, Animals, Nature*, edited by Greta Gaard, 13–59. Philadelphia: Temple UP, 1993.

Blavatsky, Helena P. *The Secret Doctrine.* Edited by Michael Gomes. New York: Penguin, 2009.

Bonet, Juan Manuel. "La forma expresa el contenido de una época." *El País, Archivo: hemeroteca Digital.* January 30, 1977. https://elpais.com/diario/1977/01/30/cultura/223426812_850215.html

Chevalier, Jean and Alain Gheerbrant. *Diccionario de los símbolos*. Barcelona: Herder Editorial, 1986.

Chodorow, Nancy. "Gender, Relation, and Difference in Psychoanalytic Perspective." In *The* Future of Difference, edited by Hester Eisenstein and Alice Jardine, 3–19. Boston: Barnard College Women's Center, 1980.

Cirlot, Juan Eduardo. *Diccionario de símbolos*. Barcelona: Ediciones Siruela, 2004.

Daniel, Yvonne. *Embodied Knowledge in Haitian Vodou, Cuban Yoruba, and Bahian Candomblé*. Chicago: U of Illinois P, 2005.

Del Villar, Arturo. *Maruja Mallo, pintora del pueblo, testigo de lo que hicieron en Galicia*. Madrid: Biblioteca.

Divulgación Republicana, 2009.

Diego, Estrella. "Retratos." In *Maruja Mallo, Vigo, Casa de las Artes, septiembre de 2009—enero de 2010/ Exposición Madrid, Real Academia deBellas Artes de San Fernando, 26 de enero—4 de abril de 2010*, edited by Fernando Huici March and Juan Pérz de Ayala, 71–87. Madrid: Sociedad Estatal de Conmemoraciones culturales, 2009.

Ferris, José Luis. *Maruja Mallo. La gran transgresora del 27*. Madrid: Ediciones Temas de Hoy, 2004.

Ginway, Elizabeth M. "Surrealist Benjamin Peret and Brazilian Modernism." *Hispania* 75 (September 1992): 543–53.

Huici March, Fernando. "Con el cerebro en la mano." In *Maruja Mallo, Vigo, Casa de las Artes, septiembre de 2009—enero de 2010; Madrid, R.A. Bellas Artes de S. Fernando, enero—abril de 2010*, 71–87. Vigo: Fundación Caixa Galicia, 2010.

Johnson, Miriam M. "Androgyny and the Maternal Principle." *The School Review* 86, no. 1 (1977): 50–69.

Jung, Carl G. *Man and his Symbols*. New York: Dell, 1968.

Luna, Melva. "La personalidad pictórica de Maruja Mallo," In *Maruja Mallo*, edited by Juan Pérez de Ayala and Francisco Rivas, 88. Madrid: Galería Guillermo de Osma, 1992.

Mallo, Maruja. "Lo popular en la plástica española (a través de mi obra) 1928–1936." In *Maruja Mallo*, 39–48. Buenos Aires: Losada, 1942.

———. "Proceso histórico de la forma en las artes plásticas." In *Maruja Mallo, 59 grabados en negro y 9 láminas en color 1928-1942*, estudio preliminar por Ramón Gómez de la Serna, 27–38. Buenos Aires: Losada, 1942.

Mangini, Shirley. *Maruja Mallo*. Barcelona: CIRCE, 2012.

———. "Maruja Mallo. La bohemia encarnada." *Arenal* 14, no. 2 (July–December 2007): 291–305.

Matory, J. Lorand. *Black Atlantic Religion. Tradition, Transnationalism, and Matriarchy in the Afro-Brazilian Candomblé*. Princeton and Oxford: Princeton UP, 2005.

O'Connell, Mark and Raje Airey. *Signs and Symbols*. London: Anness Publishing, 2006.

Omari-Tunkara, Mikelle Smith. *Manipulating the sacred. Yoruba Art, Ritual, and Resistance in Brazilian Candomblé*. Detroit: Wayne State UP, 2005.

Pérez de Ayala, Juan. "Vida vibrante." In *Maruja Mallo. Naturalezas Vivas. 1941– 1944*, 21–31. Madrid: Galería Guillermo de Osma, 2002.

Piquet, Adriana. "Maruja Mallo: Drama y verbena." *Atlántida. Ilustración Mensual Argentina*, (September 1937): 38–76. This is a magazine with no volume.

Plumwood, Val. *Feminism and the Mastery of Nature*. London an New York: Routledge, 1993.

Rivas, Francisco. "Maruja Mallo, pintora del más allá." In *Maruja Mallo*, edited by Juan Pérez de Ayala and Francisco Rivas, 15–27. Madrid: Galería Guillermo de Osma, 1992.

Rodrigues, Lia Paula. "Space and the Ritualization of Axé in Candomblé." In *Kult 6—Special Issue Epistemologies of Transformation: The Latin American Decolonial Option and its Ramifications*, 85–99. Roskilde, Denmark: Department of Culture and Identity. Roskilde University. 2009. http://postkolonial.dk/artikler/ kult_6/RODRIGUES.pdf. Accessed 11/2/2019.

Sansi, Roger. "Shires, substances, and miracles in Afro-Brazilian Candomblé." In *Anthropology & Medicine* 18, no. 2 (August 2011): 271–83.

Seligman, Rebecca. *Possessing Spirits and Healing Selves. Embodiment and Transformation in an Afro-Brazilian Religion*. New York: Palgrave Macmillan, 2014.

Sterling, Cheryl. *African Roots, Brazilian Rites. Cultural and National Identity in Brazil*. New York: Palgrave Macmillan, 2012.

Torres-García, Joaquín. *Escritos*, edited by Juan Fló. Montevideo: Arca Editorial, 1974.

———. *Estructura*. Montevideo: Biblioteca Alfar, 1935.

Turner, Victor, "Passage, Margins, and Poverty: Religious Symbols of Communitas," In *Dramas, Fields and Metaphors. Symbolic Action in Human Society*, Victor Turner 231–71. Ithaca: Cornell UP, 1974.

Van Gennep, Arnold. *The Rites of Passage*. Translated by Monika B. Vizedom and Gabrielle L. Caffee. Chicago: U of Chicago P, 1960.

Voeks Robert A. "Candomblé Ethnobotany: African Medicinal Plant Classification in Brazil," In *Ethnobotany. A Reader*, edited by Paul E. Minnis, 148–71. Norman: U. of Oklahoma P, 2000.

———. *Sacred Leaves of Candomblé. African Magic, Medicine, and Religion in Brazil*. Austin: U of Texas P, 1997.

Wilde, Lawrence. *Global Solidarity*. Edinburgh: Edinburgh UP, 2013.

Young, Iris Marion. *Justice and the Politics of Difference*. Princeton: Princeton UP, 1990.

Zahara, Helen V., "Man-the Miracle of Miracles," In *H.P. Blavatsky and the Secret Doctrine*, edited by Virginia Hanson, 57–66. Wheaton, IL: The Theosophical Publishing House, 1988.

Zambrano, María. *Persona y democracia. La historia sacrificial*. Barcelona: Anthropos, 1988.

Zanetta, María Alejandra. *La otra cara de la vanguardia: Estudio comparativo de la obra artística de Maruja Mallo, Ángeles Santos y Remedios Varo*. Lewiston: Edwin Mellen P, 2006.

———. *La subversión enmascarada. Análisis de la obra de Maruja Mallo*. Madrid: Biblioteca Nueva, 2014.

Chapter 8

Technologies of Affective Solidarity

Salvador, Brazil's Ani Ganzala and Zinha Franco

Naomi Pueo Wood

Broader access to social media and growing transnational solidarity networks has led to increased attention to racial and economic inequalities across the Americas. Through greater integration of the internet into our daily lives, cross-cultural comparative analysis of representation has also led to a deeper awareness of inequalities globally. Due to the now widely available data on the overrepresentation of black people in the prison system, for example, many people can no longer deny this modern method of racialized persecution and oppression. Brazil is in the top three countries with the highest rate of incarceration with 725 million people, third to China at 1.6 million, and the United States at 2.1 million.[1] And, among these 725 million, the population of imprisoned black women in Brazil has increased 700% since 2010.[2] This data shows ways in which Brazilian national politics (de) value certain citizens and continue legacies of slavery, settler colonialism, and exploitation in this postcolonial, former slave-system nation. And, the prison system is only one such social institution that cannot hide its blatant racial bias in a contemporary context of access to data. The availability of this information and subsequent increase in transnational solidarity is the context within which I will explore the connections between local *artivismo* and transnational, queer Afro-diasporic solidarities in the age of social media and globalized activist networks originating in Salvador, Brazil.

Artivismo, art-activism, is an identity espoused by artists in Brazil to signal their desire for social transformation. A term borrowed from the early graffiti artists of the US-based Hip Hop movement, *artivist* creators are seeking to transform society into one where they see themselves represented, included, and celebrated.[3] Or, as Argentinian activist and performance artist Paula Telis says, "el artivismo no se conforma con ser un modo de reflejar la realidad, sino que protagoniza un modo de crear otra distinta."[4] In other words, *artivism* is the basis for the creation of a new reality. While drawing concrete connections between oppressive colonial legacies and contemporary persecution is essential for understanding our present, specifically highlighting artivists who are contributing to the formation of transformed realities is the focus of this essay.

In the context of Salvador, Brazil, a regional capital city with an 80% black population, the lack of representation of the majority inhabitants is stark in popular media, as well as in politics and higher education nation-wide.[5] Throughout the past decade, the increase in globalized popular media has created a unique opportunity for artists to make transnational connections, find inspiration across linguistic and geographic borders, and sustain hope for change through seeing themselves mirrored in the work of others. In the case of the work by queer black women analyzed in this chapter, these reflections of self simultaneously affirm access to spaces previously denied locally and also empower the activism of artists in distant locations.

"TECHNOLOGIES" OF *AFETIVIDADE*

In her talk at the 2019 LAVITS (Latin American Network of Surveillance, Technology and Society Studies) Symposium held in Salvador, journalist, activist, and founder of the app "+AmorEntreNós" (More Love Between Us), Sueide Kintê described the technologies of survival that black women in slave societies have been developing and employing for centuries.[6] Kintê has researched black women's sustained methods of survival and has been speaking on sexism, homophobia, and racism for the past decade. Mutual care, community childcare and rearing, maintaining spiritual belief systems and rituals, and sustaining energies of hope, she argues, are technologies of affective survival. In her talk, Kintê introduced these strategies and likened them with innovative technologies. Technology, by her definition, is the creative and systemic response to a given environment. In the examples that Kintê notes, technologies of care responded to an oppressive and dehumanizing environment; the strategies that enslaved and recently "freed" black women innovated draw on histories of survival tactics and creative development of self-love.

Yet, our contemporary historical moment, Kintê argues, is one of dangerous competitiveness. "Competitiveness. The paradigm of success that shapes our lives today, is impossible; it is a paradigm that dilutes humanity and empties human beings."[7] So, she affirmed, black women have developed collaborative solidarity networks and continued collectivity to combat this emphasis on competition that seeks to separate and create antagonistic relationships. Kintê then proposed a paradigm shift, one that builds upon the Afro-diasporic cosmovision rooted in *Candomblé*. In her vision we must move from a combat-centered ruling head, that dominated by the *orixá* Ogúm, the warrior god, to one that is centered on community. To facilitate this shift, we must look to Oxúm, the goddess connected with maternity and one who guides births, both of new life and of change. Oxúm is fascinated by her own beauty and finds strength in asserting her stunning appearance; she carries a mirror with her to admire her own reflection. This goddess is also connected with fresh waters, rivers, lakes, and streams, places where she might also find her own beautiful image reflected. Kintê asks how it is that Oxúm, a water goddess, will pacify the warring tendencies of Ogúm, who has been the ruler of our minds. She explains that,

Deep in her self-knowledge about creation. Everything that falls in the hands of Oxúm she fertilizes and creates. It is in this way that the death that Ogúm provokes doesn't only become destruction. Because Oxúm's action makes it so that it becomes progress. What I want to say is that in the context of my paradigm, technology must be pacified. How will it be pacified? With community. With people. This is the dilemma that is presented between progress and affect.[8]

Here, Kintê is referring to the disproportionate surveillance and brutality of black people in Brazil. Kintê's theorizations contribute to critical race studies research like Ignacio Cano's "Racial Bias in Police Use of Lethal Force in Brazil" (2010) and Luana Marques-Garcia Ozemela et al., in their "Race Differences in Police Violence and Crime Victimization in Brazil" (2019) to refer to the ways black people have been policed, tracked, segregated, and disciplined for centuries.[9] Her use of the term "technology" is capacious in its definition and links technologies of care during slave times to technologies of activist organizing at present. Like the app "+AmorEntreNós" which connects a network of black women to one another so they can exchange free services, mutual care networks on and offline are technologies of survival. Reclaiming the notion of creative, innovative survival strategies at the root of her definition of "technology," Kintê links "progress" to affirmation and mutual care among black women. To defuse the systems that continue to oppress, we must count on individuals to form community. This community-building work can be found in the *artivismo* of Zinha Franco and Ani Ganzala and the technologies of affect, communication, and transnational solidarity through social media that these artists create.[10] Adopting Kintê's refashioned concept of technology, as I do in this chapter, has the dual purpose of promoting a minority, antihegemonic thinker and of furthering the artivist project of subverting and transforming our contemporary repressive order.

In a neoliberal and capitalist economy, technology in the twenty-first century represents innovative methods for problem solving, efficiency, and productivity. For Zinha Franco and Ani Ganzala, technologies encompass these characteristics and also include affect and communication as core components. Zinha Franco, founder of the band Panteras Negras and of the production firm Estação Zinha, theorizes the spiritual and economic power of these two projects. The band, Panteras Negras, and the artists whose music is produced by Estação Zinha, are all black women, many lesbian-identified. Increasing visibility of same-sex black female love through their stage performances and collaborations, and economic gains through supportive production mentoring, Zinha Franco models the affective technology of community accountability. Similarly, the watercolor paintings and graffiti art of Ani Ganzala center the black female queer experience and communities of care and affection as they encourage a new paradigm for this historically invisibilized and exploited group. A self-taught visual artist, Ani Ganzala has learned to navigate the masculinist graffiti scene and to publish her watercolors online to reach a larger black queer audience and to find ways to make her artwork her main source of income. Thus, these two artivists use social media and transnational networks as well as the affective technology of care to transform their local environments and earn a living from their art.

LOCAL CONTEXTS: SALVADOR DA BAHIA

Salvador, Bahia, as the first colonial capital in Brazil and the one-time epicenter of the trafficking of enslaved Africans, is an important site for the examination of Afro-diasporic *artivism*. It holds stories of great brutality and exploitation and also of prolonged resistance and resilience. The overwhelming number of enslaved Africans who passed through the city,[11] the diversity of ethnic backgrounds, and the longevity of the slave system in Brazil[12] make Salvador a particularly rich site for analyzing legacies of both black resistance and white supremacist racism.

The region is known for being the "heart" of Brazilian culture and the birth of many "roots," hybrid, and syncretic cultural forms. Bahia and black Brazilians from the northeast are both exotified and commodified within the local and national imaginaries. Tourism propaganda inviting people to Salvador regularly features highly acrobatic freeze-frames of slender, muscular black male bodies performing capoeira; the black female *baianas de acarajé*[13] posing in the recently renovated historic center of Pelourinho selling the secular version of *Candomblé* ritual fritters; and the young black men of Olodum beating large bass and snare drums and playing samba-reggae music as they parade through the cobblestone streets of the old town. These

Afro-diasporic cultural forms can be exploited in tourist propaganda and also can be linked to survival and the celebration of the Yoruba-inspired spiritual tradition, *Candomblé*. As tourist propaganda it posits a contradiction: it paints Salvador as a continued site for consuming and exploiting Afro-diasporic cultural productions; yet, it does so through the very artistic expressive forms that were developed and sustained as sites of resistance. In exploitative transnationalism, cultural practices are marketed and, in this case, black Brazilians are again deemed consumable. In the transnational solidarity networks focused on care and healing the continuity of *Candomblé* and other practices of care are sources of continued empowerment.

Candomblé, the West African-based spiritual belief system in Brazil, represents one of the ongoing sites of resistance to colonialism and white supremacy. It is a practice Afro-diasporic people developed and whose rituals continue to sustain spiritual communities despite violent repression.[14] *Candomblé* in Salvador reflects the fusion of multiple ethnic groups who represent neighboring regions in Yoruba-land, current-day Nigeria, Togo and Benin, who are all guided by the *orixás*, spirit-gods. While individual *orixás* are revered in isolation in villages across multiple nations of West Africa, in the colonial Brazilian context different ethnic groups were forced together and then transformed their ancestral practices into something new, which was *Candomblé*. In the Brazilian fusion, multiple *orixás* are worshiped simultaneously within the same nation rather than remaining separated and revered in separate adjacent nations as in Africa. Each *orixá* spirit guide is known for its association with specific elements of nature and particular roles in the functioning of interpersonal relations. The Dique do Tororó lake in the center of Salvador, for example, boasts statues of eight of the primary *orixás* that are revered by many Brazilians, both those who identify with the *Candomblé* religion and those who identify primarily with Christian religions. The integration of some elements of the *Candomblé* religion into secular parts of Bahian culture signals the importance of this tradition to the understanding of technologies of resistance and resilience, particularly for the black women who are the principal heads of the *terreiros*, houses of worship, and community leaders.

Through the *Ifá* divination system, *Candomblé* followers are made aware of their connection to particular orixá guides and can discover ways that they can help heal themselves and their environments. Followers are focused on the already established community and on maintaining their purity of connection with the *orixás*, listening when they are given messages and honoring the symbiotic relationship between humans and nature. For the many Afro-diasporic people who consider themselves "of *Candomblé*" this spiritual tradition is a reminder of their ancestors who were forcibly taken from their homeland; those who survived the crossing were violently subjected to slavery for centuries while others did not survive the Atlantic. The native West African Yoruba language still used in songs and prayers and the foundational reverence for Africa in the songs' lyrics make capture, slavery, and survival in the Americas fundamental referents to the lived practice of *Candomblé* in Brazil. The spiritual tradition in this context continues to serve as a method for community building, celebration of African ancestry, and resistance to the increasing diffusion of Pentecostalism and Evangelicalism, Occidental religions that continue to persecute *Candomblé* in the twenty-first century.[15]

In contemporary Brazil, the effects of the late abolition of slavery in 1888 and continued racial segregation in the major cities has impact nation-wide. In particular, the overrepresentation of black males in the prison system, as previously noted, and the overrepresentation of black women as domestic workers make clear the deficiencies in the largely nonexistent, state-sponsored efforts to reconcile and repair from the decades of violence and degradation of black people and specifically of black women.[16] In a society which continues to devalue black women's labor and their fundamental role in contemporary life, *Candomblé* has been a source of subversion and sustained relationships to *orixás* are particularly important. This spiritual site of resistance offers a continued alternative to the paradigm violently installed by the colonizing Portuguese back in the sixteenth century. And, as Kintê's reference to an African cosmovision and paradigm that centers Oxúm demonstrates, the close relationship between spirit guides and contemporary resistance persists.

ZINHA FRANCO: PANTERAS NEGRAS AND ESTAÇÃO ZINHA

Zinha Franco is the founder of both the production company Estação Zinha and the instrumental jazz group Panteras Negras. What started as a single project to create a network of black female musicians during November's black pride month (2018) turned into an ongoing collaborative project and the band Panteras Negras, Black Panthers. After playing two packed shows at Salvador's Museum of Modern Art's "Jam no MAM" (2019) the group found themselves forming part of a small but growing presence of black female musicians reshaping the music performance scene in Salvador.[17] Panteras Negras is an instrumental group, made up of Dedê Fatuma (percussion), Suyá Nascimento (guitar) e Line Santana (drums), that has collaborated with Aya Bass and other vocalists while Estação Zinha production continues to expand the visibility of black female musicians through mentoring up-and-coming artists. Their listening audience has expanded immensely in the past year as has the media publicity and attention to the group more generally. For Zinha Franco, this media attention is essential for the work that she does educating black female musicians about the production industry and, thus, furthering networks of affirmation and showcasing the continued resilience of queer black female *artivismo*. The group is being recognized in the feminist and black activist music circles in Brazil for the unique contribution they are making to the local music scene and to social justice activism in Salvador.[18] With this recognition comes further empowerment and affirmation of the transformative potential of recognition and representation.

In an interview she gave in May 2019, Zinha Franco explained the pressure that she feels to represent black women, in particular, and also the importance of helping develop an environment where Panteras Negras is not the sole example of an all-black female instrumental band. She noted that,

> This question of being a mirror, no? Of being someone in whom another can see themselves reflected, right? Well, I believe that we must be conscious of the actions that we are taking in our daily life, in our surroundings, so that others can see us an example. A positive example, an example of good things. So, in the context of the music scene, there is Panteras Negras and . . .? It is important for us to be this reflection.[19]

The fact that she is not aware of any other examples of all black female instrumental groups in Brazil also creates a certain amount of pressure or added responsibility for projecting a particular image and for responding to scrutiny of their individual actions. Zinha says that she takes this responsibility as a privilege and a challenge as she seeks to recruit more black women into the music scene and empower them to also envision themselves on stage. The notion of being a mirror, like Oxúm's mirror reflecting her own black, sensual, and powerful beauty back to herself, is central to the technology of *afetividade* that Panteras Negras and Estação Zinha foster. Transforming the images that are reflected back to young black women is a core responsibility Zinha Franco assumes in her work as a performer and producer.

Estação Zinha is meant to be a place to showcase black female musicians and also to create a mirror for what is possible. When Panteras Negras rehearse in their neighborhood and young women pass by and associate this musical talent with black women it increases their sense of life options. However, Zinha is well aware of the obstacles and criticism that awaits such audacity in the face of extremely racist and sexist social conditions.

> Many black women suffer from low self-esteem; there is racism, and other factors that make it so depression is more common for us. And, thanks to my orixá who enlightened my *orí* (spiritual intuition, consciousness), I am here. And I am

able to bring that knowledge to others. You know? The idea of the band came during that moment of depression, the moment of rescue, of me seeing and finding purpose in my life, you know? To have a purpose. So, really, it was a rescue. I am here, I am alive, I can.[20]

The relationship between depression and the sense that she could make a difference in the lives of other black women remains essential in the efforts of Estação Zinha and Panteras Negras. In both producing and showcasing black female musicians, Zinha Franco uses the technology of survival that Sueide Kintê recommends. She is creating communities of affect and sustaining a sense of communal survival as a central purpose for her *artivismo*.

ANI GANZALA: WATERCOLOR AND GRAFFITI

Survival has been a key word in historical and sociological accounts of colonial and postcolonial black experience in the Americas. The rebellion of survival has oftentimes emphasized daily struggles and persistence to live. However, life-affirming paradigms of thought and daily pleasures are also essential to survival. To survive, for Ani Ganzala, required transforming her lived environment into one that reflected her life and to literally paint the walls around her to modify the official historical record to reflect the realities of queer black women. A self-taught painter and graffiti artist, Ganzala chose to abandon public school teaching, where the required textbooks ignore or misrepresent the realities of black resistance, survival, and resilience, and instead use her artwork to document and disseminate a more robust representation of the lives and histories of black Brazilians.

While Salvador boasts of many public murals and sanctioned graffiti art, these are still mostly male spaces and works of art that exclude the intersecting identities of black, female, lesbian of *Candomblé* that Ani Ganzala inhabits. As she embarked on her artistic process, she became acutely aware of the sexism involved in learning this art form and also the lack of opportunities and safety experienced by female graffiti artists. In an interview she explained:

So, yes, I faced this problem [of sexism and learning opportunities], but over time I realized that, for example, some things that I graffitied on the street ended up not being accepted, like graffiti with LGBT and queer relationships . . . because what I do is all about the things I believe, who I am . . . and so I started to watercolor paint. I started to paint and publish it on social media. There, I was able to reach a much larger audience, and especially other black lesbians anywhere who looked at what I was doing and felt . . . identified. So that was the process. It was technology. The graffiti wall is a technology of communication, the oldest in the world. What we see today are cave paintings. We can understand that they are the first works of graffiti—when human beings felt the need to talk about their history through drawings on walls, on stones.[21]

Ganzala confronted the additional censorship of her art through turning to wider networks on social media and through seeking out queer-identified and feminist spaces where she encountered a celebratory audience who rejoiced at seeing their histories and identities represented. These technologies of communication she cites, from premodern cave paintings to contemporary graffiti in the city, to shared copies of watercolor paintings through social media, are also technologies of care and survival. These images affirm that existence, resilience, and pleasure are central to black queer womanhood. The literal erasure of her work from public spaces offers a blatant metaphor for the erasure and silencing that black lesbians have experienced for centuries. When graffiti art that seeks to mirror these identities within a community are vandalized or completely painted over, artivists like Ani Ganzala innovate new technologies of solidarity and community care.

Ani Ganzala's artwork is dominated by images of black women, mothers, daughters, and lovers and expressions of the relationships between these identities and contemporary social realities. Her art reflects the identities of black women who have not historically been included in the dominant

Figure 8.1 Ani Ganzala, "Sem título 5" (2016). *Serie Erotismo*, 2016. Watercolor, 18 3/4 × 13 3/8 in. (47.6 × 34 cm). *Source:* © Ani Ganzala.

narrative of the Brazilian nation. Tanya Saunders questions institutionalized research methods and archives and asks,

> I ask myself if now is the time to turn inwards and access all of these previously existing bodies of knowledge in order to articulate a Brazilian conceptualization of emancipation, knowledge that would be different than in other geographical contexts, but that have the power to contribute to decolonial processes in such a way as to redefine human-ness.[22]

Ganzala's paintings and graffiti art represent an insight into knowledges formerly ignored, hidden, or rendered unintelligible. Her artwork illustrates emancipation through pleasure, joy, and self-narration.

In her "Sem título 3" and "Sem título 5" (2016), for example, she paints black women into lesbian sexuality with emphasis on their pleasure, vulnerability, and agency. Each of these two images showcases a different sexual position. In "Sem título 5," the sixty-nine position emphasizes the blending of the two women's bodies, the way that their brown skin becomes one as the watercolor paint that links their abdominal areas shares the same color and has no separating lines. The tenderness shown through the curved legs and embracing arms highlights the intimacy and closeness and takes the perspective of a nonpornographic onlooker. While the sexual position and act are clear, Ganzala does not emphasize the genitals or even the facial expressions of pleasure but rather relies on the feeling of the pleasure that this intimate act between lovers and viewers evokes. In "Sem título 3," Ganzala paints the act of penetration and, again, the ease and comfort the two women feel together. With her arm draped back behind her head and her legs comfortably held up and resting on her penetrating lover, the two women peacefully close their eyes as their thighs and pelvises unite. The image is a clear celebration of black female sexuality and the power of erotic, sensual encounters. Able to reach a larger audience via her Instagram, Facebook, and social media networking, Ganzala circulates these mirrors to a broader network of Afro-diasporic and LGBTQ-identified people.

In these images, Ganzala paints a background that is absent of referents or specificity; the outside world of racist sexism is not in focus. In "Sem título 5," the two lovers are surrounded by repeated patterns of tiny circles and squares, making their rounded shapes stand out, and in "Sem título 3" the lovers are portrayed in the middle of an explosive galaxy of colors. Thus, viewers are invited to observe and, perhaps, see themselves reflected in these spaces of pleasure and comfort. The technology of communicating affect through art is powerfully developed in Ani Ganzala's artwork. To defuse the violence and continued discrimination experienced by so many black lesbian women, Ani Ganzala paints images of community and of women loving and celebrating one another.

Figure 8.2   Ani Ganzala, "Sem título 3" (2016). *Serie Erotismo*, **2016. Watercolor, 18 3/4 × 13 3/8 in. (47.6 × 34 cm).** *Source*: © Ani Ganzala.

Ani Ganzala reaches a broader audience through publishing her artwork online and thus continues to strive to fulfill her purpose as an artist of expanding the archive of images available to affirm black lesbian love. While her work is sometimes erased or marginalized in the male-dominated graffiti world, she has found social media and watercolor painting as supplementary methods for establishing a larger transnational network. Simultaneously, she forms part of a broader care network where she paints alongside other black female graffiti artists and appreciates the music of Panteras Negras as part of the soundtrack to her community building.

TECHNOLOGY OF AFFECT AND REPRESENTATION

For Zinha Franco and Ani Ganzala, participating in collaborative feminist projects has provided mirrors for affirming their work and simultaneously highlights the need for greater visibility of black female identities in the midst of a highly exclusive and discriminatory dominant consumer culture. In their "El populismo cultural revisitado," Jim McGuigan and Pere Muñoz theorize the relationship between consumerism and elitism in popular culture. The construction of passive or active consumers reflects the framing of the dichotomous popular versus culture of the masses. They note, "el consume comenzó a no ser algo visto como el momento 'pasivo' de la circulación cultural, sino como algo 'activo' y nodal, que involucraba la apropriación popular de artículos y la interpretación diferencial de textos."[23] How will we disempower the technologies of competition, asked Sueide Kintê; how will black female artists assert their active creation and consumption in the realm of popular culture? Through community, Kintê says. Rather than coming up in a highly competitive art scene, where resources and recognition are limited and standards of "art for the masses" can be exclusionary and elitist, these artists have sought out collaborations to affirm the power of black (and often lesbian) women. In an interview published in *Vice i-D*, Benoit Loiseau spoke with trans artivist Ariel Nobre and other queer artists on identity, censorship, and survival. Nobre noted that she "feel[s] that we're living a war. The conservatives are trying to recreate the environment of the 70s and 80s, during the dictatorship. But it's another society now, and they don't realize that. The elite doesn't accept that black people are in universities, that transgender artists are in museums, that the poor have more access. They can't accept that we can speak for ourselves."[24] Nobre's sentiment echoes the work of Franco and Ganzala and other artivists who are targeting one another as their core audience and affirming the reality social transformation from within black LGBTQ creation.

Panteras Negras's collaborations with a variety of rising black female vocalists contribute to a narrative of black women reflecting one another's images to multiply representation. In their work with Aya Bass (a collaboration between Luedji Luna, Xênia França, and Larissa Luz), Panteras Negras performed this communal affect in their stage presence. A play on the word "Yabás," the name Aya Bass is the collective name of the female *orixás* of *Candomblé*. These *orixás* and, by extension, these artists demonstrate the collective power of black women reflecting one another's beauty and strengths. In her interview for AlmaPreta.com, Larissa Luz notes that she and many other rising black singers are confronting a Brazilian Nationalist music industry that has a long history of celebrating and appropriating Afro-diasporic culture and promoting ideologies of racial democracy and harmony. In Axé Bahian carnival music, in particular, the principal singers have been white while the music almost always features secular *Candomblé* rhythms.[25] So, Zinha Franco and Panteras Negras break through not only as black female musicians in a music industry that perpetually appropriates black cultural traditions, but also as an instrumental group that insists upon the recognition and celebration of black female musicianship.

At the January 2019 "Sangue Nova" show, the three female vocalists along with Zinha Franco on bass presented their first collaborative performance. The content was focused on covers of songs by black singers from Bahia and the United States and was accompanied by a clear political message: this city is black and must be appreciated as such. Larissa Luz noted that,

They want black music, but they don't want black people; they want black dance, but they don't want black people; they want black hair, but not black people. It's time to make concessions, to stop speaking from a place that is not yours . . . black in spirit does not exist. If you are black, you are black and if not, not.[26]

All dressed in white, one by one the women take the stage, tenderly embrace, then find their positions. The clear reference to *Candomblé* both in the name of their group and in their all-white costuming links them to the forces of the female *orixás*. Again to Kintê's question: how will we allay destructive competition? Through community.

Aya Bass is committed to citing black artists and, like Panteras Negras, featuring only black female musicians. As they stated in their opening musical interlude, they are singing for all of the yabás, for black women (*orixás*). As Ani Ganzala paints her celebratory watercolors of black lesbian sexuality, her repertoire also includes a multitude of references to *orixás* and *Candomblé* spirituality. These strong natural, spiritual, and often female forces form part of the broader network of care that contributes to the formation of transnational solidarity networks. Even as 2020 spirals into an international pandemic, Zinha Franco has taken her musical audience on a daily exploration of consciousness-raising regarding inequality, racism, and public health during this unprecedented global moment.[27] The networks of engaged listeners, producers, and fellow-artivists affirm their commitment and engagement through these mutual care networks.

The affective impact of attending a performance by Panteras Negras or viewing a painting or graffiti by Ani Ganzala highlights the transformational capacity of collaborative artivism in the face of the environment of competitiveness that Kintê identifies. Focusing on black female beauty reflected in Oxúm's mirror facilitates the birth of new paradigms in the face of violent and repressive legacies of colonialism and slavery. In this reflection we can witness the birth of a transformed society and the pacification of oppression-centered social frameworks.

NOTES

1. Fernando Caulyt, "Brasil, terceira maior população carcerária, aprisiona cada vez mais" *Carta Capital*, September 12, 2018 https://www.cartacapital.com.br/soc iedade/brasil-terceira-maior-populacao-carceraria-aprisiona-cada-vez-mais/

2. Mateus Araújo, "Dina Alves: O cárcere é a maior expressão do racismo" *Pastoral Carcerária* January 10, 2019 https://carceraria.org.br/combate-e-prevencao -a-tortura/dina-alves-o-carcere-e-a-maior-expressao-do-racismo

3. Eva Aladro-Vico, Dimitrina Jivkova-Semova and Olga Bailey "Artivismo: Un nuevo lenguaje educativo para la acción social transformadora" *Comunicar*, XXVI, no. 57 (October 2018): 9–11.

4. Paula Naanim Telis. *Mujer Basura: Performance y Feminismos* (Buenos Aires: Milena Caserola, 2016), 40.

5. Instituto Brasileiro de Geografia e Estatística (IBGE) ibge.gov.br

6. Sueide Kintê, "Tecnologia, cuidado e interseccionalidade." Presentation at the *VI Simpósio Internacional LAVITS: Assimetrias e (In)visibilidades: Vigilância, Gênero e Raça*, (Salvador, Brazil, June 26, 2019, Video, http://lavits.org/assista-mais -um-video-do-vi-simposio-internacional-lavits/?lang=pt.

7. Kintê, presentation. "Competitividade, o paradigma do sucesso que a gente tem hoje, é um paradigma impossível; é um paradigma que dilui a humanidade e que esvazia-se o ser humano."

8. Kintê, presentation. "No fundo no conhecimento de si mesma sobre criaçao, tudo que cai nas mãos de Oxúm ela fecunda e gera. É assim que a morte que Ogúm provoca não vira somente destruição. Porque a ação dela gira que vira progresso. O que eu quero dizer com isso e que no meu paradigma a tecnologia precisa ser apaziguada. Como é que ela vai ser apaziguada? Com a comunidade. Com pessoas. Esse é o dilema colocado entre progresso e afeto."

9. Luana Marques-Garcia Ozemela, Alessandra Conte, Guilerme Sedlaceck and Leopoldo Laborda. *Race Differences in Police Violence and Crime Victimization in Brazil*. (Inter-American Development Bank, 2019). https://publications.iadb.org/ publications/english/document/Race_Differences_in_Police_Violence_and_Crime _Victimization_in_Brazil_en_en.pdf and Ignacio Cano, "Racial bias in police use of lethal force in Brazil." (*Police Practice and Research*, 11, no. 1, February 2010), 31-43.

10. As this volume was going to print, Zinha Franco initiated their gender affir- mation transformation. His new name is Ziati Franco and he uses he/him pronouns. "Banda Panteras Negras" continues to be the only known LGBTQ instrumental group.

11. Estimates cite approximately 500 million versus 5 million enslaved Africans were brought to the United States, for example.

12. Abolition of slavery in Brazil was in 1888, the last nation in the Americas.

13. In the 2020, Netflix Series "Street Food: Latin America" Acarajé is one of the featured foods highlighted in the second episode centered on Salvador, Brazil.

14. Nathália Fernandes de Oliveira, "A Repressão Policial às Religiões de Matriz Afro-Brasileiras no Estado Novo (1937-1945)" (2015):1–172 https://ww w.historia.uff.br/stricto/td/1903.pdf & "Diálogos da fé: Candomblé: religião de resistência" Carta Capital (November 2017) https://www.cartacapital.com.br/blo gs/dialogos-da-fe/candomble-religiao-de-resistencia/ and Marileide Alves Povo Xambá Resiste: 80 anos da repressão aos terreiros em Pernambuco (Recife, Cepe Editora, 2018), 13.

15. See Carly Machado's article "Evangélicos, Mídias e Periferias Urbanas: Questões para um diálogo sobre religião, cidade, nação, e sociedade civil no Brasil contermporâneo" for a discussion of evangelical political and religious action with

regards to civil society and culture in Brazil specifically through the use of religious propaganda in the media.

16. In her "Mujeres andinas, movimientos feministas y proyectos de Desarrollo," Maruja Barrig discusses the ways that black and indigenous women have been systematically invisibilized or ignored within the white feminist movements in Peru and Brazil. While domestic workers allow newly liberated white women to work outside of the home or participate in other social movements, the women caring for the well-being of the home (including childcare) are deemed "dirty" and inferior. Cited in *Género, Etnicidad y Educación en América Latina* edited by Inge Sichra Mejía Lequerica (Madrid, 2004), 101–12.

17. The "Jam" is part of the city of Salvador's regular programming. The two shows played by Panteras Negras (in March and May of 2019) both boasted packed audiences.

18. Their debut performance in São Paulo (July 2019), for example, accompanied the exhibition "Ounje—Alimento dos Orixás" which boasted immersion into African culture through traditional foods of Candomblé terreiros and hybrid rhythms from Bahia.

19. Zinha Franco, personal interview, June 2, 2019. "Essa questão de ser espelho, né? De ser alguém em que o outro se possa espelhar, né? Então eu acho que a gente precisa pensar quais ações a gente está movendo, no nosso cotidiano no nosso ao redor, para que os outros nos vejam como exemplo. Um exemplo positivo, um exemplo de coisas boas. Então, pensando no âmbito musical, existe a banda Panteras Negras e . . .? É importante que a gente faça essa reflexão."

20. Franco, interview. "Muitas mulheres negras sofrem de autoestima; existe racismo, existem fatores que contribuem para que a depressão se aproxime mais em nós. E, graças ao meu orixá, que iluminou meu orí, eu tô aqui. E consigo também levar à gente isso. Sabe? A ideia da banda foi nesse momento da depressão, nesse resgate, de eu ver o propósito da minha vida, sabe? Tem um propósito. Então realmente foi um resgate. Eu estou aqui, eu estou viva, eu posso."

21. Ani Ganzala, interview, June, 25, 2019. "Então, sim, tinha esse problema, mas aí com o tempo eu percebi que por exemplo algumas coisas que eu grafitava na rua acabavam não tendo aceitação, como fazendo grafite de relações LGBTs e queer . . . porque o que eu faço tudo está ligado às coisas que eu acredito, a quem eu sou. E, [assim] comecei a fazer aquarelas. Comecei a fazer aquarela e publicava nas redes sociais. Aí consegui chegar a um público muito maior assim, e principalmente para outras lésbicas negras em qualquer lugar que olhavam pro o que eu 'tava fazendo e sentia . . . sentia identificada. Então aí foi o processo, né. E teve como tecnologia, né. O muro é uma tecnologia de comunicação, a mais antiga, né, no mundo. O que a gente vê hoje é o que é uma pintura rupestre, né. A gente pode entender que ali são os primeiros grafites—que quando o ser humano sentiu necessidade de falar sobre a sua história através de desenhos nas paredes, nas pedras."

22. Tanya Saunders, "Epistemologia negra sapatão como vetor de uma praxis humana libertária" (Periódicus 7, no. 1, May–October 2017), 115–16. "Me pergunto se é hora de se voltar para dentro e acessar todos esses corpos de conhecimento existentes para articular a(s) noção(s) brasileira(s) de emancipação humana, uma(s) que será

diferente daquelas existentes em outros contextos geográficos, mas que tem o poder de contribuir para processos descoloniais de modo que redefinam o ser humano."

23. Jim McGuian and Pere Muñoz, "El populismo cultural revisitado," (*Guaraguao* 4, no. 10 Summer 2006), 32.

24. Ariel Nobre and Benoit Loiseau, "5 Queer Brazilian Artists on Identity, Censorship and Survival." (*i-D.Vice.com* April 25, 2018), https://i-d.vice.com/en_us/article/9kg7gv/queer-brazilian-artists-censorship-politics

25. Guilherme Soares, "Proyecto Aya Bass reúne as potências de Larissa Luz, Luedji Luna e Xênia França" (*AlmaPreta*, January 28, 2019), https://www.almapret a.com/editorias/realidade/projeto-aya-bass-reune-potencias-de-larissa-luz-luedji-luna -e-xenia-franca.

26. Soares, "Proyecto Aya Bass." "Querem a música negra, mas não querem os pretos; querem a dança negra, mas não querem os pretos; querem o cabelo dos negros, mas não querem os pretos. Esta na hora de fazer concessões, de parar de usar um lugar de fala que não é seu . . . preto de alma não existe. Quem é preto é, quem não é, não é."

27. In her "Live Conscientização Popular- 20 minutos do seu dia!", Zinha Franco hosts activists, scholars, and artists from within the community to reflect daily on mental health, economic impact, popular music, public health safety, among other themes. During the first week she reached eight thousand people. These are broadcast on her Instagram Live account, @aquelaqueproduz.

BIBLIOGRAPHY

Aladro-Vico, Eva, Dimitrina Jivkova-Semova and Olga Bailey "Artivismo: Un nuevo lenguaje educativo para la acción social transformadora" *Comunicar XXVI*, no. 57 (October 2018): 9–18. https://www.revistacomunicar.com/ojs/index.php/comunica r/article/view/C57-2018-01

Alves, Marilede. *Povo Xambá Resiste: 80 anos da repressão aos terreiros em Pernambuco*. Recife: Cepe Editora, 2018.

Araújo, Mateus. "Dina Alves: O cárcere é a maior expressão do racismo." *Pastoral Carcerária*, January 10, 2019. https://carceraria.org.br/combate-e-prevencao-a-to rtura/dina-alves-o-carcere-e-a-maior-expressao-do-racismo

Aya Bass "Sangue Novo Festival." January 29, 2019. https://www.youtube.com/w atch?v=qSgTpVz7Xzk

Barrig, Maruja. "Mujeres andinas, movimientos feministas y proyectos de desar-rollo." In *Género, Etnicidad y Educación en América Latina*, edited by Inge Sichra, 101–112. Madrid: Mejía Lequerica, 2004.

Cano, Ignacio. "Racial bias in police use of lethal force in Brazil." *Police Practice and Research*, 11, no. 1 (February 2010): 31–43.

Caulyt, Fernando C. "Brasil, terceira maior população carcerária, aprisiona cada vez mais" *Carta Capital*, September 12, 2018. https://www.cartacapital.com.br/soc iedade/brasil-terceira-maior-populacao-carceraria-aprisiona-cada-vez-mais/

Fernandes de Oliveira, Nathália. "A Repressão Policial às Religiões de Matriz Afro-Brasileiras no Estado Novo (1937–1945)." Diss. Universidade Federal Fluminense, 2015. https://www.historia.uff.br/stricto/td/1903.pdf

Franco, Zinha. Personal interview with author. June 21, 2019. Unpublished.

Ganzala, Ani. Watercolor Paintings. "Sem título 3" and "Sem título 5". From the series *Erotismo* (Watercolor, 2016). Photo credit, Mitra Ghaffari.

Grabe, Shelly and Nicole M. Else-Quest. "The Role of Transnational Feminism in Psychology: Complementary Visions." *Psychology of Women Quarterly* 36, no. 2 (2012): 158–61.

Kintê, Sueide. "Tecnologia, cuidado e interseccionalidade." *VI Simpósio Internacional LAVITS: Assimetrias e (In)visibilidades: Vigilância, Gênero e Raça*. Salvador, Brazil, June 26, 2019.

Lugones, María. "Toward a Decolonial Feminism." *Hypatia* 25, no. 4 (Fall 2010): 742–59.

Machado, Carly. "Evangélicos, Mídias e Periferias Urbanas: Questões para um diálogo sobre religião, cidade, nação, e sociedade civil no Brasil contermporâneo." *Debates do NER, Porto Alegre* 19, no. 33 (2018): 58–80.

Marques-Garcia Ozemela, Luana, Alessandra Conte, Guilerme Sedlaceck and Leopoldo Laborda. *Race Differences in Police Violence and Crime Victimization in Brazil*. Inter-American Development Bank, 2019. https://publications.iadb.org/publications/english/document/Race_Differences_in_Police_Violence_and_Crime_Victimization_in_Brazil_en_en.pdf

McGuigan, Jim and Pere Muñoz. "El populismo cultural revisitado." *Guaraguao* 4, no. 10 (Summer 2006): 30–53.

Nobre, Ariel and Benoit Loiseau. "5 Queer Brazilian Artists on Identity, Censorship and Survival." *i-D.Vice.com* April 25, 2018. https://i-d.vice.com/en_us/article/9kg7gv/queer-brazilian-artists-censorship-politics

Saunders, Tanya. "Epistemologia negra sapatão como vetor de uma praxis humana libertária" Periódicus 7, no. 1 (May-October 2017): 102–16.

Soares, Guilherme. "Proyecto Aya Bass reúne as potências de Larissa Luz, Luedji Luna e Xênia França." *AlmaPreta* January 28, 2019. https://www.almapreta.com/editorias/realidade/projeto-aya-bass-reune-potencias-de-larissa-luz-luedji-luna-e-xenia-franca

Telis, Paula Naanim. *Mujer Basura: Performance y Feminismos*. Buenos Aires: Milena Caserola, 2016.

Index

About the Contributors

Raysa E. Amador, a professor and Chair of languages and literature at Adelphi University in New York, holds a doctorate in Spanish from New York University. She has more than two decades of experience teaching and researching Latin American culture, civilization, and literature. Dr. Amador is the chair of the Languages and International Studies Department and the director of the Latin American Program at Adelphi. Dr. Amador is the coauthor of *The Female Body: Perspectives of Latin American Artists* (Greenwood, 2002). Prior to this research she undertook a programmatic investigation of a series of questions pertaining to the Chronicle of Indies and the law and published the book *Una aproximación histórica a Los comentarios reales* (Editorial Pliegos, 1984). In addition, she is the author of numerous articles on Spanish and Latin American literature. A member of the honor society *Phi Beta Kappa* as well as former member of the New York Council Speakers of the Humanities Program, she has lectured extensively on the literature of the Discovery of the New World and on Latina writers in the United States.

Leslie Bary teaches Latin American literature and culture at the University of Louisiana at Lafayette. She has scholarly publications on César Vallejo, Oswald de Andrade, Emilio Adolfo Westphalen, Rubén Darío, the question of cultural identity, and other topics, and she has lectured widely on representations of race in Latin American writing. Her current book project is *That Discerning Eye: Race and the State in Modern Latin American Literature*. Her translation of Pedro Granados's *Roxosol* is forthcoming from Artepoética. Her political work includes the movements for postconviction relief and the abolition of immigrant detention.

Olga Bezhanova is an associate professor of Spanish Literature and chair of the Department of Foreign Languages and Literature at Southern Illinois University, Edwardsville. Her articles on the subject of modern and contemporary Hispanic literature have appeared in *Romance Quarterly, Bulletin of Spanish Studies, Hispanófila, Revista Canadiense de Estudios Hispánicos, Letras hispanas, Anales galdosianos*, and so on. Her book *Growing Up in an Inhospitable World: Female Bildungsroman in Spain* was awarded the Victoria Urbano Prize for the Best Critical Monograph by the Asociación Internacional de Literatura y Cultura Femenina Hispánica. Dr. Bezhanova's second book titled *Literature of Crisis: Spain's Engagement with Liquid Capital* was published by Bucknell University Press in the Fall of 2017 and was released in paperback in 2019. In 2019, Dr. Bezhanova was awarded the Panteleimon Kulish Medal by the Literature, Art and Communications Academy of Ukraine for a significant contribution to the promotion of Ukrainian literature in the United States and Hispanic countries. In 2020, she became the recipient of Internationaler Medaille Heinrich Böll (wegen des Große Erfolges in der Literatur und Kommunikation) awarded by the German branch of the Literature, Art and Communications Academy of Ukraine.

Barbara Minter is a PhD candidate in Spanish at the University of Alabama. Her dissertation focuses on contemporary Spanish television that reinterprets the first half of the twentieth century, with an emphasis on various female protagonists that embody postfeminist identities in several recent programs that reinterpret women of the past. Her research interests include television studies, film studies, postfeminist studies, women writers, transnational studies, and identity studies. She has several articles published or accepted for publication and has presented at conferences both nationally and internationally.

Sowmya Ramanathan is a scholar of twentieth-century literature and visual arts of the Latin American Southern Cone, working at the intersections of aesthetics, critical theory, and gender and sexuality studies. She is currently a PhD candidate in the Department of Spanish and Portuguese at Princeton University and holds a bachelor's degree from the University of California, Berkeley, in Sociology and Spanish Language and Literature. Her dissertation, titled, "Diamela Eltit: Textures of Reading and Writing in Times of Danger," explores the Chilean writer's dialogues with prominent figures of the Latin American cultural tradition, such as José Donoso, Severo Sarduy, and Paz Errázuriz, illuminating a politically situated literary and aesthetic practice that examines new forms of collective rationality during the rise of neoliberalism in Chile.

Rosita Scerbo is an assistant professor of US Latinx Culture at Allegheny College, PA. Her research interests include Latin American and Chicanx Visual Autobiography, Digital Humanities, Visual Disability Narrative, Corporeal Invisibility, and Feminism, and Gender Studies. She received her bachelor's degree in Foreign Languages and Literatures (Anglo-American and Hispanic-American) from the University of Calabria in 2013. In 2016, she obtained her master's degree in Hispanic-American Literature and Linguistics from West Virginia University. In May 2020, she obtained her PhD in Latin American/Latinx Visual Studies from Arizona State University. In addition, Rosita is also a trilingual published author/writer, ethnic minorities ARTivist, and online pedagogy specialist, and has worked as HASTAC Communications and Digital Content Development Intern.

Java Singh received her PhD in Latin American literature from Jawaharlal Nehru University, India. She teaches graduate and postgraduate courses at the Spanish department in Doon University, Dehradun. Her most recent publications are *Gendered Ways of Transnational Unbelonging* (coeditor, Cambridge Scholars Publishing, 2019), a chapter on women's crime fiction in *Papeles del crimen* (University of Barcelona Press, 2020), and an article on science fiction in *Qvadrata* (Autonomous University of Chihuahua, 2020). Her research interests include Southern Cone women writers and filmmakers, comparative literary and cultural theory, and speculative cinema and fiction. She also holds an MBA from the Indian Institute of Management, Ahmedabad.

Naomi Pueo Wood is an associate professor of Spanish and Portuguese at Colorado College. Her most recent work "O arquivo corporal: aquarelas e graffitis de Annie Ganzala" in *Latin American and Latinx Visual Cultures* (2019) highlights the usage of the erotic in the paintings and graffiti art of Annie Ganzala. Her prior work "Publicando el placer: los gestos queer en la música y el performance de Kumbia Queers y Krudas Cubensi" in *Letras Femeninas* (2016) shows how queer/lesbian musicians emphasize pleasure in their lyrics and music videos as a political act which deemphasizes protest and struggle as the heart of lesbian/queer activism. Her ongoing research is focused on Critical Race Studies and Gender and Sexuality Studies in the Americas.

María Alejandra Zanetta is distinguished professor of Spanish Literature and Culture at the University of Akron. She earned her PhD in Spanish Literature from the Ohio State University and joined the University of Akron faculty in August 1995. Dr. Zanetta is the author of *La pintura y la prosa de Santiago Rusiñol: un análisis comparativo* (Universidad de Valladolid, 1997), and numerous journal articles in such areas as comparative studies between Juan Ramón Jiménez's paintings and poems, Ramón del Valle Inclán and Santiago Rusiñol, Rosa Chacel and Remedios Varo, Carmen Martín Gaite and Eduardo Arroyo. Currently her research focuses on the artistic and literary production of Latin-American and Spanish avant-garde women painters and writers. In *La otra cara de la vanguardia: estudio comparativo de la obra artística de Maruja Mallo, Ángeles Santos y Remedios Varo* (Edwin Mellen Press, 2006), Zanetta comparatively analyzes the visual manifestations of these women painters that result from the competing theories of gender and sexuality central to the various ideological struggles of their period. Her latest book *La Subversión Enmascarada: Análisis de la Obra de Maruja Mallo* (Biblioteca Nueva, 2014) is an interpretive study of the most important symbols of the personal iconography of the Galician painter Maruja Mallo in relation to the context in which they were created and the personal readings and experiences that had a profound impact on the personal and professional formation of the author.

www.ingramcontent.com/pod-product-compliance
Lightning Source LLC
Chambersburg PA
CBHW050641280326
41932CB00015B/2740